EVIL
BEYOND
BELIEF

HOW AND WHY
DR HAROLD SHIPMAN MURDERED
MORE THAN 300 PEOPLE

EVIL
BEYOND
BELIEF

WENSLEY CLARKSON

JOHN BLAKE

Published by John Blake Publishing Ltd, 3 Bramber Court,
2 Bramber Road, London W14 9PB, England

This edition published in paperback in 2005

ISBN 1 904034 46 2

British Library Cataloguing-in-Publication Data: A catalogue record for
this book is available from the British Library.

Printed in Great Britain by Bookmarque, Croydon

3 5 7 9 10 8 6 4 2

Pictures reproduced by kind permission of News International and Press
Association. Every attempt has been made to find the original copyright-
holders, but some were untraceable. The publishers would be grateful if
the relevant people could contact us.

Papers used by John Blake Publishing Ltd are natural, recyclable
products made from wood grown in sustainable forests. The
manufacturing processes conform to the environmental regulations of
the country of origin.

Nottingham, England, 21 June 1963

Moonlight bathes the night in hazy shadows. Grey skin on a shapeless, bloated face. Lying flat on her back … staring over the top of her sheet.

He looks down at her – he can't take his eyes off her. He hears her little dry coughs, like the whimperings of a small dog. She desperately wants more morphine to ease the pain.

Oh my God. She's going to die? he asks himself as he turns his head away with great effort. Seconds later, he glances back at her again, lying in that bed. He rolls his head from side to side, looking for the morphine that might help her. But there is none left. Nothing.

Everything remains moonlit. Black and white.

The animal murmurings continue from deep within her. Then the sounds end. He leans down and presses the palm of his hand across her mouth, before rolling his eyes upward. He watches her lips for movement – is she dead? He calls to her but she doesn't reply. She just stares straight ahead. Then the whimperings begin again.

Her skin looks matt. Her face is taut and harsh. But her eyes catch the moonbeam and sparkle for a beat. Dry spittle encrusts her lips. The muted sound of pain, barely audible.

'I'm sorry … I'm sorry,' he says. But her eyes never acknowledge him. They stare straight ahead out of the window.

Speaking shoots his mind into space once more. His thoughts drift away. Then he blinks hard and returns, brushing her bare hand with his fingertips. Her eyes remain fixed … straight ahead.

His face is just two feet from her. Again, his mind floats high up into the starry sky.

Then he snaps back into reality. Her watery eyes gaze out towards the forest. The lights of the city sparkle in the distance … overhanging trees cut long finger shadows across nearby fields. Everything remains bathed in moonlight. She's gasping as the last few breaths struggle from within.

He so wished he could simply pick up the syringe and put her out of her misery.

In memory of every single one of Fred Shipman's victims – may you all rest in peace.

'If he came back this afternoon, I would be there on his doorstep. Dr Shipman was wonderful with my second husband. He tried everything to save him. I will never believe he did it. He has been wonderful to me – and others. I am heartbroken.'

One of Fred Shipman's patients, 1999

'He wants to control situations. He likes to have control over life and death.'

Detective Chief Superintendent Bernard Postles, head of the team that investigated Fred Shipman, 2000

'Lots of old ladies have died under Dr Shipman. They say he's a lovely doctor but you don't last long.'

One of Fred Shipman's oldest living patients, 1998

Author's Note

The central figure in this story, Harold Frederick Shipman, was always known to family, friends and patients as 'Fred'. In an effort to avoid confusion, throughout this book he will be referred to by that name.

Quotations from written material appear, with few exceptions, without the editorial '(sic)'. When it seems that a word was inadvertently missing, it has been added for the sake of clarity. Mistakes in punctuation, grammar and spelling have been corrected in certain instances, but in others it was felt that retaining an error helped convey the flavour of a document and the style of the person being quoted.

'I will use my power to help the sick to the best of my ability and judgment; I will abstain from harming or wronging anyone by it. I will not give a fatal draught to anyone if I am asked, nor will I suggest any such things.'

From the Hippocratic Oath taken by Harold Shipman
when he qualified as a doctor in 1973

Preface

There is a kind of poetic injustice in the fact that Fred Shipman, the intriguing subject of this book, really does exist. He should be found only in horror fiction – the wiry, bearded, sharp-tongued medic who strode to the rescue of countless patients only to cut short their lives with cold indifference.

Unlikely as his life story sounds, it is essential to examine it in minute detail in order to get a handle on the twisted mind of this extraordinary killer. You will read details here that will shock and amaze you. To be sure, Fred Shipman was no ordinary man, but a doctor whose superb bedside manner helped him gain the confidence of hundreds of patients before he cruelly cut them down. But was Fred Shipman psychotic or insane? From his life and crimes, I hope to reconstruct the development of his criminal brain – not only his nature, but even his appearance and personal idiosyncrasies and, in some instances, his charm and kindness. To watch Shipman at work is to imagine oneself back in a trusting middle-class world where the doctor is given Godlike reverence and respect.

I first came upon the crimes of Fred Shipman when I, along

with millions of Britons, heard about the first excavation of one of his victims in the dead of night in a cold, isolated graveyard in Hyde, Lancashire, in the summer of 1998. It soon became clear that police had failed in their original investigation some months earlier. They, like so many of Shipman's patients, refused to believe that such a respected, almost idolised figure could be a cold-blooded killer. By the time investigators produced a criminal profile it was way too late.

All of Fred Shipman's victims deserve a mention because each, in their own way, is highly unusual. But I hope that most of all, this book will inform the reader about the doctor himself. What sort of man could stoop to killing on such a massive scale? How did he come to find a taste for death? What drove him to kill in increasingly large numbers? How did he hide these murderous instincts from the outside world?

I hope I can answer these and many other questions in an easy, non-technical style but – and the reader should be prepared for this – in relatively explicit language. There is shocking material in this book and I cannot gloss over certain, disturbing facts. In some murders, Shipman was more successful in covering up the facts than others, but I hope I have managed to get to the bottom of the truth.

There is a lesson to be drawn from the Fred Shipman case. What I have long found fascinating, and what I will underline so sharply, is the fact that the motivations behind the acts of a madman possess their own twisted logic. The psychotic murderer never acts with complete irrationality. There is a method to his madness. A rationale hidden behind what he has done and how he does it, however bizarre and completely without reason it appears to be. The challenge to me, as an author, is to find that logic. And it is this hunt – this seeking out of the hidden mathematics of the disturbed mind, this reconstruction of the chess moves made by a madman – that I hope will unravel on the pages you are about to read.

I will also make this point; it is astonishing that so many of us are sane, and remain sane. That the human mind works at all, that anything so fantastically complex could even begin to operate as a unit, is itself remarkable. That most of us manage to keep this intricate and enormously variable mechanism under some sort of control most of the time, living with one another in tolerable harmony, is more remarkable still.

In *The Good Doctor* I have tried to probe the innermost feelings of a man now labelled one of the most prolific serial killers of modern times. Doctors play a very special role in our society. So often, people trust them without question. Doctors are rated as more 'special' than the rest of us. Yet they are prone to guilt, depression, anger and – in the case of Fred Shipman – murder.

But what makes Fred Shipman's crimes so extraordinary is the coldness with which he snuffed out people's lives, as though flicking a switch. But then doctors are trained not to show their true feelings to their patients. In Shipman's case, he seemed to bottle up those emotions so much that his only means of 'escape' was to kill.

I've interviewed countless people during the course of my enquiries into Shipman. But it was his family and friends who were to provide me with the opportunity to delve inside his mind and soul to explore the motives that drove him to kill. I have deliberately set out to inform and provoke in the hope that next time such a crime occurs, you will be alert to it. The tragedy of Shipman is that he carried on for so long without even being suspected of his crimes.

In trying to present the facts in this dramatic fashion, there is no doubt that some readers might discover discrepancies between my version of events and what has been reported elsewhere. I can assure you I have tried only to rely on information that I believe to be entirely accurate, but if I have erred in any way then it was entirely in good faith.

In parts, the Shipman story has been adapted to read as near to fiction as possible. That is what makes it all the more frightening … and realistic. That has meant I have had to make some informed deductions for dramatic purposes. But the actual facts are as they occurred.

Here, then, is the truth about Fred Shipman – the man, the murderer, the father, the trusted doctor. It promises to shake your trust in human nature to the core.

Wensley Clarkson, 2005

Prologue

Hyde Cemetery, Hyde, North of England, November 1998. The rusting black-and-gold gates, proudly emblazoned with the town's crest, are rarely shut. Fresh yellow lilies lie alongside a gravestone: 'To loving dad, Stan'. A few yards away fading daisies for a 'mum gone but not forgotten'. Elsewhere, numerous ivy-choked tombstones of generations long departed. Wire mesh garbage cans hold old bottles of beer from the people who sometimes slip into the cemetery to drown their sorrows. Across the way, a park worker with a rivet gun fixes tiny metal plaques to a stone wall in the garden of remembrance.

The 104-year-old Hyde Cemetery provides a backdrop more befitting a horror movie than real life. Gnarled old oak trees flash long thin shadows across the ground. Large ornate monuments erected in memory of some of the area's richest families create an almost gothic atmosphere. November is the month of the Holy Souls, when parishioners of the nearby St Paul's Church pray for the dead at every Mass. If ever their prayers were needed, it was now.

Just 100 yards away, residents sleep peacefully in their homes as cars and vans creep quietly along the cemetery pathway in low gear. In the starry sky, half a moon spreads long fingers of darkness across the grass. The smooth blankets of turf that covered the graves of Marie Quinn, Bianka Pomfret and Ivy Lomas have been peeled back and replaced with churned mounds of earth which now scar the once neat and tidy graveyard. The stark image of a white tent covering a desolate grave indicates that something is wrong. It's pitch dark. The grumbling sound of a generator cuts through the cold night air. Powerful spotlights strike beams of white across the gravesites. The old mill town of Hyde, in Lancashire, is about to unearth yet more evidence of the death and destruction wreaked by Fred Shipman.

A total of seven bodies would be exhumed from this same cemetery over the following months. A large white tent has been erected around the plot of Irene Turner. This once proud grandmother-of-four, described as 'exquisite' by her family, was always dressed to the nines, never a hair out of place. Yet she was about to undergo a final, humiliating fate.

As the inquiry team gathers, Father Denis Maher whispers a prayer in the freezing air, his breath sending out small slivers of vapour through the cold, damp air. Maher has been asked to attend by many of the families whose loved ones have been disinterred. Back in their homes they lie awake wondering what horrific sights are greeting the investigators and their hand-picked priest.

Each suspected victim has been assigned two detectives dedicated to the case, including the task of exhumation. All forensic officers wear green plastic department bodysuits. Just beyond them, uniformed officers patrol the perimeter of the graveyard checking for ghoulish onlookers, their torches flashing. For all the investigators, it is a most distressing time. It's just as bad for the freelance workmen contracted at double the pay rates to dig up the graves. They usually find most of their employment digging up roads.

Father Maher explains, 'Nobody enjoys doing this. Nobody

wants to do it, but they know it must be done and they do it with dignity and sensitivity.'

The priest repeats the prayers and service as each body is returned to its final resting place in a new coffin with a new name plate, usually within 24 hours.

'It consoles the families,' says Father Maher. But that reburial only comes after investigators have completed their grim task in a far corner of the graveyard where the rows of new marble tombstones glisten like black, shiny teeth.

The Catholic section bore the brunt of it with four exhumations. Flowers and a modest brown marble gravestone – inscribed 'a dear wife, mum and nana, always in our hearts and sadly missed' – are removed from Mrs Turner's well-tended plot as the mechanical digger starts up.

One officer stops by the fence and pours a cup of tea from a flask while another lights a cigarette.

'I'm glad I'm not over there,' he says.

The entire operation will take at least two-and-a-half hours, the sodden ground and waterlogged grave making the task more difficult than in previous exhumations. At hourly intervals a church bell tolls. Eventually, lights begin to come on in nearby homes as early risers awaken.

An hour later, the digger falls silent, leaving an unearthly hush; the operation is complete. The tent is removed to reveal the work team carefully clearing away their equipment and debris from the grave and surrounding plots. But these exhumations have struck fear and horror into the hearts of the people of Hyde. One woman, whose house backs on to the cemetery, says, 'You hear noises and half wake up, then realise what it is. It makes you shudder.'

As Father Maher later pointed out, 'It's pretty normal to die. You have the funeral, and that gives a natural completion to death. But this reversal – it has a profound effect on everyone involved. For a big town, Hyde is very close-knit. Everyone is either related or knows someone whose death is being investigated. Quite frankly, I don't know if the place will ever get over it. It's like a cancer eating away at the heart of the community.'

But where and how did that cancer begin?

CHAPTER ONE

Mummy's Boy

Harold Shipman and his young wife Vera's first home was 163 Longmead Drive. The newly-built Edwards Lane estate in the city of Nottingham was in the district of Sherwood, named after the nearby famous forest where Robin Hood, according to legend, robbed the rich to help feed the poor. At the time, Nottingham successfully developed new industries such as bicycles and tobacco.

The Edwards Lane estate was a very close-knit community because it only consisted of a couple of dozen roads lined with new red-brick houses.

Harold Shipman's slightly built wife seemed exotic in comparison to her overweight husband. Her neat home and polite children were considered as 'a credit to her'. Harold Shipman was a hosiery warehouseman who drove a Bedford tipper truck, moving stones and broken tarmac for local building companies. His favourite hobby was his flowers in his back garden and he smoked a pipe and wore a trilby hat over his thinning grey hair.

The couple's first child, Pauline, was born in March 1938.

9

Harold set off to fight with the Sherwood Foresters regiment less than two years later in the Second World War. Vera, still in her teens, had to fend for herself and baby Pauline. Her next child – Harold Frederick Shipman – wasn't born until after the war ended on 14 January 1946. The newest arrival was called Fred to avoid confusion with his father.

Fred attended the Burford Infants School, close to Longmead Drive. Fred is pictured wearing a bow-tie while most of his classmates do not. Vera made him wear it. Shy Fred struggled at school because of his left-handedness, but Vera insisted he work even harder until he had more than compensated for it.

By the time Fred was eight, he was considered so bright, he was bussed out to a new school called Whitemoor Primary on the nearby Whitemoor council estate to study for his all-important 11-plus examination which would gain him entry to two of the city's finest schools.

The Shipman home in Longmead Drive had three bedrooms with a downstairs bathroom, a small front yard with a larger 60ft back yard. With a sister seven years older, Fred, in effect, found himself with two mothers doting on him. The Shipmans seemed a happy, functional family. But neighbours later recalled that the family were rather insular and rarely communicated with other residents.

Vera undoubtedly wanted her children, especially Fred, to believe they were better than all around them. Fred never seemed interested in joining in with all the usual street games played by most children on the estate. As one contemporary recalled, 'He just didn't mix much with the other lads.'

Many kids visited the local cinema at weekends to watch Roy Rogers, Tarzan and the Robin Hood films. Fred rarely went because his mother insisted he stay at home and do some extra school work. Young Fred Shipman watched the world having fun from the window of his bedroom which he shared with his younger brother Clive, two years his junior.

Classmate and neighbour Alan Goddard travelled every day on a double-decker bus to Whitemoor Primary School with

Fred. Both boys were outsiders when they first arrived at the school.

Fred failed at most sports but he did excel at stool ball, a sport unique to Nottinghamshire which was a cross between baseball and cricket, played with a large paddle which looked like an oversized table-tennis bat. Fred even posed in the team's photograph, dark-haired and dark-eyed, proudly dressed in the school T-shirt issued to the team. One school friend later recalled, 'Freddie was a complete loser.'

At home, Harold Shipman was a patient and decent father. But it was Vera who had the stronger personality. Vera, born illegitimately to a local lace clipper, wanted security and happiness for her children. She wanted her children to eventually beat a path off the estate. And the estate was becoming livelier and noisier. Drunken brawls between teenagers and wife-beating incidents regularly occurred.

Young Fred Shipman sailed through his 11-plus with such good results that he won a scholarship to High Pavement, a highly respected grammar school. He was one of only a handful of boys from the estate to make it to High Pavement.

Fred was carrying big hopes on his shoulders. He had to get up before 7.00am each morning to get to High Pavement and other boys on the estate teased him because of his 'fancy school uniform'. It was usually dark by the time he got home most evenings, and he continued to spend all of his waking hours poring over books.

Vera Shipman's determination to move up the social ladder prevented them from making a lot of close friends in the neighbourhood where they lived. They did spend some time with the Cutler family who lived directly opposite them on Longmead Drive, but one neighbour later explained, 'The Cutlers said they weren't easy by any means.'

High Pavement's motto was: 'Virtus Sola Nobilitas' (virtue is the only nobility) and Vera saw it as the making of young Fred. The school, founded in 1788, was renowned for sporting and academic prowess.

High Pavement was so-called because of its original location between the city's castle and the middle of Nottingham. Lord Byron's mother worshipped at the chapel while her son, aged ten, was treated for a deformed foot at the local hospital. DH Lawrence later used the chapel as the meeting place for his fictional characters Paul Morrell and Miriam Leivers in *Sons and Lovers*.

High Pavement was one of the first non-sectarian schools in England and also became the first school in the country to teach practical science 100 years later became a boys-only establishment. Nearby Manning School provided education for girls. When Fred Shipman started in September 1957, school premises opened in Bestwood, less than a mile from the Shipman home. Fred and his neighbour, Alan Goddard, walked to school together in brown blazers trimmed with brown and yellow braid, brown caps, ties striped in brown, yellow and blue, and school socks.

Fred's family invited Alan Goddard over each year for Bonfire Night parties in their back garden where they ate toffee and cakes made by Vera Shipman. Alan Goddard even watched the local professional football team Notts County with Freddie and his dad.

Another friend from Fred Shipman's High Pavement days recalled, 'Fred was a wise head on young shoulders; always focused on something and he worked so hard,' and another classmate, Bob Studholme, said, 'No one really knew Fred Shipman. He was always in a crowd but I couldn't honestly say that Fred had a real friend.'

In his first year, in form 1C, young Fred Shipman had a story published in the school magazine, *The Pavior*.

> *When Uncle Ted visited us last year he brought*
> *along his little puppy, Soot, who was of course*
> *black. While he was here we had a budgie given*
> *to us and Soot grew very jealous of him when we*
> *tried to make the bird talk. One day he knocked*

over the cage and broke Joey's wing so we took
him to a vet and he put a splint on the wing. One
day Joey went and had a bath in Soot's water and
pecked at his bone. Now Soot's fond of Joey and
lets him ride on his back and pull his tail and
have a bath in his water. Joey says 'Naughty Soot,
naughty, naughty Soot' and Soot goes and barks at
Joey as if to say, 'Naughty Joey, naughty naughty
Joey.' Wherever Joey goes, Soot goes. How's that
for being friends.

Fred never rose above the C stream in the four-class stream at High Pavement. School bells marked the end of lessons, desks were arranged in rows, strict no-talking rules in class, and masters wore black gowns. Headmaster Harry Davies was renowned for his strong sense of social justice which he passed on to many of the working-class kids who entered via scholarships. He'd even take a boy back to his home to talk to his mother and father if there was a problem.

Harry Davies was not a keen proponent of corporal punishment but he was capable at times of 'giving a good stroke of the cane' when punishment was required. Fred's High Pavement classmate Bob Studholme was beaten by Davies for throwing stones at the groundsman's tractor. After inflicting the punishment, his headmaster then shook Studholme's hand.

Back home, Fred's homework remained the most important thing in the Shipman household. His sister Pauline had left school at 15 and worked at a company manufacturing knitted garments. Then younger brother Clive didn't get into High Pavement, so Fred's academic progress was even more celebrated.

Fred Shipman remained a particularly quiet student. While many students swore, farted and got into mischief, Fred was nowhere to be seen.

By the age of 13, Fred was so physically mature that he began shaving. He sported sideburns which gave him an air of superiority which meant most students looked up to him.

When the students told a filthy joke in the sports changing rooms, Fred Shipman sat on a bench smiling faintly. Another student later recalled, 'It was a condescending smile, as if he was looking at a gang of kids and thinking, You'll grow up one day.'

Fred Shipman was an excellent rugby player, fly-half at first and later as a centre or wingback. In October 1961, he even won the prize for most improved student, a back-handed compliment that was one of the few highlights of his school career.

Young Fred was well aware that his mother in many ways resented the fact that his father was a simple workman. She dreamed of Fred making a successful career. Fred, the quiet lad noted for his politeness to adults, preferred in many ways to play with the younger children at school. Even back then he seemed in an odd, subjective frame of mind which included a total lack of interest in anything apart from his school activities.

But he was so proud to be able to wear the uniform of the best school in the area that he often passed himself off to strangers as a rich, well-spoken student. In a way, he became a kind of conman – but without actually deceiving anyone for monetary gain. Being a good-looking and plausible young man, he enjoyed being accepted as this 'other person' as opposed to the true Fred Shipman.

And Vera Shipman did little to dissuade her favourite son from his own self-delusion. In many ways, she and Fred were cut off from everyone else in the family, inhabiting their own little world. They shared a mental telepathy in which each always seemed to know what the other was thinking. It now seems entirely possible that mother and son became closer than is natural. Certainly, Vera pampered and protected Fred more than her other children. And there was a growing resentment from the other family members, including hard-working Harold Shipman.

Some believe that Fred was seduced by his mother –

certainly mentally if not physically – from the time he was about 12 or 13 years of age. This would not have been such an unusual occurrence. Certainly, Fred was in the habit of sneaking into his mother's bed at night if his father was out at the pub or working late. As one relative later explained, 'Fred and Vera had this unusual telepathy between them. Sometimes we were all a little worried as to how close they really were.' But most nights, Fred's bedtime companion was a huge fluffy pink toy pig – his favourite animal. 'Fred's bedroom was filled with toy and china pigs. He was obsessed by them,' recalls one childhood acquaintance.

Sometimes, Harold Shipman would return home late at night to find young Fred sprawled out on his side of the matrimonial bed with only that fluffy pig separating him from his mother's warm embrace. But Harold thought nothing of it and would gently lift young Fred into his arms and carry him through to the bedroom he shared with his younger brother. The following morning, there would be no mention whatsoever of what had occurred.

In the winter of 1959–60, young Fred – stocky and tough with an agressive streak – even played rugby for Nottinghamshire Schools Under-15s. During one inter-schools match, Fred carried out a vicious tackle. It was not illegal, but everyone certainly noticed the crunching.

During school cross-country runs, Fred and his classmates would stop off for cups of tea at the home of one boy called Michael Heath. Heath later recalled that Fred never stayed for long.

Fred Shipman succeeded through sheer hard work and determination. Fred often walked to school because he couldn't afford a push bike and wanted to save the cost of a bus. He carried a huge backpack of books like a snail. Fred eventually became a Pavior, a prefect in charge of young students.

Mike Heath later recalled, 'Some of us had it easy but he really worked hard. I remember he had a long, loping stride as he still does.' Fred Shipman was always most comfortable at the back of the class, absorbing the teacher's words but also glancing occasionally into another world. He was also just about the only student without a nickname. He preferred to keep out of the groups of friends who gathered in the school yard between classes.

Fred eventually passed seven 'O' Levels and found life in the sixth form (aged 16 and over) more relaxed. The boys still wore blazers, but were allowed to wear waistcoats (vests) of any style or colour. Fred favoured a bright mustard-yellow waistcoat which gave him the air of a dandy, which seemed strangely at odds with his quiet personality.

Sixth-formers also had more contact with girls at the nearby Manning School. But Fred was so shy and awkward with girls that he barely spoke to any. Yet, physically, he remained far more mature than many of his contemporaries. With his sideburns he was often teased about similarities to Elvis, although most of the High Pavement boys preferred Buddy Holly, regarded as the 'thinking man's rocker'. Studious, hardworking Fred Shipman had little time for pop music. He was more interested in pleasing his mother by getting good grades in his Biology, Physics and Chemistry A-levels.

She was clearly the driving force in his life.

CHAPTER TWO

Lessons in Loss

Just after Fred Shipman's seventeenth birthday in January 1963, something happened to him that would completely alter the course of his life; his beloved mother Vera was diagnosed with cancer. Active, house-proud Vera Shipman would soon be a mere shadow of her former self. She became emaciated, gaunt and debilitated. Seeing Fred at the end of each day when he walked in from school rallied her, but as the weeks went by she was soon struggling even to walk. With Pauline – now 25 – and Fred's father Harold at work, and youngest son Clive just 13, it was only natural that Fred would become his mother's main carer.

The family's GP, Dr Andrew Campbell, gave Vera injections of morphine in ever-increasing dosages to try to ease the pain, during house visits. Fred noticed how morphine seemed to make his mother happier. As the doctor injected his mother, her pain-lined face positively lit up after the drugs kicked in. Vera Shipman spent much of her time sitting in the front room of the family's immaculately clean council house, gazing out of the window trying to ignore the agony that wracked her withering body.

Vera had undoubtedly been a very controlling influence throughout young Fred Shipman's childhood. She had originally set about isolating him, not letting him play with the other children. She'd encouraged him to go to grammar school, which isolated him further from those around him. Even when he was good at sports, it somehow didn't provide him with a bridge to other people.

Now she was about to leave Fred – her pride and joy – just when he was beginning his life. Vera Shipman said little to the other family members but neighbours recall her spending hours talking to Fred as he sat next to her in the front room. Vera got Fred to promise that he would continue his studies. She wanted him to escape from the poverty trap and make a real success of himself.

Vera died on the afternoon of Friday, 21 June 1963, shortly after saying her final goodbyes to the family. Fred got home from school after she'd already gone. A harrowing weekend for the teenager followed although, he dared not show any of his emotions to the outside world.

Older sister Pauline was the only other woman he had ever known. But his mother was the one he had felt most comfortable with. She was his driving force; the one person who seemed to understand what he was thinking. Now she was gone. A storm raged inside young Fred's head about his mother's death. It all seemed so unfair. It wasn't just an empty void he felt. He was shattered, mentally and physically, after staying with her through so many painful nights as she lay close to death.

A strange, silent stillness came over the tiny room as young Fred realised that his beloved mother had gone for ever. The hush was only broken by the quivering of his father's voice as he tried to make Fred step outside, away from his mother's corpse. The atmosphere was unimaginable; it just didn't seem possible that such a thing could happen … it was so unfair.

But outside the Shipman house in the hours following her death, a different storm raged as it poured with rain. Fred Shipman – the athlete who had played rugby for the city's

Under-15s side – now had distinctly unmanly tears streaming down his cheeks. He walked out of the front room where his mother's corpse remained and into the hallway, laced up his track shoes and rushed out into the deluge to run. Shipman pounded the streets, water streaking down his cheeks, diluting the endless flow of tears.

The teenager was working out his grief alone, shedding tears in the rain, torn by sadness and relief. Running and running and running to escape the atmosphere at home. However, he was also pounding the pavement in order to gain mastery of his emotions, to take control and lose himself in physical endurance. His mother had told him to be strong and not let her death ruin his chances of escape.

But he found it hard to suppress feelings of grief, loss, relief, guilt, anger, helplessness and they all came out as he ran through the driving rain. Fred Shipman continued right through that night and did not arrive home until 3.00am. He was emotionally and physically spent.

Fred, his sister Pauline and brother Clive put on a brave face for the sake of their father but it wasn't easy. Fred believed his mother would want him to be strong. His sister cried frequently, as did his younger brother and it fell to teenage Fred and his father to organise the funeral arrangements; Vera's coffin was set up in the downstairs room where she had taken her last breath. The room was filled with flowers from friends and neighbours.

When Fred walked to school the following Monday, classmate Mike Heath asked him, 'What did you do at the weekend?'

'Oh,' replied Fred a little nervously, 'my mum died.'

Mike Heath didn't even know that Vera Shipman had been ill. 'I'm so sorry – are you all right, mate?'

'Yeah, I went for a run,' came the reply.

* * *

On the morning of the funeral, Fred helped to carry the coffin, which was placed on a horse-drawn carriage. Fred didn't hold his brother or sister's hands at all as the family stood in their appropriate place in preparation for the one-mile walk to the cemetery. As the carriage pulled out of Longmead Drive, the pavements contained a few neighbours and inquisitive residents, who wanted to give Vera a good send-off; some even joined in the procession and walked solemnly behind the family but young Fred knew that his mother would never really have approved of that.

They first walked half-a-mile down the road to the church. A local policeman stopped and stood on the street corner and courteously raised his helmet as the procession passed by. On reaching the church, a small group of half-a-dozen other friends and relatives awaited the coffin.

After the service, the mourners followed the carriage another half-a-mile to the cemetery where Vera was buried alongside her mother and grandparents.

Fred hardly mentioned his mother's death to his classmates, but he wore a black armband over his blazer for a while. And he couldn't stop visualising her during those last few days of her life. He now knew that he had to become a doctor because then he could try and save people like his mother from the sort of painful, lingering death that she had suffered. No one should ever have to go though that, young Fred Shipman thought to himself.

Fred's overall numb response was typical of his personality at that time even though his dark broodiness made him a figure of respect inside the school. Many considered him more mature than most of his classmates, while he was actually very under-developed in many ways.

'I can't think of one really close friendship he struck up,' said classmate Bob Studholme who also remembered that, despite him being a handsome teenager, 'I can't remember seeing Fred with a girl.'

For the final month of that school summer term, Fred continued wearing a black tie and armband. He later admitted to classmate Michael Heath that taking that long run through the night following her death 'was how I got it out of my system'.

But the reality was that Fred Shipman never worked out his highly complicated feelings about his dearly departed mother. That image of her dying would stay with him for ever. It wasn't just an occasional flashback. It came to him every single day without fail and she dominated his dreams as well.

His father was a decent, hard-working man who liked a flutter at the bookies and had simple tastes and few ambitions. He continued driving the local council's vans in the summer and their gritting trucks in the winter. But it was his wife Vera who'd been behind Fred's success and now she had gone. In a sense, Fred felt abandoned by her but he also felt an obligation to fight on to show her what a success he would become. But his few friends at the time never forgot how – after her death – not one of them was ever invited back to his home again.

Not surprisingly, the entire family was in a serious state of shock following Vera's death. They had to face the painful reality of life without her, knowing that they would never again come home from work or school and find her cooking tea. To young Fred, it seemed so strange that people in the outside world were continuing to go about their business as if nothing had happened.

Fred felt he did not have anyone to comfort him. His sister and brother had been well aware that he was Vera's favourite child and that they had shared a much closer relationship with each other. Fred was stuck in the middle and he felt incredibly lonely. And the memories of his mother wouldn't fade.

Fred rarely ventured out apart from going to and from school in the months following Vera's death. He hated the way other people looked at him with such pity and sorrow. They didn't even know her, he thought to himself. They don't know just how special she really was.

Both Pauline and Clive realised that Fred was taking his mother's death the worst. One day, Pauline even knelt down in front of Fred in the house and looked at him with her sad puppy-dog eyes and tried to get him to talk about it, but he just got up and walked away. His only way to deal with the loss was to bottle it up. And Fred believed there had to be something more than this humdrum existence, and how he longed for it. His mother had been completely right; he had to get away.

* * *

Back on the rugby field, Fred Shipman still showed no fear which made him a terrifying opponent. He clearly revelled in the rougher aspects of the game. Sports were clearly important for him. It was a means of letting off steam and Fred certainly managed that.

Fred Shipman was also a very good long-distance runner and became vice-captain of the school athletics team in his final year. He even merited various accolades in *The Pavior* student magazine for his contributions to school and house teams for both rugby and athletics. But many noticed that following the death of his mother, Fred Shipman became increasingly disassociated from his classmates. He refused to meet up with any of them at local pubs at weekends. Many presumed he had never even tasted alcohol.

However, Fred had an interest in something more intriguing than booze; he had become secretly addicted to sniffing Sloan's Liniment. Fellow cross-country runner Terry Swinn recalled that Shipman became obsessed with using Sloan's Liniment, a pungent-smelling ointment used to ease aching muscles. 'Fred loved the smell of it. Some at the school suspected that he was addicted to sniffing it. We all used it but he was addicted,' said Terry Swinn.

Fred Shipman adored the feeling of relaxation that came over him as he sniffed the ointment in a similar way to how others sniffed glue. It was the only time when he could forget about his mother and all the trials and tribulations of his home life. Fred Shipman's addictive personality was already beginning to take shape. It was an ominous sign for the future.

Back on the rugby field, Fred's fearsome reputation began to fade as many of his contemporaries caught up with his height and weight. However, Fred remained very aloof and serious compared with most of the other sixth-form boys. 'We were often flash and stupid, running around twanging girls' suspenders and all that,' Bob Studholme later recalled. 'But Fred wouldn't take part. He was always on the edge of our group. He'd never demean himself with a dirty joke. Fred was serious; we were stupid. We thought he was old-fashioned.'

Classmate John Soar agreed, 'Fred didn't mix much but he didn't suck up to authority, so people admired him.'

On one occasion, the class went on a field study course to a nearby town called Slapton-Lee. Fred shocked his classmates by taking part in a massive beer-drinking session. It was the first time any of them had even seen him with alcohol. 'He wasn't a stick-in-the-mud. Fred was not in the inner circle but he was not on the outside looking in. He just did his own thing and we admired him for it,' remembers John Soar.

Getting drunk – like sniffing that ointment earlier – enabled Fred Shipman to overcome his shyness. He liked being drunk and having that brief respite from the relentless pressure to succeed. Shipman began thinking about alcohol and drugs and how they conveniently provided escape for people with emotional problems.

But Bob Studholme now, on reflection, believes that Fred was 'too quiet. I was an open book; he was a closed soul. Fred never came to any of our houses and we never went to his. We just didn't know his family.'

Perhaps, not so surprisingly, Fred Shipman got very poor grades in his three A-levels and agreed to stay on an extra year at High Pavement and take them all over again. And there was something about Fred Shipman that even back then commanded enough respect for him to be made Head Boy at High Pavement in that extra year he stayed on to get those better grades.

Fred even took on such important roles as readings at the school's Unitarian church in Nottingham city centre. He'd been elevated to Captain of the School following Terry Swinn's departure early in the new school year after passing his examination for entry to Cambridge. Terry Swinn recalls that Fred Shipman was a firm but fair deputy. 'Very straight up and down. If you asked him a question, he would give a straight answer.'

One of the most chilling things his contemporaries do remember about Fred Shipman is what one later described as a 'certain cold stare'. It was a look of icy indifference which, years later, others would recall replacing the bedside softness of the GP when yet another elderly female patient was close to death.

Fred's sister Pauline even became young Fred's 'date' at the twice-yearly rugby club dances in the school hall. Most found it amusing that he brought his elder sister and danced with her. Eight years older than her brother and somewhat taller, they made a strange-looking couple. Fred was clearly ill at ease with most girls.

Fred Shipman appeared detached from the everyday pursuits of a typical bunch of teenage classmates. On a rugby tour he wouldn't join in all the sing-songs.

Not surprisingly, Fred's sister Pauline became a substitute mother back in the Shipman household. Fred Shipman's aunt, Dorothy Emerson, who still lives in Nottingham, recalled, 'Fred was so young when Vera died and it hit him hard. Pauline virtually took over as his mother. She did the ironing, the cooking, everything, for his father as well.'

At the Shipman family home on Longmead Drive, the three children provided the bedrock for grieving Harold Shipman to survive. Neighbour Ursula Oldknow still has fond memories of old Mr Shipman to this day. 'He lived for his family. Most round these parts throw as much ale down their throats as possible, but not that family. They had real pride and determination.'

And the family remained extremely proud that young Fred

had made it to the top-notch grammar school. 'Harold knew Fred wanted to be different,' recalled Hannah Cutler, now 83, who knew the Shipman children well.

Shipman's contemporaries believe that young Fred's seeds of resentment emerged as he struggled to keep pace with the academic high-flyers at High Pavement. Such fears of inadequacy followed him through life. It was only when he became a GP that he gained standing and respect in the community and then began to show real self-confidence.

Fred left High Pavement in 1965 and he never once revisited his old school. His earlier feeling of pride at being at the school had been replaced by a gradual resentment about the formality within which he always felt a complete outsider. Few classmates were impressed by Fred.

Fred's A-level results were a B grade in Physics, C in Biology and D in Chemistry and he was accepted into Leeds University – 70 miles to the north of Nottingham – to read medicine (senior British Labour politician Jack Straw arrived at the same time to read Law). In 1965, there was a serious shortage of doctors in Britain so generous student grants were available. Fred qualified for a full student grant which amounted to £340, the equivalent of £3,720 in 2000.

Fred Shipman's family were still devastated by Vera's death and the house had become a joyless place. Old Harold Shipman spent many hours sitting alone in the front room sucking on a pipe, staring into oblivion, thinking back to the happy days when his beloved Vera was alive.

Fred Shipman's mother hoped medical school in Leeds would provide the escape she so desperately wanted for him. The outside world was changing with alarming pace. The swinging 1960s and the Beatles were the 'in thing'. Mini-skirts and mini cars dominated Britain.

Straight-laced Fred Shipman – who'd never had a girlfriend, disapproved of dirty jokes, never served a school detention and was even afraid of sneaking a cup of tea during a cross-country run – was about to get the ultimate wake-up call.

* * *

At medical school in Leeds, the difference between Fred Shipman's age – he was nearly 20 because he'd had to retake his exams – and the other more academically attuned 18-year-olds again marked him out as different, making him even more of a loner. And Fred Shipman seemed strangely obsessed with casting off his former life in Nottingham. He never played rugby again. He buckled down to his studies, constantly driven by the thought that this was what his mother would have wanted.

By this time, Fred Shipman was thinner but extremely dapper. One student at Leeds even went so far as to describe him as 'rather spivvy, wiry and dark'. But despite Fred's swarthy, almost Latin, good looks, he was still shy, introverted and definitely not one of the boys at medical school, although plenty of girls noticed him because of his handsome features.

Most presumed that Fred Shipman would probably start enjoying life to the full when he got to Leeds University. But if he did hang out in bars and nightclubs, it certainly didn't last long because, within a few months of starting his degree, at the age of 20, the next major change in his life was about to occur. Her name was Primrose Oxtoby.

CHAPTER THREE

A Clandestine Marriage

Primrose Oxtoby was named after the beautiful flowers that lined the steep Yorkshire lanes and blossomed in the hedgerows near her family home. Her birth, on 19 April 1949, was supposed to represent new hope and joy for the Oxtoby family. Parents Edna and George, who managed a farm at Huttons Ambo, near York, in the north of England, were already the parents of two other children and, at 39 and 44, they were old-fashioned in both age and values.

By the time Primrose reached school age in 1954, the young Elizabeth II had been crowned Queen of England and the family had moved to the tiny hamlet of East Rigton, between Leeds and Wetherby, where father George continued his career as a farm foreman. They lived in a small tied cottage at the bottom of a lane near the farm where he worked.

Primrose's mother Edna hated her daughter playing in the yard with friends. Edna saw it as 'unnecessary'. If Primrose got her dress dirty she was in real trouble. Edna believed her youngest daughter would be contaminated by other people's relaxed attitudes. When children did play with Primrose, it had to be near her home and playmates had be personally approved by Edna. At primary school in nearby Bardsey, little Primrose rarely joined in with the other children.

At home, if Primrose's friends made any noise, her mother would insist they went home immediately.

At home, Edna Oxtoby remained a strict disciplinarian. Primrose sometimes burst into tears at school; but most of the time she kept it all bottled up inside herself, which can't have been healthy. Primrose escaped her misery by retreating into her own little world. She felt alone, battling against her parents and the sneers and teasing of many of her classmates. It was an attitude that would persist in later life as well.

When Primrose was eleven, her parents inherited some money and moved the family from their tiny tied cottage to a substantial stone-built, semi-detached house in the nearby town of Wetherby. Primrose started at Wetherby County Secondary Modern in 1960. It was a five-minute walk from the family's new home, which perched on a hillside overlooking the town centre. The 1876-built property was in a row of four matching pairs, each referred to as 'villas' to attract professional, middle-class people who might commute to nearby Leeds. Wetherby attracted many visitors with the River Wharfe forming a picturesque southern boundary for the town plus the nearby racecourse and the beautiful Yorkshire Dales. George Oxtoby eventually got a job as a road labourer earning £10 a week. It was just enough to support his family.

Although Primrose was considered a bright child before she hit her teens, she failed to make the grades to be offered a place at one of the area's better schools. That meant Primrose was destined to leave school at 15 without even taking any of the elementary British qualifications, such as O-Levels.

Primrose was certainly different from most other children. With few real friends, often she'd end up alone in the corner of the school yard.

On Sundays Primrose, her mother, Edna and her sister, Mary, attended the 10.00am service at the Methodist Church in Bank

Street. Afterwards at the church hall they'd to listen to parables and sing hymns. Sometimes there were even lectures on morality. There was also Sunday School, where children discussed the meaning of Bible stories.

Edna Oxtoby's most important priority for her two children was that they had proper and decent lives. Primrose was forbidden from attending the local youth clubs where they played rock and roll and twisted the night away. There were no visits to the local cinema or any question of her talking to boys. Primrose must have been frustrated but she never confronted her mother. Visitors to the house said the atmosphere was always tense. Meanwhile Primrose's older sister Mary was training to be a nurse at a local hospital near Wetherby. Primrose did a newspaper round from the age of 13 which enabled her to get free comics. She adored girly stories of horses and fairytale princes in magazines like *Bunty*, the only publication her mother permitted into her home. There was a piano, which Primrose struggled to play. Father George Oxtoby loved tending to his rows of vegetables in the back garden, in his flat cap and with a roll-up cigarette in his mouth. While Edna's home-made pies and cakes encouraged weight problems in the house.

Primrose was rarely allowed out to play at weekends. She sat with her parents reading or doing needlework. Primrose did have pet rabbits in a hutch in the garden and the family had a small black poodle dog.

Primrose thrived on the local Girl Guide troupe which held weekly meetings, as well as days out and occasional weekend camps. Primrose, in her navy-blue sweater, slacks and wellies, joined in and got on with things. She adored it. With short hair, and tomboyish in appearance, she loved organising food for the rest of the troupe.

The most daring thing Primrose ever did at Girl Guides was asking for a cigarette from a group of young police cadets whom they met while out hiking. But she only took a couple of puffs at it and never smoked again.

Primrose's mother Edna was a tough uncompromising sort of woman. When one neighbour asked the family to stop building work on a fireplace at midnight, they received a handwritten note from Edna in their mailbox next morning stating that from that moment on she would have nothing more to do with them. They were never spoken to again.

While many of Primrose's classmates adored pirate radio stations, saved up for Beatles records, and dolled themselves up for dances in local village halls, Primrose remained at home with her parents trapped in a twilight world.

Primrose was a real plain Jane back then, tortured by her own lack of charisma. With her pudding-basin hairstyle, scrubbed face, twinset and pearls, pleated skirts and clumpy flat shoes is barely remembered. Her name was the only thing which stood out. She was renowned for her stubbornness.

At 15, Primrose was 5ft 4in tall with a sturdy build that attracted glances from the teenage boys of Wetherby. However, Primrose knew times were changing and was determined to show her mother she had an independent spirit, unlike her.

Older sister Mary settled into a job as a nurse in an old people's home but never married. Mary later developed multiple sclerosis and moved into a care home because she could not look after herself.

Primrose's sex education was non-existant as neither of her parents ever discussed the facts of life with her. There was no mention of pregnancy or contraception, or even what a period was, leaving Primrose to probe these subjects with other girls at school.

In September 1964, Primrose was just fifteen-and-a-half years old and about to start a college course in Leeds after winning herself a place on an art and design course. She did one painting of hats which was so good it is remembered to this day.

Primrose and a group of her school and Girl Guide friends rode by bus into Leeds for their various jobs and colleges. They talked about clothes, make-up, music ... and boys.

Those 40-minute bus rides into Leeds were exciting for

Primrose, especially since she knew her mother didn't like her being out in the big wide world. That year at college helped Primrose become more independent of her parents. Sometimes, she even defied her mother by coming back late in the evening from college after stopping for a coffee with a friend.

At the end of that year, Primrose was awarded a college certificate and got a job as a window dresser. She soon even bought new, modern clothes and make-up. She also went to the cinema with friends. And each morning she caught the number 38 bus into the centre of Leeds. Then one day, she spotted a handsome, dark-haired young man sitting at the back of the bus.

* * *

Medical student Fred Shipman was living in digs at 164 Wetherby Road, Wetherby, in an area called Wellington Hill. Landlady Mrs Copley took in students as a sideline to supplement the takings from the family greengrocery business. Fred and another student at the same digs, Peter Congdon, dressed immaculately as they travelled on the 38 bus to medical school each day.

Towards the end of his first year at medical school, Fred Shipman caught Primrose glancing across at him. Shy Fred Shipman looked away. For many weeks he didn't speak to her, but Primrose was determined. She even told one friend in a giggly voice, 'He keeps catching my eye on the bus …' By the end of that month, she predicted to the same friend, 'We'll marry some day.'

Primrose began loathing this snotty young student with his wavy black hair and was on the verge of giving up her attempts when suddenly he began talking to her. Primrose's friends on the bus had watched as shy, plain Primrose fell for the dark stranger. Primrose had no one to ask advice about this blossoming relationship. She didn't even dare tell her mother she had met a boy.

Teenage Primrose, just 16, knew absolutely nothing about

sex. She hadn't been given any sex education at school and she'd never even had a boyfriend. Back in the mid-Sixties less than 8 per cent of all babies were born out of wedlock, compared with five times that amount today.

In many ways, Fred and Primrose were made for each other. There were many subjects they simply knew nothing about. They were both nervous – almost afraid – of the ever-changing world around them. Even photos in newspapers of scantily-clad women brought embarrassed responses from Fred Shipman.

Fred and Primrose shared furtive glances on top of a double-decker bus and little else.

* * *

When losing one's virginity, said Queen Victoria, one must close one's eyes and think of England. Attaching a little more lyricism to the act, the great romantics, from Cervantes to Byron, saw virgins as roses and their deflowering a poem to passions that would saddle lions.

Fred Shipman's first and only taste of real romance – not necessarily the actual act of making love, but certainly a beginning – came within a few days of meeting his first ever girlfriend Primrose Oxtoby. After all those brief exchanges on the double-decker bus, Primrose found herself with no choice but to make the first move. She'd even told the shy medical student, 'Are you going to take me to the pictures or what?'

Primrose found him an attractive but not exactly cool operator. He even had a chipped tooth from an old rugby scrap, but all it did was add to his demeanour.

The night of their first date, Fred and Primrose met secretly at the end of her street before jumping on a bus to the local cinema in Wetherby. However, as Primrose later told one of her few friends, they hardly touched each other that night and conversation between the two was strained because of Fred's shyness. But Primrose was not easily deterred.

A few nights later, she and Fred shared a few beers in a local pub and once again she had to make the first move. She got things going by casually dropping a hand on the seat beside him. Then she started playing with his fingers. Minutes later, they finished their drinks and lunged at each other in a nearby alleyway, sort of kissing, only they didn't seem able to put their mouths in the right place at first.

Fred's head was spinning and he could hardly breathe with excitement. Primrose could hear her heart banging away in her eardrums. Once or twice, she opened her eyes to make sure his eyes were closed, and they were, so she reckoned he must have meant it.

After that, the couple felt as if they had already made love and could talk more easily together. Things soon got pretty hot and heavy between them. Fred and Primrose were floating along, clinging to each other for dear life. They knew there was no one and nothing else that mattered from that moment onwards. Primrose quickly found herself contemplating a future with this shy, awkward medical student. Fred was still hiding the pain and anguish of losing his mother, so being romantic was a welcome diversion, although he remained terrified of rejection.

One day Primrose astonished her parents by bringing Fred Shipman home. She'd never had a boyfriend before and now here she was standing with a fully-grown medical student in the dark and austere living room of the Oxtoby house in Wetherby. Fred was usually silent and moody in company, but on this day he tried to be more animated, making small-talk about his plans for the future. Primrose's parents were deeply suspicious of this handsome-looking young man with his wavy, jet-black hair. He talked very quietly and properly and his voice was so gentle they found it difficult to understand what he was saying.

By the time Fred had departed, Primrose's parents had already turned against their daughter's first boyfriend. Mr Oxtoby told Primrose he was too old for her and she should have nothing more to do with him. But within weeks they were inseparable, although Primrose never again brought Fred back to meet her family.

Eventually, heavy kissing soon led much further for Fred and Primrose. Making love was a new joy that neither knew much about previously. But despite Fred Shipman's medical training, he made no attempt to use a condom, although he later admitted to being so shy that he couldn't bring himself to go into a chemist for a packet of three. Fred and Primrose were reckless and inexperienced.

Primrose was only three years younger than Fred but that gap was huge back then at 19 and 16 respectively. Primrose was deeply impressed by Fred's university status and his profound dislike of her parents was based entirely on their dislike of him. They saw through him and were suspicious of his motives.

Fred and Primrose were soon quite domesticated. Primrose cooked for friends at Fred's digs and guests later recalled that the food was excellent, but the atmosphere in the house was depressing.

It was hardly surprising when Primrose got pregnant, although their few friends were shocked. In Britain at that time, the legal age for sex was 16. Years later, Shipman claimed to a friend it had all been an awful mistake. Would Shipman have ever married Primrose if the pregnancy hadn't happened? We will probably never know.

But this child would give Primrose the perfect chance to escape from her disciplinarian mother. And Fred Shipman seemed happy to marry Primrose, despite later misgivings.

Primrose shared the news of her pregnancy with a couple of close girlfriends, who were stunned that their gentle, overweight friend had been sleeping with the man. They were particularly worried about how Primrose's parents might react to the news.

Primrose still hadn't told her mother at that stage. She knew they wouldn't be exactly thrilled but this was her opportunity to start her own life.

In fact, both families were horrified by the news. Harold

Shipman even told his son he was relieved his wife was dead. Fred was mortified because he would never have done anything to upset his dearly departed mother. And his sister Pauline simply refused to talk about the 'scandal'. Fred would never forgive them for their cruel response at his time of need. Things had been building up to this ever since Vera Shipman's death. Fred Shipman now felt completely estranged from his family. He just wished his mother was still alive to give him some help and support.

Primrose's parents Edna and George were equally upset about the pregnancy. Pregnancy out of wedlock was shameful even though the young couple had already announced they were arranging a wedding. Edna wouldn't even let Fred and Primrose get married in Wetherby in case people might see Primrose's bump.

Fred Shipman was a hated figure, despite his bright future as a doctor. There was something unpleasant about young Fred. Neither Edna nor George could put their finger on it. He seemed morbid and non-communicative. And his eyes always seemed so shifty.

But Fred and Primrose decided their wedding should go ahead and they set a date for 5 November 1966 when Shipman would have just completed his first year at medical school.

* * *

Hand in hand, the young lovers climbed the steps of the Barkstone Ash Register Office on 5 November 1966. The bride wore a long blue dress. The groom wore a white shirt, a dark tie and an ill-fitting black suit that would have more befitted a funeral than a wedding. Once inside, streams of light from the stained-glass dome highlighted the shine of Primrose's dark page-boy hairstyle. She was a tad on the plump side. Fred and Primrose clung to the iron-rail banister as they ascended the stone steps to the ground-floor office of the registrar of Births, Marriages and Deaths.

From the large windows that spanned the spacious room, they could see the vast trees of the adjoining park, as well as some of the civic buildings that dated from before Victorian times. Within minutes, they were husband and wife.

Fred and Primrose pledged each other complete and utter loyalty before retiring to a nearby pub without any of their few relatives and friends, who had already dispersed. Primrose's mother and Fred's father were present but they barely exchanged glances. That was it; the start of married life. No honeymoon. No gifts. No smiles from dozens of guests. No speeches. Just a functional marriage for a functional reason.

It hadn't exactly been the type of wedding that every young girl dreams of, but that didn't matter one iota to Primrose. She couldn't have been happier; all that mattered to her was that she had married the man of her dreams. To complete the day (and night) he took her back to his digs and carried her over the threshold.

Primrose was a quietly spoken, shy window-dresser whose family came from similar working-class stock to the Shipmans. Primrose might not have had the same high-flying ambitions as her young husband, but she was fiercely loyal. Some of Fred's fellow students at Leeds University recall Primrose getting 'quite aggressive' whenever anything negative was said about her husband Fred.

Primrose's pregnancy at the age of 17 had opened a gaping wound between her and her strict Methodist parents which would never heal.

Primrose lived the final few weeks of her pregnancy at her parents' home in Wetherby. Fred never once made an appearance at the house and the couple usually met at nearby cafés.

On 14 February 1967, at Harrogate General Hospital, Primrose had a baby daughter, Sarah Rosemary. But her parents' relations with Primrose and Fred remained difficult. The young family eventually found an apartment in the Woodhouse district of Leeds, a student area filled with small houses converted into flats and bedsits on narrow streets.

Fred and Primrose presented a picture of contentment and normality to the outside world. Primrose respected him for doing the right thing and marrying her when she fell pregnant and trusted him totally. She believed he would make a fine doctor, encouraging him not to be distracted by baby Sarah as he laboured over lecture notes at night. Primrose believed she and Fred could take on the world. Nothing else mattered.

Primrose, not yet 18, enjoyed running a home; she knew about cleaning and cooking, and she adored baking cakes and pies.

One of the first students to encounter Mr and Mrs Shipman was Dr Susan Pearson – also married and with a baby while still a student at Leeds. She and a couple of other students were invited by Fred for tea. Primrose quickly laid out tea, sandwiches and cakes within minutes of their arrival.

Baby Sarah was by now a toddler, and toys were scattered about the room, which was clean and well cared for. It was more homely than the usual student flat, because of the baby's things. Primrose said little, busily offering guests drinks and food.

But Primrose's emotionally immature husband's views about his own mother's death were still omnipresent in his own mind. He still couldn't forgive Vera Shipman for leaving him at such a young age. Was this why he rushed into that relationship with Primrose?

The Pressure Bottle

CHAPTER FOUR

The Pressure Builds

M an is an evolving creature, with various levels of need. His evolution tends to happen in so-called 'leaps'. When he first tries to master a skill it doesn't come easily, then suddenly it becomes demotified and, eventually, natural.

The same is true of anyone's personal evolution: we quite suddenly care about something that was a matter of total indifference a few days earlier. A child who has always thought nothing of stealing wakes up one morning to find he's outgrown those urges. But in Fred Shipman's case, he'd failed to grow up.

Basic moral common sense just did not evolve in young Fred Shipman. Many might say that, because his main guiding light – his mother – left him at such an early, impressionable age, he didn't know where certain behavioural boundaries existed. It meant he was capable of anything, irrespective of whether it was good or bad.

Fred Shipman was an impoverished 20-year-old medical student facing the intense pressures of being a husband and father. Occasionally, he escaped it all by slipping down to the local pub and downing a few pints of beer while Primrose stayed at home with their baby daughter.

Fred and other medical school students, working in pairs, were encouraged to carry out experiments on themselves. These included measuring each other's oxygen consumption, swallowing tubes to monitor gastric juices and even drinking gallons of water to measure its intoxicating effect, plus a grisly experiment in which blood was taken from earlobes.

This was when Fred Shipman encountered morphine for the first time since it had been used by doctors to ease the pain of his mother's cancer. Fred Shipman was soon fascinated with morphine and carried out his own 'experiment' to discover if his mother really was 'put out of her pain' as the Shipmans' GP had said as he administered the drug to her during the last few weeks of her life. One night after downing a few pints of beer at his local pub, Fred pitched home to find Primrose fast asleep and decided it was time to find out if morphine really did work.

The following morning, Primrose found her husband slumped asleep on the armchair in the living room. She presumed he'd fallen asleep after drinking a few beers. He didn't tell Primrose that he'd injected himself with one of the most potent drugs known to mankind. It had been a wonderful feeling. All his fears disappeared. He didn't get high. He didn't get stoned. He just didn't give a damn.

* * *

At the end of Fred Shipman's second year at medical school in Leeds, he was put into specific groups, usually of four, on two-month cycles, so that students got to work with a cross section of their contemporaries once they began the practical part of their studies in specific hospitals around the area for the following three years. Much of Fred Shipman's time was spent at the Leeds General Infirmary, but there were also stints at St James's, in Menston, and the Highroyd Hospital, in Leeds. There was even one stint in Wakefield, 30 miles to the east of the city.

Other students noticed at the time that Fred Shipman was particularly fascinated with corpses, which were often used during lectures and for practical experimentation. 'Fred had absolutely no qualms about handling a body, while many of us were a bit squeamish to say the least,' one Leeds student later recalled.

On one occasion, Shipman was found in the hospital morgue at Wakefield some hours after all his fellow students had gone home. He later said he'd stayed behind to spend more time studying the body. But then he was one of those slightly geeky types anyway, so no one was that surprised.

At the end of that three years came a month of final exams. Shipman graduated as a Bachelor of Medicine/ Surgery and was registered as a doctor with the General Medical Council, number 1470473, on 5 August 1971.

In fact, Shipman had scraped a pass and immediately began looking for a position as a pre-registration doctor. Many of Fred's fellow students found proper placements in Leeds hospitals, but married students like him needed to get a junior housemanship position, where there might be accommodation for his young family.

Shipman eventually got a position at a hospital in the nearby town of Pontefract which had the perfect accommodation for Primrose and little Sarah, now a lively three-year-old. Working as a houseman at the Pontefract General Infirmary involved long hours, low pay and numerous emergency room incidents. It was the ultimate test of character.

Nine months after starting at Pontefract, the Shipman's second child, Christopher Frederick Shipman, was born at Wakefield Maternity Hospital on 21 April 1971. The family lived in the grounds of the hospital in a red-brick 1930s-built house. Living within the hospital made life much easier for Fred Shipman because of the long hours he worked. There were plenty of shops and amenities for Primrose and their two young children.

The course at Pontefract was incredibly intense, leaving students with little spare time. The early years at medical school had meant visits to wards to meet real patients, but now Fred was out on his own. He had to learn how to deal with people, to treat patients with respect, be polite and understanding and honest.

However, Fred Shipman wasn't exactly a medical high-flyer. His leap into marriage and fatherhood had been made partly to help him avoid the more lively social scene favoured by many medical students. Most junior doctors at Pontefract popped over the road to the Victoria, the local pub, for a chat and a pint of beer, while Fred would wearily pack up his books and shuffle off home to Primrose. The only time he drank was alone at another pub where he knew he wouldn't bump into any other medics.

Shipman never openly complained about his predicament. In fact, he'd often proudly refer to his two young children and wife in the most glowing terms. 'It was almost as if he felt a little superior to us because he was already at a more adult stage of his life,' recalled one former student.

Fred Shipman retained that burning ambition to do well in the medical profession. He was single-minded. It wasn't going to be easy to succeed after coming from an under-privileged background but he really wanted to make it. Having a young family and keeping up his studies required a very focused attitude. He was under severe pressure, struggling financially. But Fred Shipman firmly believed he could overcome such obstacles. In any case, he felt his mother Vera was watching over him the whole time and he didn't want to let her down.

At Pontefract General Infirmary, Shipman worked under general surgeon consultant Mr L C Bell, aural surgery consultant Mr K Mayll and medical consultant Dr J Turner. After two years, he would be qualified for full registration with the General Medical Council. And while still living in the hospital accommodation at Friarwood Lane, Pontefract, he also took a diploma in child health and a Royal College Diploma in Obstetrics and Gynaecology.

Throughout this period, Fred Shipman's interest in drugs continued to grow. Thanks to the long hours and gruelling work schedule at Pontefract, Shipman began using another easily available narcotic called pethidine. It was a dangerous move for someone who undoubtedly had an addictive personality.

Fred Shipman was first attracted to pethidine in order to 'come down' after his adrenalin-filled casualty department shifts so that he could get some sleep. He worked incredibly long hours before going home to Primrose and the children. But once he'd started using pethidine, he soon needed more and more. He enjoyed the sensation that pethidine produced – a 'wide open' state of mind, as if he could not 'pull down the shutters against the blazing light of reality that was beating through the window', one regular user later explained.

Pethidine, similar to another opiate, morphine, was known in the medical profession as a strong narcotic analgesic. Pethidine tended to be used mainly in hospitals to relieve severe pain felt during labour and after operations. Sometimes, it was used as a premedication before surgery.

Shipman adored the rapid rush that pethidine caused. As one who has taken it frequently explained, 'It takes effect quickly but its effect lasts only for a short time. But it takes you to such heights that it's worth the ride.'

That meant Shipman could inject himself just before he knew he was going to have 30 minutes alone after work. Then he would sit down, roll up his sleeve and deliver the pin prick, his nerves already tingling with expectation.

Pethidine quickly proved itself habit-forming for Fred Shipman. As one user explained very clinically, 'Both tolerance and dependence can develop when the drug is used regularly.' In other words, using pethidine for anything other than a genuine medical reason was highly risky.

Hospitals recommended using a maximum dosage of 150mg every four hours. Shipman was soon taking doses every two hours. But he knew only too well what to look for in terms of an overdose reaction. As one medical reference book pointed out,

'Seek immediate medical advice in all cases. Take emergency action if there are any symptoms such as muscle twitching, nervousness, shallow breathing, severe drowsiness, or loss of consciousness.'

Driving under the influence of pethidine was a highly risky undertaking. And any use of alcohol could seriously increase the sedative effects of the drug. If it had not been for the discovery of drugs, Fred Shipman later surmised, he might not have got through medical school and the pressures of being a father at such a young age. Pethidine seemed to remove the usual 'filters' from his normal perception of life. It felt as if he was playing a record player at full volume, with all the tone controls turned up to maximum level. But that filter was there to aid his mind to work and grasp at a strange kind of reality.

Pethidine weakened his willpower while undoubtedly strengthening his incoming stimuli, which meant that he immediately experienced an increase in intensified perception. It was the perfect drug to enable him to continue his long, arduous hours in Pontefract. But injecting himself with drugs was a risky business because it weakened certain elements of his self-control. It was all a question of maintaining a balance.

Shipman rapidly became frightened and fatigued by his over-use of illicit drugs. He was subjecting his body to endless abuse and with those drugs came a general mistrust of the world around him. Life was already becoming confused for Fred Shipman. Work was strange and impersonal. He wanted to simply withdraw inside himself, roll up in a ball, like a child in a warm bed, and pull the blankets up. But he couldn't do that because he had already burdened himself with so many responsibilities.

The strain of his job as an overworked, underpaid junior doctor was producing an inner revulsion for all around him. He talked to few of his colleagues and seemed guarded most of the time. He'd long since decided to mind his own business which is, in fact, a mild form of schizophrenia, a self-chosen state of isolation that was on the verge of turning into complete alienation from people in general. In many ways, Shipman was already close to committing 'mental suicide'. The drugs had encouraged this impersonal state of mind and he was living what could be described as an air-conditioned nightmare. His mind had become a wasteland of confusion.

But his use of drugs did give Fred Shipman the confidence to begin looking for a job as a general practitioner. He and Primrose both agreed that they wanted to stay in the Yorkshire area. Eventually, he spotted a job advertisement in a medical magazine for a position at the main medical centre in the town of Todmorden.

It seemed the perfect place for a young, ambitious doctor to make a name for himself.

CHAPTER FIVE

Pillar of the Community

Todmorden was a quiet, unassuming market town sitting on the edge of the Pennines amongst countryside of high moorlands, limestone slopes, steep-sided valleys and plunging waterfalls. Its plentiful supply of water provided the basis for a thriving cotton industry in the mid- to late 1800s when much of the income from manufacturing was ploughed back into the community. Todmorden lay in the shadow of vast Whirlaw Hill and, at the end of the day, the sun dropped behind the hill as gusts from the craggy slopes shook the red and pink seasonal decorations at the top of the town's main road called Halifax Street.

Todmorden was a self-contained town, a ribbon of dark Victorian millstone grit in a narrow defile where the River Calder cut deep into high, wild moors. There was barely enough room for the main road to Burnley and the Trans-Pennine railroad to squeeze through the gap. As a border town, Todmorden was governed by a Yorkshire local authority but had a Lancashire postal address. Up the valley was the once mighty cotton capital of Burnley; downstream was Halifax. In all other directions nothing but bleak moor – the kind where Cathy Earnshaw might be found calling for her Heathcliff.

Todmorden's damp, bronchial climate, exacerbated by clinging mists that lingered in the steep valley, made it one of England's great cotton towns, with 1,800 looms clattering through the Victorian fog.

In Todmorden, as everywhere else in the industrial North of England, the basic industry set the pattern of life; steel in Sheffield, coal in Barnsley, wool in Bradford and Huddersfield. In Todmorden – up until the First World War of 1914–18 – cotton had been Britain's most successful industry. That industry gave Todmorden a Lancashire way of working and living carried over to Yorkshire's steep valleys. Red-brick mills rose across the horizon back then; and life centred on those mills.

Todmorden's physical decay in the mid-1970s reflected its industrial heritage of the 1800s and the early 1900s. Yet there was a wealth of sturdy Victorian buildings and the once picturesque Rochdale canal waterway flowed right through the town. The population of Todmorden had fallen by 50 per cent and was standing at around 12,000 by the time Fred Shipman got his first job as a GP. There had been little investment in the town centre for many years and the poverty of many residents had even attracted European and Government funding for the rundown districts of the community. Todmorden needed to maintain its rail link, to renovate its canal, secure a stronger market town identity and refurbish a lot of buildings in the town centre if it was going to thrive as it had done during those boom years of the cotton industry 100 years earlier.

Civic pride, however, was still everywhere in Todmorden thanks mainly to the Fielden family, a powerful and benevolent mill-owning dynasty that gave tiny Todmorden a Grade I listed town hall which would not look out of place in a major city. By now its main use was as a ballroom and the venue for Monday afternoon tea dances.

Todmorden remained a hard place in many ways; the

churchyard contained numerous examples of child mortality. Many were laid beneath the earth in their twenties and thirties from climate, disease or the toil and danger of the Industrial Revolution. But the town had a long tradition of looking after itself. Maybe that is why newly-qualified Dr Fred Shipman found it so easy to blend in with the surroundings.

There was no cinema. Just 50 pubs and a club. The streets of Todmorden were usually deserted by 5.00pm. A few modern buildings had replaced the mills and the number of churches had shrunk to three. Yet much of the grey-stone housing remained as did many of the shops and businesses. It was just the type of place that Fred Shipman would feel at home in. In Todmorden, they liked to think that all their hard work in the cotton mills helped the south get even more prosperous, while they and the rest of the north of England fell further and further behind.

In March 1974, Fred was taken on as a junior GP at the Todmorden Group Practice run by Dr Michael Grieve. The handsome young doctor and his family were initially greeted as a breath of fresh air. Within a month, 'young Fred', as Grieve called him, was promoted from assistant to principal GP. He immediately rolled up his sleeves and began working day and night for the good of the practice. As Dr Grieve later recalled, 'Young Fred fitted in well. He was enthusiastic and interested in every stage of the medical profession. He was almost too good to be true.'

According to Dr Grieve, most patients adored him. 'He had a lot of fans. I remember there was one girl, whose baby he delivered, who still, to this day, thinks the world of him.'

The Shipmans purchased a picturesque grey-stone house on a street called Sunnyside on the hill overlooking the centre of Todmorden. It was a comfortable four-bedroom semi commanding excellent views, yet within walking distance of the surgery and all the town's main stores.

And Fred Shipman's treatment of patients went from strength to strength. When ten-year-old Karen Shepherd was diagnosed by another doctor as having blood poisoning, Fred Shipman stepped in and said it was osteomyetis. He was absolutely correct and, in effect, saved little Karen's life. Some months later, Karen's younger sister was diagnosed by Shipman as having a hole in the heart after other doctors had failed to pick it up. Senior partner Dr Grieve later recalled, 'He made that extra special bit of effort to find out what was wrong with a patient and it paid off handsomely.'

Another patient, lorry driver Frank Scott, never forgot how Shipman rushed over to his home to deliver Frank's wife's baby. A year later, he repeated the delivery with a second Scott child. 'The man was a saint, a really good person. He treated us so well. I'll never forget what he did for this family,' Frank Scott later recalled.

'Young Fred' even helped teach his colleagues how to fit intrauterine devices, which were then coming into use for the first time. 'He was very good technically and very good clinically,' recalled senior partner Dr Grieve. 'He'd got all the right qualifications and worked well. Mothers thought the world of him. Mind you, he was good with everyone.' Also, Shipman's strong Nottingham accent had a soothing effect on many patients. The fact that he didn't speak with a 'posh accent' made many feel less intimidated and more able to relax in his presence.

It was also noted inside the Todmorden practice that Fred Shipman was constantly pushing himself to the limit. 'He was always rushing around like a maniac. Always everything last minute. He never stopped,' recalled one patient. 'You couldn't keep up that pace without something happening. He was on course for a major burn-out.'

Fred Shipman had continued prescribing himself pethidine following his dabbling with the drug while at Pontefract General Infirmary. For the moment, no one in Todmorden had any idea their new young doctor was an intravenous drug addict, but some of the town's younger residents did hear other rumours.

Around this time – in 1974 – many of Shipman's younger patients heard that the handsome young doctor was willing to prescribe slimming tablets containing speed – amphetamines – even if the patient was clearly not overweight. The drug culture that had been sweeping Britain's youth for the previous ten years meant that many people under the age of 30 were willing to experiment with just about any narcotic.

One local girl who was supplied with amphetamines (she's now a happily married mother-of-three) recalled, 'We were all in our early 20s and you know what you're like, and someone said we could get these slimming pills off Dr Shipman. It was only him at the practice who was willing to supply them. He'd give them to you. All we had to do was go in and just ask him, simple as that. He didn't even bother weighing you to see if you were overweight. I went to see him at least once a month. He used to give me a big bottle with 100 amphetamine tablets. I'd take one and be up all night doing whatever. I can't remember how many times I went to see him but he never once bothered to examine me. Nothing. He was never awkward about supplying them and never made any comment about what they were really for. I'd be in and out in a minute. He'd just say "How Many?" Very cavalier attitude. When I realised afterwards what was in those tablets I thought it was strange.'

But it was the expression on Shipman's face that the woman patient never forgot. 'It was a really weird look, a kind of smirk would wipe across his face then it would return to doctor mode within a split-second. He looked so satisfied with himself. I'll remember that look for the rest of my life. When I thought about it later, it was obvious he knew exactly what he was doing. He just didn't talk about it directly. It's only afterwards I realised he must have known.'

But senior partner Dr Grieve wasn't surprised when he heard about Fred Shipman's illicit prescribing of slimming pills to some of the town's youth. He said, 'Most people prescribed sleeping pills easily at this time. He'd come from Pontefract which was where there was a big drug problem.'

At one stage, the surgery was given regular patrols by the local police following an incident when two men walked into the practice armed with a knife which they pointed at a pharmacist and then demanded drugs. Moments later, one of them tried to overdose in the treatment room. Many of the doctors in the practice had been physically attacked at some stage.

Meanwhile, the patients and staff had no idea that Fred Shipman was himself on a regular fix of pethidine at that time. 'He never seemed out of it. He was very nice. He was very, very popular,' recalled the woman who was prescribed the amphetamines.

She and her gang of friends used to visit all the nightclubs in nearby Wigan where the speed tablets would help them to stay up all night to dance. 'There wasn't much to do in Todmorden at the weekends, so it was a welcome relief to get out to Wigan. It was mainly young girls who took them, but when I decided to stop, I handed them over to a guy I knew who went and sold them off in one of the clubs in Wigan. I suppose Shipman might have thought he was living his youth through us.'

* * *

Behind Shipman's own drug addiction was another 'respectable' side to the young GP's life. He had become a much valued member of the Rochdale Canal Society, specifically set up to help preserve the local waterway that ran through the Todmorden valley. Society secretary Brian Holden explained, 'I was in awe of Fred in many ways. After all, he was a doctor and they were treated with the utmost respect in a place like Todmorden.'

Holden didn't discover until many years later that Shipman – who had already started to age at an alarming rate – was 15 years younger than him. 'I always presumed he was close to my age because he seemed to stoop and his reactions were like that of an older person.'

Even in his late 20s, Fred Shipman felt the pressures of

responsibility as a father, husband and local practitioner. 'He moved in a virtual shuffle, like a man approaching his fifties,' explained Brian Holden. 'I had a great deal of respect for him. In fact, we all tended to bow and scrape to Fred because he seemed such a caring doctor.'

Shipman was extremely reliable at turning up with Primrose at the Canal Society's Saturday afternoon sessions by the waterway during which volunteers helped clean out the canal and rebuild some of the worn-away brickwork. Holden also recalled, 'Fred would do the digging and Mrs Shipman would brew the tea which was very nice of her. They certainly were not afraid to muck in and help out.'

Brian Holden found it difficult to call Primrose by her first name. As he later explained, 'I couldn't bring myself to call her that because it seemed such a silly name. I always called her Mrs Shipman and she certainly did seem much younger than him but I always found her perfectly polite.'

Brian Holden and his fellow society members were at the time working on a strip of canal between Todmorden and the nearby town of Littleborough. The waterway cut a line right through the middle of the town as it kept to the long thin valley northwards. The society also held monthly meetings in the winter at information centres located between Manchester and Darby Bridge at each end of the canal. Fred Shipman paid £1 a year in subscription to be a member of the canal society.

Shipman was particularly interested in helping improve the riverside walk and specific buildings labelled 'blots on the landscape' which had been identified for attention. Some in Todmorden believed that, with the right facelift, the community could be made an attractive destination for tourists. There was also a feeling that anything which improved the appearance of the town would help reverse the decline in population. 'But in those early days, we were still considered part of the lunatic fringe,' Brian Holden later explained. 'Most people in the town thought we were crackers. But Fred didn't seem to mind in the slightest. In fact, I think he rather enjoyed telling people he was a member of the society because it made him seem more interesting.'

Eventually, Shipman even purchased a small dinghy, which he used in the society's occasional boat rallies held to help raise money for the organisation. 'Anything from a canoe to an inflatable was used for the rallies. Basically, it could be anything you could throw in the water and later recover.'

The first Rochdale Canal Society regatta in 1975 was a huge success and the supposedly 'unsociable' Shipmans played a major part in it; Primrose provided numerous delicious cakes and kept huge brews of hot tea on the boil. Earlier, Fred Shipman had even sent away a sample of the water from a tap by the side of the canal to see if it was clean enough to drink. 'He was most concerned that we didn't end up being poisoned by the water,' Brian Holden later recalled. 'If anything, he was almost too helpful.'

Fred Shipman was genuinely interested in the Canal Society because it presented him with an opportunity to do something 'normal' and integrate himself and his family into the community. He was desperately fighting an addiction to pethidine on one front and, with it, a series of strange urges in regard to his patients. Fred Shipman was in a deeply confused state. He wanted to rid himself of these demons and lead the life of a fine, upstanding citizen in Todmorden.

But the more pethidine Fred Shipman injected into his bloodstream, the more unhappy he became. The pressure of long hours at the surgery and the confusing messages that had continued to haunt him ever since the death of his mother were converging on each another. He needed a release. The drugs were not enough to help him get through the day. Another type of urge was increasing its power over him and he felt that the death of his mother lay behind it all.

CHAPTER SIX

A Taste for Death

One of the first patients to find themselves on the receiving end of Fred Shipman's rapidly deteriorating physical and psychological state in Todmorden was a 72-year-old woman called Ruth Highley, who lived in Maitland Street, in the Walsden area of the town.

Her death in the early summer of 1974 was unexceptional. On the death certificate, Shipman gave the cause of death as, '(a) hypothermia and (b) kidney', which were incredibly vague descriptions.

That first death was, in Fred Shipman's eyes, a 'mercy killing'. He had broken the taboo of inflicting death for justifiable reasons. Significantly, it was the first death certificate ever signed by Fred Shipman. He signed another 21 during his 18-month stay in Todmorden. But he was so perturbed by the ease with which he'd killed that patient that he immediately increased his use of pethidine in order to avoid being tempted to take the life of anyone else.

The only other way to deal with those urges was to succumb to sexual activity, but all that did was delay the moment of truth.

Sometimes, Shipman stopped off at an anonymous pub well away from his patients' catchment area and downed a few pints before heading towards the red-light district of Bradford, just 30 miles to the north of Todmorden.

One retired Bradford police officer recently recalled that Shipman's name came up as someone who was cautioned for kerb-crawling on 'at least two or three occasions' around this time. 'But he was never actually apprehended in the presence of a prostitute. I just happened to remember his name when it came up years later,' explained the retired officer.

Some years later, the same vice area became the epicentre of the search for the notorious Yorkshire Ripper.

* * *

On 4 August 1974, Fred Shipman, the friendly doctor already renowned as Todmorden's most popular baby specialist after successfully overseeing some very awkward births, visited the home of Susan and Mark Orlinski just after the premature birth of their son Christian. The Orlinskis lived in Holme Street, in the Lydgate area of Todmorden.

'Christian was born so early we didn't have a cot or a nappy or anything ready,' Mrs Orlinski recalled. 'Shipman then turned up – it was a Sunday morning – looked the baby over but made no comment about his health other than to say he was OK. He didn't even suggest he should be taken to hospital for some basic check-ups since he was rather premature.'

The Orlinskis never heard from Shipman again. Their baby son died the following morning. Mrs Orlinski now says, 'I have absolutely no doubt that Shipman was on drugs at the time and forgot all about our baby. He would be alive today if Shipman had bothered to come back to see us.'

The Todmorden coroner signed the death certificate after Shipman told him that the child had died of 'sudden death in infancy syndrome'. It would be another 25 years before it emerged that Fred Shipman had killed the child.

To this day, the Orlinskis find it painful to speak about their infant son's death, but they have no doubt that Shipman is guilty. 'We just wish we had never laid eyes on the man. Why did he have to do that?' Mr Orlinski later asked. 'Why? What sort of sick and twisted man is he?'

Fred Shipman was supposed to be a doctor trained not to kill people, but to care for them. However, Shipman considered all medical treatment as a form of controlled violence. It was obvious in surgery as well as during medical treatment. Shipman knew that he prescribed drugs all the time which were poisonous if taken wrongly. Fred Shipman had made the transition from being a carer to a deliberate killer. He'd been put on a pedestal by the local community. He felt immortal. He was master of the universe. He was so invincible he could do anything he wanted.

On 21 August 1974, just a couple of weeks after the death of the Orlinski baby, attractive Elaine Oswald decided to visit Fred Shipman because of a severe pain in her left side. The GP was immediately very concerned and thought that it might be a kidney stone problem. He gave her a prescription for Diconal, a painkiller, and told her to take two tablets and go home to bed for three or four days.

Shipman insisted he would call on her personally after surgery to take a blood sample. 'Leave your front door unlocked so that I can walk in without disturbing you,' Shipman told 25-year-old Elaine, who agreed to the GP's request without even questioning his authority.

But, later, Elaine felt slightly better, so she ignored his advice and went shopping in Todmorden town centre. Then she went home and rang her husband and her boss at the local Department of Social Security to let them know of her illness. 'I curled up in bed with one of my novels. I was just getting drowsy when Dr Shipman called "Hello" and came upstairs. I sat up, we chatted and he told me he had just picked up his wife and child they were waiting outside in his car. As we talked, he took blood from my arm.'

Then Elaine passed out. Shipman told her later that she had

stopped breathing for five or six minutes, although he said her heart did not stop. She later recalled, 'All I remember is coming to on the bedroom floor, bruised, battered and bleeding from the mouth, surrounded by Shipman, two paramedics and Shipman's wife and child, who were watching the proceedings.' Elaine was then dragged outside to the waiting ambulance and forced to stand upright and 'move my unco-operative legs'.

Shipman then accompanied his young patient on the eight-mile trip to the Victoria Hospital in Burnley. 'Inside the ambulance, someone's hand slapped my face every time my eyes closed,' she recalled. Elaine's ordeal continued at the hospital where she was thought to have overdosed on the painkillers and was forced to have her stomach pumped. As her mother, Joyce Taylor, later recalled, 'At the time, we believed that Dr Shipman had saved her life.'

In fact, Fred Shipman went to the hospital to ensure that he covered all his tracks, and he told staff what he believed had happened. Fred Shipman said Elaine had suffered an allergic reaction to the painkillers and, from that day onwards, she never touched any drugs for fear of an adverse reaction. Elaine Oswald remains completely traumatised by the incident because she insists she only took two tablets. Her mother says today, 'We now wonder what he did to her. Did he inject her with something or what happened to her?'

In fact, Fred Shipman's failure to satisfy his urge to kill on that occasion convinced him to stick to older, more vulnerable patients. They were much easier to dispense with.

And no matter how much pethidine Fred Shipman consumed, it wasn't enough to quell that urge to kill. On 21 January 1975, 73-year-old widow Lily Crossley died in Todmorden half-an-hour after a home visit by the young GP. Her brother Douglas Redmond later recalled, 'She was slightly ill and had anaemia, but she was not ill enough to suddenly die like she did.'

Lily was a retired weaver and one of a family of seven brothers and sisters. 'She thought he was a wonderful doctor and trusted him completely,' added Mr Redmond, who only linked the death of his sister to Shipman many years later. I suddenly thought, 'Oh my God, did he kill her?' The death certificate signed by Shipman stated that Lily had died from cancer and pernicious anaemia.

Later that same day, Fred Shipman went out again to 84-year-old Elizabeth Pearce. She died minutes later and Shipman put her death down to a cerebral haemorrhage. Shipman then went to the Todmorden home of Robert Lingard, 63, who died minutes after the GP's arrival. Mr Lingard was a heavy smoker and drinker but his sudden death came as a shock. His daughter-in-law Margaret Lingard, a nurse, later recalled, 'It was out of the blue. Shipman said, "He has had a heart-attack."'

And Mrs Pearce's grandson, George Dobby, later said, 'I was shocked to learn that Shipman signed two more death certificates on the same day that my grandmother died.'

All three of these patients had been in reasonable health until Fred Shipman came calling. They all died on the same day – 21 January 1975 – just seven days after Fred Shipman's twenty-ninth birthday.

* * *

Fred Shipman's desperate attempt to retain a reasonably high level of self-esteem showed a preoccupation with the idea of intellectual and creative eminence in his field as a doctor. At home, he treated his wife and children in a mildly despotic manner and expected total, unquestionable obedience, becoming highly abusive at the least sign of resistance. Fred Shipman was obsessed with being in the right all the time. He lacked a self-critical faculty and would storm and rage about the most trivial matters, completely unaware that all he was really doing was over-indulging himself and wasting everyone else's time.

His attitude was that Primrose should truly respect him at all times and she should not tell him when he was in the wrong. If she ever dared to do that, then he took it as the ultimate insult.

Later in 1975, a Shipman patient called Hubert Dobson went to see him after developing boils all over his face and neck.

Shipman told 44-year-old Dobson he was suffering from diabetes and prescribed 250mg of Diabinese tablets.

The following day, Dobson, his wife and two children headed off on a driving holiday to the West of England. He was towing a caravan behind his car. He later recalled, 'I was driving along some narrow country roads when my vision started going and I was on the point of a black-out. My eyelids kept dropping and it then became a desperate struggle to stay conscious at the wheel long enough to find a lay-by.'

Dobson eventually swerved off the road before collapsing across the steering wheel. When the family returned to Todmorden, he went to see Fred Shipman who simply dropped the dosage of tablets after he heard what had happened. For the following ten years, Hubert Dobson continued taking the tablets on a regular basis, but then he started getting such serious tingling and trembling from the pills that he stopped taking them altogether.

Some time later, he had to go to hospital for a routine check-up and when his blood was tested it was discovered he wasn't even suffering from diabetes. Dobson concluded that Shipman had taken a guess at his original diagnosis when other doctors told him that the GP should have taken all sorts of tests before diagnosing the disease.

* * *

On 9 August 1975, Fred Shipman was called to the bedside of 89-year-old William Shaw at his house on Stansfield Road, in Todmorden. His daughter Eunice later recalled, 'Dr Shipman came along, as our usual GP was about to go on holiday. It was the first time I had ever clapped eyes on him.'

Shipman seemed in a hurry and told Eunice that his visit was a mere formality which would prevent the necessity for a post mortem examination. 'He was saying all this very loudly in front of my dying father and I shooed him away saying I didn't want him to hear things like that,' she later explained. 'I thought that Dr Shipman was extremely callous in the way he behaved.'

William Shaw died shortly afterwards but Fred Shipman's unpleasant bedside manner was never forgotten by other members of the Shaw family.

Shortly after the death of William Shaw, Fred Shipman started blacking out at the surgery. Concerned staff presumed he was working long hours and was simply exhausted from his gruelling routine. Primrose was so worried about her husband's 'black-out problems' that she offered to chauffeur him around on his house calls just in case he collapsed at the wheel of his car.

No one at that stage – including Primrose – realised that the black-outs were as a direct result of the GP's addiction to huge doses of pethidine. Fred Shipman had rapidly used up all the available veins on his arms and legs in a desperate attempt to stay high enough to get through his day's work which often began at 8.00am and didn't end until 9–10pm. But suspicious deaths and heavy drug-taking were the last things on the minds of Fred Shipman's fellow doctors in the overstretched practice. Many just presumed the black-outs would stop once he learned to pace his workload more carefully.

In fact, the only serious problem about Fred Shipman as far as the other doctors at the practice were concerned was Primrose. She was still only in her mid-twenties and extremely defensive of her hard-working husband. Many found her to take offence at the most harmless remarks. Primrose even made it known that she reckoned senior partner Dr Michael Grieve did not appreciate her husband enough. She claimed Dr Grieve preferred the receptionists to her husband.

On one occasion in 1975, Dr Grieve's wife heard yet another of Primrose's bitter outbursts and told her in no uncertain terms to 'shut up or else'. She concluded that Primrose would never last the course as a doctor's wife.

One of Shipman's other partners in Todmorden, Dr John Dacre, later recalled, 'Fred was a reasonably immaculate man, but the same couldn't be said for his wife. She was obese, scruffy and looked more like a bag lady than a doctor's wife. She was rather on the uncouth side and we didn't really have much to do with her.'

However, Fred Shipman the control freak so feared being crippled by anxiety and self-doubt that he attempted to continue to exercise total control over his life. That need for control continued to extend to his immediate family. He always had to call the shots because he couldn't live with himself unless he did. It wasn't about him being cruel – it was simply about the needs that he felt.

And there were other aspects to his marriage to Primrose that put him under even more pressure. Fred Shipman undoubtedly found intimacy with Primrose painfully uninteresting so the couple's sex life was characterised more by a lack of activity than anything else. Shipman was only capable of having a relationship that looked normal on the condition that it was on his own terms. That was why Shipman so desperately needed to dominate the world around him. Illicit phials of pethidine were not enough in themselves to help him overcome his mother's painful end. Maybe the deaths of his patients would help.

At the surgery, Shipman spent longer and longer hours alone in his office, avoiding going home until late most evenings. He'd increased his dosages of pethidine to 300mg a day (most people could not withstand more than 100mg) and gave himself a last 'booster' injection at around 7.30pm to keep him going until it was time to walk home for dinner.

Throughout this disturbing period in his life, Shipman's only real confidante was Dr Brenda Lewin, the sole female doctor in the Todmorden group practice. Lewin had problems of her own that were associated with alcohol.

Practice head Dr Michael Grieve later explained, 'Fred and Brenda had a very interesting relationship. In some ways, they were both tragic people. Thinking back on it they obviously both recognised something in each other.'

Another doctor who has long since retired from the Todmorden practice says that Fred Shipman and Brenda Lewin – who was 15 years older than him – enjoyed a very close relationship. 'They were always going into each other's offices and closing the door. Fred only ever seemed to open up to

Brenda. It was as if she was the only one who truly understood him as a person.'

Dr Lewin was a well-respected doctor who'd worked all over the world before she arrived in Todmorden and had been considered, according to Dr Grieve, as 'something of a high-flyer'. Dr Grieve later explained, 'Brenda sympathised with Fred in many ways. It says a lot about both their characters.'

One doctor at the practice believed that Fred Shipman and Brenda Lewin were romantically involved at one stage. 'I saw them out together one evening in a local restaurant,' said the doctor. 'They didn't see me but they seemed very animated with each other.'

Dr Lewin was married to an invalid at the time and Shipman's wife was by all accounts not on his wavelength when it came to certain subjects. 'They were obviously thrown together. Brenda was incredibly loyal about Fred and was always referring to how concerned she was that he was overworking,' added the doctor. 'I really think that he was the true love of her life.'

But while Fred Shipman's close relationship with Dr Brenda Lewin enabled him to pour out his thoughts to a 'soul-mate', it also helped pile the pressure on his psyche. He knew that she suspected he was taking drugs because of the way he was behaving.

'I understand that, at one stage, Fred broke down and told Brenda about the pethidine. She wasn't even shocked by it. She simply told Fred that he must sort himself out before it was too late. If anything, it brought them even closer together.'

But following his confession, Fred Shipman cooled his friendship with Brenda Lewin because he feared she might inform the head of the surgery about his drug habit. But as one of its former doctors later explained, 'Brenda just wasn't that sort of person. She was an incredibly discreet, understanding woman. She simply wanted what was best for Fred.'

As Dr Grieve later explained, 'Brenda had problems with alcohol which actually meant we were more aware of her situation than anything concerning Fred Shipman at that time.

I even used to get complaints about her. It's no surprise they formed such a close relationship.'

And Dr Lewin's sister, Carol Scott, later said, 'My sister recognised Fred's problems and could see he was in trouble. She wanted to help him. They clicked in a very special way.'

Carol Scott even met Shipman socially when he was out with Dr Lewin. 'We all knew him as Fred and he was an extremely amusing young man. I understood what my sister saw in him. We all did.'

* * *

Until those first few 'kills' in Todmorden, Fred Shipman had a blurred self-image which was synonymous with feeling weak and passive. But as soon as he'd started taking the lives of other human beings, he experienced a sense of power and purpose, his self-image became clear and everything suddenly had a true meaning.

Shipman's need for purposive action was acute, for it made his image re-appear in the mirror. Instinctively, he began constantly looking around for something that would galvanise him back into action. In many individuals it is a sexual instinct, but in Shipman it was purely a dance of death that he sought so desperately.

But then Fred Shipman was not an excessively brutal man; he projected a good impression of decency and efficiency to most of his patients. But that softer aspect of his personality prohibited him from expressing the violent feelings that lay beneath the surface. By killing a patient, he could ignore their personality and concentrate on the release of the desire to watch someone die. In some ways, Shipman saw his behaviour as magical – a violent and unsubtle solution to an extremely subtle problem.

Shipman was rapidly concentrating narrowly and obsessively on killing people and with that he ran the risk of him dehydrating his soul. Human beings have the power to relax, to fling open their senses as if they were windows and allow the air of the outside world to blow in. But Shipman had unhitched his mind from its normal purposes and allowed it to wander freely.

Shipman had already taken it all much too far because that was the only way his urges could be fully satisfied. Shipman had stepped into an obsession from which he could not escape. He was a man who had deliberately made a decision to satisfy those urges by killing his patients. Now, with his most important memory banks filled with images of death, how could he avoid continuing his obsession? In some ways, he was like a man suffering from such a serious head cold that he could neither see nor smell nor hear nor breathe properly.

Back in the real world, Fred Shipman was trying his hardest to make a niche for himself in his first group practice, as well as bring up and support an ever-growing young family on a modest salary. There was no support from his in-laws who'd continued their feud with Primrose after her decision to marry Fred while pregnant. And the couple rarely visited Harold Shipman Snr or Fred's brother and sister, all of whom still lived in Nottingham.

Fred Shipman convinced himself that he'd been driven to take bigger and bigger doses of drugs and even kill a few people after suffering depression because of opposition to his ideas for improving the Todmorden practice. And that stress was taking an appalling toll on his health. His black-outs became so serious that he had a nasty fall in the bath as he and Primrose were decorating the family home. Primrose continued ferrying her husband to his home visits because of his ill health. For six months he had been constantly injecting pethidine into his arms and legs – his veins were now on the verge of collapse through over-use. He was also taking extra doses orally.

But did Primrose begin to pick up clues as to what her husband was doing during some of those home visits? She certainly walked into patients' houses with Shipman. At least two witnesses recalled seeing her and the couple's two children as the GP attended a sick patient.

'She'd walk in with him as if she was his assistant, but it certainly seemed a bit unprofessional when she brought the children in as well,' recalled one of Shipman's Todmorden patients. 'She must have realised he was up to something, surely?'

Then, one day, Shipman announced to his colleagues at the practice in Todmorden that he was suffering from epilepsy. No one disputed his self-diagnosis and his partners were most sympathetic. But Fred Shipman assured them all he would be fine and that he'd deal with the illness himself.

Fred Shipman was now a full-time junkie, snatching a few minutes alone in the practice toilet in order to 'jack up' more pethidine at least three times a day. As the quantities increased, so did his desperation to mask his hopeless addiction. He would stay at the practice until long after all the other doctors had left for the day so that he could feed his habit in isolation and carefully calculate the names of patients through which he could continue to claim prescriptions.

Then, a few weeks later, a local chemist noticed for the first time that Shipman was prescribing a vast amount of pethidine. Shipman had actually forged more than 70 prescriptions to feed his own 700mg-a-day habit. The GP often used part of those prescriptions on a patient and then retained the rest for his own use. But on other occasions, none of the drugs he prescribed actually went to the patient for whom it was intended.

Shipman forged the signature of Nancy Harris, matron at the Scaitcliffe Hall Nursing Home in Todmorden, on many prescriptions. He even signed the back of the prescription forms to obtain exemption from charges.

Nancy Harris never forgot how Fred Shipman called round at the nursing home one evening. 'He rushed upstairs and a moment later rushed downstairs and out of the building. I thought, well, 'That's strange!' she later recalled. 'There must have been something wrong at the time. He was not like the rest of the doctors, he was like a flash of lightning.'

Shipman had only been at the Abraham Ormerod Medical Practice, in Todmorden, since March 1974, but during his time in the Pennine town he signed a total of 22 death certificates, more than double any other doctor in the practice.

In July 1975, a Home Office drugs inspector questioned Fred Shipman at the surgery about discrepancies in prescriptions. He completely denied any wrong-doing and, for the moment, the inspector went away convinced that perhaps it was all a 'misunderstanding' just as Shipman had claimed. The Todmorden chemist who'd first alerted the authorities was furious. He had no doubt that Fred Shipman was fraudulently feeding his or someone else's illicit drug habit.

One morning, a receptionist at the practice telephoned the same chemist to mention she would be calling round to pick up some bandages and dressings. The chemist decided to leave the drugs book open for her to see. She fell for the bait and was horrified to notice that it was filled with pages and pages of entries, all in Shipman's name, all for pethidine, a drug rarely used in day-to-day health care.

Partner Dr John Dacre later recalled what happened. 'The receptionist came hot-foot across to the surgery. I went back and saw all the entries in Shipman's name. There were thousands of ampoules. It was excessive. We never use it except for labour pains or as a painkiller before you go on to morphine. Everyone was absolutely horrified,' said Dr Dacre.

Dacre and his colleague Dr Lewin discussed the matter later that day and decided to investigate further and then confront Shipman on the following Monday morning. When senior partner Dr Michael Grieve was eventually told the news, he was stunned. 'I was fed up quite honestly, I knew nothing of it. I had been sat in a surgery with him all that weekend then it was all sprung on me.'

At a dramatic practice meeting that Monday, one senior partner, Dr John Baker, confronted Fred Shipman, who was sitting to one side. Baker said, 'Now, young Fred, can you explain this?'

Baker placed before him the evidence that showed Shipman had been prescribing pethidine to patients who had never received it.

From Fred Shipman there was no denial, no embarrassment,

no remorse. He simply said softly, 'I will stop – can you give me another chance?'

The partners refused. That was when Shipman flew into a rage. Dr Dacre later recalled, 'We were astounded, amazed to find out what was going on. It was shattering. It was the first time I had seen him lose his cool. He stormed out, saying he resigned.'

But that wasn't the end of the matter.

Less than an hour later, Primrose Shipman walked into the meeting of GPs, who were still deciding what to do next. She immediately declared that her husband would not be resigning. 'You'll have to force him out,' she said.

It took the practice six weeks to remove Fred Shipman from the partnership for breaching practice rules by misusing drugs. In all that time, although not working, he remained on full pay.

Then, in November 1975, the same inspector visited the Todmorden surgery accompanied by a policeman. Shipman was told that it was alleged he'd been dispensing drugs 'in other than proper circumstances'. Shipman stunned the two investigators by immediately standing up and saying that he had been injecting himself with pethidine for more than six months. He also said he was in the habit of taking up to 600 to 700 milligrams a day and explained he had been depressed when he started taking the drug, and had taken more and more as he became increasingly depressed.

Senior partner Dr Dacre advised him to seek immediate help or risk being struck off as a doctor. Fred Shipman accepted the advice gratefully and went into hospital immediately after being given police bail following his arrest on charges of forging prescriptions and stealing drugs.

One consultant psychiatrist who treated Shipman at the time concluded that his drug habit was associated with the GP's feeling of 'total failure in his personal and professional life'. What none of those doctors or investigators realised was that Fred Shipman was already hiding a dreadful, dark secret which was tearing him apart. He was also hooked on killing.

CHAPTER SEVEN

A Tarnished Reputation

Primrose Shipman later admitted to one close friend that those two years in Todmorden were the best days of their lives and she acknowledged that much of that was down to her husband's addiction to pethidine. 'It turned him from being a morose, quiet, shy sort of person into a bubbly, funny man in many ways. He was like a different person. It was truly amazing,' she said.

And Shipman's addiction to pethidine certainly improved the couple's social life. Countless party photos of Fred Shipman during this period show the GP drinking chilled wine and laughing with other guests. Yet the need to kill ran through his veins alongside those drugs, although Shipman consumed glass after glass of wine to try and mellow out his hyped-up response to pethidine.

In many ways, Fred Shipman had fitted perfectly into Todmorden. Its vast catchment area enabled him to go out and make numerous house calls – and he did not hide the fact that, unlike many of his colleagues, he liked making personal visits to patients' homes. He relished the privacy of seeing them in their own homes away from the prying eyes of receptionists and other doctors.

But Dr Michael Grieve, the doctor who first appointed Shipman, later recalled, 'Everything was perfect. He'd been working very hard, then we discovered about his illness and periods of unconsciousness. It was a tragedy in many ways. He'd been such a fine doctor at first.

'A great deal of the pethidine was prescribed on our account. Most of these patients received nothing from Fred. It's easy to be wise after the event. How could I have been so dim? He was being driven around by his wife. She knew he was blacking out but had no idea about the drugs.'

Fred Shipman never did give a proper reason as to why he got hooked on pethidine. He later repeated his claim that he'd been driven to taking the drugs to get himself over the stress of not getting his own way in the practice.

But Michael Grieve says, 'Looking back on it, Shipman was working very maniacally before all this was discovered. He got through an enormous amount of work surmising records and putting things on to the computer. The public don't seem to realise that GPs are expected to do the work of ten other people with appallingly inadequate resources. Even the practice computer was paid for by a charity but all the work was done free of charge. Fred's day was spent getting up, walking to work and then coming home late. He even took the records home at night to do even more work. No wonder he caved in under the pressure.'

Grieve is still full of admiration for the way Fred Shipman volunteered to work on the Rochdale Canal. 'He'd even bought that little rubber boat so his family could enjoy the canal,' recalled Dr Grieve. 'I had a boat at Skipton and I was touched by that because he was so proud of his boat.' But he added, 'Fred was playing a role in the community, except that he was fuelling it with this bloody pethidine. Mind you, he probably couldn't have done any of these things without the drugs to keep him going. Other members of the practice were not well – two sick partners had to go part-time. It was tough by anyone's standards.

'How on earth is a doctor expected to work 24 hours a day, 365 days a year to cover all his patients any time of the day or night? You drove your own cars. These days they go out with a man in a car with a mobile phone. There was a lot of snow back in those days and it was so tiring. Even your medical bag was heavier in those days. It was an exhausting job.'

Immediately after Shipman had been fired, members of the practice went through all their medical records and found that pethidine had been, according to Dr Grieve, 'going out at a rate of knots'. Dr Grieve finds it impossible to this day to concede that Shipman's killing habits began in Todmorden. 'I don't agree that he was killing people here. How could he have been doing that? It would have come out when they originally went through the books.'

Grieve added, 'Look, Fred Shipman was not easy-going by any means. He was very uptight. Fred pleaded with us to cover him while he tried to get off drugs but I said, "You have to go into hospital. Everything must be out in the open. You cannot go around trying to conceal things."'

Within weeks of Shipman's dismissal from the Todmorden practice on 10 October 1975, a local real estate agent was instructed by Primrose Shipman to put the family's beloved house on Sunnyside up for sale. The details were published in the Todmorden *News and Advertiser*. They stated, 'Penrhyn, Sunnyside, Todmorden. Excellent semi-detached property commanding good open views yet within walking distance of Todmorden town centre. Accommodation: Small hall, through lounge, living room, kitchen; 3 first-floor bedrooms; de luxe bathroom. Garage space. Full central heating. Price includes many extras. Viewing by appointment.'

Back in Todmorden, the young woman and her friends who had been turned into amphetamine addicts by Fred Shipman had to be weaned off them by a replacement doctor who was shocked to discover that Shipman had been prescribing the slimming tablets to perfectly healthy patients. 'I never touched another drug after Shipman left. I was stunned to hear he'd been on drugs himself,' that woman explained years later.

Meanwhile, Primrose and the children headed over to Wetherby to stay with her parents while Fred went for full-time treatment for his addiction to a drugs clinic near his favourite city of York. But the one colleague Fred Shipman clearly adored – Dr Brenda Lewin – still thought the world of him despite his drug addiction. She even visited him at the rehabilitation centre, called The Retreat, in York, numerous times following his dismissal from Todmorden.

'I'm not surprised they kept in touch. They really respected each other and Brenda refused to turn her back on Fred even after his drug addiction was exposed,' explained practice head Dr Michael Grieve.

But behind her genuine concern for Fred Shipman, there lay a very personal tragedy for Dr Brenda Lewin. Her drinking problems had become so acute that she was sent off to Leeds to attend a special course. Dr Grieve explained, 'Unfortunately, she suffered a breakdown and I had to get her committed to a hospital. She never worked again.'

And one of the other doctors in the practice added, 'Brenda was heartbroken by what happened to Fred Shipman. Combined with the health problems of her very sick husband, it all proved too much for her to cope with.'

Yet for at least another five years, Fred Shipman stayed in close contact with Brenda Lewin. As one now retired doctor from the Todmorden practice later explained, 'Fred never forgot Brenda and he even visited her when she was in hospital. It's really sad because in many ways they were much better suited to each other than their respective partners and perhaps it could all have been so different if they had formed a proper stable relationship.'

As Dr Lewin's sister, Carol Scott, later said, 'Fred had no one else to turn to except my sister. He needed an outlet and Brenda was there for him. He opened up to her about every aspect of his life but she was so loyal she would never have blown the whistle on him.'

But in The Retreat, Shipman became something of a *cause célèbre* thanks to his status as a doctor. But getting the GP to expand on his problems during psychiatric sessions was not easy. 'It was almost as if Fred was playing a game with every psychiatrist who tried to counsel him,' one of his friends later explained. 'He just didn't like giving away anything of himself.'

However, during one psychiatric session, Fred Shipman did let slip his killing urges, but then laughed them off as something he suffered nightmares about. Explained one former member of staff at The Retreat, 'After some months of treatment he began to relax more and seemed to be coming to terms with what he had done. He even referred to nightmares he'd suffered ever since his mother's death, but, of course, no one realised that he'd already turned those nightmares into a reality.'

Fred Shipman had already decided to do everything in his power to convince psychiatrists that he was fit to continue practising as a doctor. He knew he had to give them some information about himself but he wanted to make sure it was only the bare essentials. He needed to get back to being a doctor in order to satisfy the lust to kill.

On 13 February 1976, at Halifax Magistrates' Court, Fred Shipman pleaded guilty to forging prescriptions and stealing drugs, and asked for 74 other offences to be taken into consideration. Psychiatrists recommended to magistrates that Fred Shipman be allowed to continue as a doctor. Of course, they had no idea he'd already killed a number of patients. Dr Hugo Milne – who years later would examine one of Britain's most notorious serial killers, Yorkshire Ripper Peter Sutcliffe – wrote to the court, 'It would be to his advantage if he were allowed to continue to practise. Conversely, it would be catastrophic if he were not to be allowed to continue.'

Fred Shipman – the small, bespectacled, shy GP – had brilliantly duped some of the most respected medical experts in Britain. None of them got even a hint of the fact that he was already killing patients. Safe in the knowledge that he had escaped justice, Fred Shipman's self-esteem and arrogance began to re-emerge. Shipman wasn't even asked to appear before the British General Medical Council's Professional Conduct Committee. He was told by letter about the consequences of any further misconduct.

The court also heard how, on release from his six-month treatment programme, Shipman was due to take up a post as a medical assistant in County Durham in which he would have no access to drugs. Health officials had been told of his conviction and that he must remain under supervision while he worked under a district physician conducting baby clinics.

Presiding magistrate Dr Maurice Goldin told Shipman, 'It is indeed a very sad case, that almost at the beginning of your career you should find yourself in this position. It is something which, it seems, has been going on for a long time and no one could be more aware of the dangers involved than yourself.'

In court, Shipman blamed the surgery for his crimes. He told magistrate Dr Goldin how he'd taken drugs as he descended into depression caused by difficult relationships with his colleagues. The court heard from two impressive character witnesses – Ken Fieldsend, the managing director of a Todmorden engineering firm and local musical conductor Dr Ben Horsfall. Both said they had confidence in his ability. Chairman of the Bench Dr Goldin advised Shipman to 'get better and get out of medicine'.

Shipman was fined £600 and ordered to pay £57.78 to Britain's National Health Service in compensation. By now he had lost his job, spent many months in 'rehab' and was seeing a psychiatrist. But at least Shipman had helped the Home Office with their enquiries, said Dr Goldin.

Todmorden's *News and Advertiser* local newspaper reported Fred Shipman's court appearance in such a low-key manner it did not even warrant a front page mention:

DOCTOR FINED £600 FOR DRUG OFFENCES

Dr Harold Frederick Shipman (30), a former partner in a group practice at the Abraham Ormerod Medical Centre,

Todmorden, was fined £600 at Halifax Magistrates' Court last Friday for drug offences.

Primrose Shipman's hopes of reconciling with her estranged parents were ruined by her husband's court appearance on the drugs charges. The couple were once again outcasts just as they had been after their hastily-arranged marriage. But that isolation helped them forge an even closer relationship. It remained an 'us against the world' situation which kept Fred and Primrose one step removed from reality much of the time. Primrose remained unflinchingly loyal to Shipman, especially while he was suffering from acute depression following his dismissal from the Todmorden practice. Their marriage was described by one psychiatrist who counselled them in 1976 as 'very happy and stable'.

But the highly respected Dr Hugo Milne, who examined Shipman while he was in the drug addiction clinic in York, later claimed Shipman's 'melancholy' state had put the relationship under immense strain. Dr Milne said that Primrose had been 'quite unable to understand her husband's withdrawal from normal behaviour'.

Essentially, Fred needed Primrose desperately, despite the huge gap in their intellectual capabilities. He wanted someone to be dependent on him. He'd been over-indulged by his mother, who thought he could do no wrong, and he needed his wife to adore him and bow to his every whim. While Primrose was undoubtedly overwhelmed in many ways by her more intelligent husband, the relationship suited him perfectly. He didn't want anyone questioning him and he certainly did not take kindly to any criticism. Fred Shipman needed women to be utterly dependent on him – his mother, his wife and his female patients. To Primrose, he was the provider and mentor. In many ways, they were addicted to each other.

* * *

Back in Todmorden, Fred Shipman's former colleagues were

still stunned by the revelations about his 'dark side'. Senior partner Dr Michael Grieve dismissed Shipman's claims about the other practice members. 'He was enthusiastic and hard working and we were pleased with him. I had sympathy for him, even after the case. We did talk and listen to him. I think it was his own depression that caused all these problems. He worked incredibly hard to summarise our notes, harder than was physically possible. Now we know why – to find out who was on pethidine.

'Being a doctor is a hell of a job, it's not easy. You get blamed for deaths anyway, even when you've tried to save them. That's why you get drug use with doctors and midwives; it can be because they have to try what they're giving their patients.'

Before Fred Shipman could bounce back as a GP, he had to suffer a few indignities. After his treatment for pethidine addiction was completed, he, Primrose, ten-year-old Sarah and six-year-old Christopher moved into a small council house on the Burnhill Estate in Newton Aycliffe, County Durham. In many ways, Fred Shipman had come full circle back to the type of life he had had as a child growing up in Nottingham. But at least the Burnhill Estate was brand new. The houses were modern, clean-cut properties set among wide grass verges and alongside privately-owned bungalows with pretty gardens surrounded by thousands of acres of countryside.

Sarah and Christopher settled into the local schools and one neighbour recalled, 'They were friendly enough; they would say "Hello". They just seemed nice and normal.'

But Fred Shipman went out of his way to keep a distance from his neighbours. 'I didn't even know he was a doctor,' said another local resident. The Shipmans only stayed on the estate for about a year, but another neighbour Margaret Norms, later said residents were sorry to see them go. 'They were a good family and he was a lovely man.'

On 12 September 1977, after a break of one year and 264 days, Fred Shipman landed himself a job as a clinical medical officer for children of the South-West Durham Health Authority, where his role included liaison between the health authority, GPs and community groups.

However, that job lasted just 18 days, before he left for Hyde, near Manchester, and the Donnybrook House group practice. Fred Shipman expected eventually to break back into general practice. He saw an opportunity and even told the eight partners at the Donnybrook Group in Hyde about his drugs conviction, but insisted he was clear of his addiction. He got the job.

'All I can ask you to do is trust me on this issue and watch me prove my worth,' he told the doctors in Hyde. They were impressed by his honesty. They took him at his word and he repaid their trust by immediately throwing himself into the job with great energy and enthusiasm.

Within two years of his shameful expulsion from the Todmorden practice, Fred Shipman was back in general practice with the keys to the medicine cabinet once again.

How could the practice have known that they'd just employed a mass murderer who saw Hyde as the perfect killing ground in which to recommence his sick and twisted habit.

CHAPTER EIGHT

Another New Start

Hyde, a suburb to the south-east of England's third-largest city, Manchester, was located on the edge of the Peak District National Park. A few miles down the road were the county borders into Derbyshire, Cheshire and Yorkshire. Many of the buildings of Hyde had sprung up during the town's rapid expansion in the eighteenth and nineteenth centuries when the dark, Satanic mills of the cotton industry were the key to the area's prosperity. Hyde had been a wealthy mill town thanks to the boom years of the Industrial Revolution. By the time Fred Shipman and his family descended on Hyde, it was far less prosperous.

The town had still retained its old-fashioned dignity in a close-knit community with families going back many generations. Churches and chapels were always full on Sunday.

Hyde's 1960s-built shopping mall contained local traders selling off cut-price products such as cheap clothes and fruit and vegetables. Employment prospects for local youngsters were poor and most travelled into the centre of Manchester to seek work. The local authority which covers Hyde is called

Tameside and has since been the birthplace of a couple of well-known soccer stars and rock singers, but nothing else of any real note.

Although there is one pair of infamous and notorious former residents who will never be forgotten. Myra Hindley and Ian Brady lived on the Hattersely housing project when they carried out the final two of their depraved murders of schoolchildren in the early 1960s.

Shipman believed Hyde represented his last chance to make it as a respected GP. The family immediately rented a pretty, semi-detached house on Lord Derby Road, Hyde, on a year's lease. The modern-style home, with its lawned gardens and nearby schools, was perfect for him and his young family. The property had vast picture-style windows which allowed plenty of light to pour in – and it stood on top of one of Hyde's many hills overlooking the old chimneys and dying mills to the distant, rolling fields. Here, the Shipmans believed they had a chance to settle down and put the past behind them, to wipe the slate clean and start all over again.

The partners at the new practice at Donnybrook knew about his drug problems but that was 'all in the past'. They didn't even bother informing the local area health authority because they were convinced that Fred Shipman was no longer a liability.

How wrong could they have been?

Meanwhile, Fred Shipman's domestic life seemed relatively 'normal'. Babysitter Jenny Unsworth looked after the Shipman children during the family's first months in Hyde, including New Year's Eve when Fred took Primrose to a party in Leeds. Jenny found Sarah and Christopher very well behaved. They both went to bed without any fuss, leaving Jenny to tuck into sandwiches and coffee provided by a charming Primrose. Jenny noticed Fred Shipman had a home-brew beer in vast plastic bottles behind the settee. He enjoyed a pint or two at home after his long and exhausting days in the surgery. The Shipmans were so grateful to Jenny for babysitting at short notice they presented her with a plant as a thank you some days later.

Another babysitter was Mary Burgess, whose daughter Jennifer was a receptionist at the Donnybrook practice with Dr Shipman. Mary and Shipman's wife Primrose began working together as registered child-minders and became firm friends within months of the Shipmans' arrival in Hyde. Primrose's choice of jobs seemed bizarre considering she had her hands full with her own children, but she seemed happy to utilise her skills as a mother and add some much-needed money to the family's weekly income. Soon she was minding at least a dozen children in the house each morning but they never arrived until after Fred Shipman had left for work.

One who visited the house just after the children had arrived one morning described it as 'disorganised chaos'. The neighbour added, 'The house was untidy but it was hardly surprising considering the number of kids running riot there every day.'

Ironically, Mary Burgess might never have started babysitting for the Shipmans or become Primrose's friend if it hadn't been for Fred Shipman's calming bedside manner as a doctor. For Shipman had found her first husband dead at home from natural causes. During the visit, Shipman showed such kindness and sensitivity that he even gently advised Mary to leave the house rather than become upset further looking at the body. No one to this day knows if Mary's husband was one of Fred Shipman's early victims.

'The babysitting really helped me,' Mary Burgess later recalled. 'I could talk to them both at any time; they were wonderful. Primrose was bubbly then, we used to have a laugh. The children were lovely, very bright.'

Later, Fred helped Primrose do the catering at Mary Burgess's daughter Jennifer's wedding. Mary Burgess recalled, 'I can still see them buttering bread. Fred is not one of those snooty doctors; I can't do with them, especially when you are not well. He was human, not stiff and starchy.'

Mary Burgess's assessment of the Shipmans certainly provided another insight into their character. But it did not reflect the truth as far as his 81-year-old patient Josephine

Carroll was concerned. Just one week after starting at the Donnybrook practice, Shipman visited the nearby home of Mrs Carroll. Minutes later, he called her relatives to say she had died of natural causes. His killing urge had well and truly kicked back into gear and he was deliberately 'homing in' on elderly women, who'd been lucky enough to live to old age, unlike his own dear mother.

Fred Shipman and Primrose socialised occasionally with other doctors from the Donnybrook practices. But when one doctor's wife asked Primrose if she was close to her family, Primrose responded coldly, that she had nothing to do with them.

Many of Fred Shipman's colleagues speculated about Primrose's skill as a child-minder. As one pointed out, 'She wasn't exactly charming and we all wondered how on earth she found the patience to look after so many children.' But somehow Primrose continued to cope with her own children and her job as a child-minder.

Around this time, it became clear that the Shipman children didn't exactly have the best of relationships with their parents. One Sunday, a friend of Sarah's fell off a bicycle during a charity ride organised by the Shipmans' local pub, The Dog and Partridge. Shipman, who was called to the scene by a frantic Sarah, scrubbed away the dirt and loose skin with a viciously heavy hand. 'He was awful,' Sarah's friend later recalled. 'I almost cried he was so rough. It was bloody painful.' Moments later, Shipman walked off in a huff because he considered himself to be 'off duty'.

Yet Fred Shipman's children were obviously an essential part of his life. They provided him with a feeling of normality as his mind grew increasingly twisted. The pressure he felt under to provide for them gave him the perfect excuse to work long hours. And despite his drug rehabilitation treatment, the stress was sometimes alleviated by an occasional shot of pethidine.

Fred Shipman continued to seek forms of escape from the mundane routine of his life. He believed the evils of drugs were far preferable to the other instincts eating away at his mind; the urge to continue killing had to be quelled. If it meant going back into the dark abyss of drugs, then so be it. But the reality was that Shipman needed constant doses of both drugs and death to survive his environment.

* * *

By this time, Fred Shipman was only in his early thirties but looked older thanks to a grey beard and dark grey thinning hair. He was smallish, thinnish with a middle-aged paunch and tended to wear grey-brown suits, conservative ties and thick-lensed spectacles. With his dry and narrow face, his scratchy, pedantic voice and his tetchy manner, he was more like an old-fashioned schoolteacher or a middle-ranking civil servant.

In the surgery, he often drummed his fingers impatiently in the presence of certain patients. His prescriptions were written with neat precision which only he seemed to be able to decipher, but he had a tendency to frown irritably or sarcastically when someone was annoying him. All these characteristics made him seem as respectable and English as a rainy Sunday afternoon. Yet to his older female patients he was diligent and courteous, polite, a perfect gentleman; the embodiment of a good doctor.

Fred Shipman liked lists, he liked organisations, he liked order – and he was brilliant at Trivial Pursuit. His passion was clearly for objects, things; people became items in his catalogue. He was in urgent need of controlling. The addiction to kill was once again rearing up inside him.

Shipman had become like a magician with his mysterious bag of tools and potions, his secret vocabulary, his impenetrable handwriting, his hidden knowledge. He could cure and listen. He understood people's pains and indignities. He knew about the body's intimate details and his patients' lives. However, some of those patients were getting on his nerves; they needed tidying away. They were not real people in his drug-addled mind but symptoms and problems; a cold, a cancer, heartburn, an ache, an irritation and a worry. For Fred Shipman, patients really were as meaningless as that. His fixes of drugs and death were all that really mattered.

Soon after moving to Hyde, Fred Shipman joined the St John Ambulance brigade, where he taught dozens of young members the importance of first-aid. Through the organisation, he also trained registered child-minders. He was known as a charming, patient instructor. His very light-hearted teaching manner was supposed to help his 'pupils' remember their lessons better. Amongst the audience of child-minders was Primrose, whom many recall sitting listening adoringly to every word her husband uttered with a proud smirk on her round face.

However, some pupils later recalled that Shipman occasionally belittled people who gave him the wrong answers to his 'test' questions. One of them, Janet Redfern, recalled, 'His attitude was just below arrogance. He had a superior air about him – "I know I'm better than you but I won't rub your noses in it. I will let you know that so you like me a lot." But he wasn't really offensive and we did learn a lot.'

During one of Fred Shipman's first-aid lessons, he claimed that he was allergic to bee stings. He told his audience he kept a syringe of antidote in his car at all times. In fact, it was a phial of pethidine and Shipman had got into the habit of keeping the drug in his car in case his craving for a fix became all-consuming. The secret life of Fred Shipman clearly had not ended when he was hauled before those magistrates in Halifax following his problems at Todmorden.

Meanwhile, Shipman's professional work continued to thrive. He took on numerous roles in the hope of gaining gravitas. Besides the St John Ambulance, he was also treasurer of the Small Practitioners Association, a national support group for surgeries with three doctors or less. He was also on the Tameside Local Medical Committee, whose secretary Dr Kailash Chand later described him as 'no diplomat but a good doctor'. He added, 'I would have been his patient, happily.'

* * *

The Donnybrook practice where Fred Shipman worked had been a major innovation when it was set up in 1967; 14 doctors in two practices serving a whole town from one building. And Fred Shipman was soon considered an important part of that set-up. 'He was very assertive,' recalled now retired Dr Bill Bennett. 'He didn't like people opposing him very much as I remember. But he certainly worked hard.'

Dave Owen, chief officer of the Tameside and Glossop Community Health Council, explained, 'Dr Shipman could come across as abrupt and rather arrogant. This was no major concern, though; in fact, it was a bonus when it came to negotiating services for his patients. He was very good at that.'

But Donnybrook practice manager Vivian Langfield found herself regularly on the receiving end of Fred Shipman's 'assertiveness'. And she was horrified when the GP began snapping at her beloved team of receptionists, known as 'the girls'. When she defended them, he turned on her. She later recalled how he would literally turn white with rage, just because one of them had forgotten to get him a cup of coffee. Explained Miss Langfield, 'I am always frightened of people who turn white, not red, with temper. He would be very calm, not raise his voice. That was even more scary.'

On one occasion, when Shipman was irritated by a particular member of the surgery staff, he asked Miss Langfield, 'Who was that girl?'

She replied, 'You know who it is.'

And then he responded, 'Tell her to leave on Friday.'

Numerous receptionists later claimed that Shipman created a bad atmosphere. He talked down to people, they said. And Fred Shipman was just as hard on his fellow doctors. He told one doctor in front of the reception staff, 'If you can't show an interest in the practice, then leave it to those of us who can.'

But other doctors found nothing wrong with Fred Shipman's

behaviour. One GP concluded, 'We felt he was only doing his job, if a little forcefully at times.'

However, Fred Shipman was extremely sensitive about his junior position within the pecking order of the group practice. He felt he should have been promoted soon after his arrival in the town. And he was so irritated by this oversight that he usually didn't even bother attending any of the surgery's social events.

* * *

In 1979, Fred and Primrose bought a modest three-bedroom, semi-detached house in a leafy enclave called Roe Cross Green, in the village of Mottram, ten minutes' drive from Hyde town centre. The Shipmans also added to their brood of children; on 20 March that year, their second son, David, was born.

David represented a new start for Fred and Primrose following the drug problems; the children would provide a pathway into the community's heart. People liked the Shipmans. How could anyone dislike a large, happy young family working hard and keeping themselves to themselves?

Soon Primrose was known in Mottram as 'the Childminder', always trailing a crocodile of children. But as 'the doctor's wife', everyone also gave her a measure of respect despite her obese, chaotic appearance. Meanwhile, Fred Shipman still kept that 'bee-sting antidote' in his car – just in case he needed a fix.

By 1980, Fred Shipman had become, in the words of some of his staff, 'a complete bitch' towards some of his colleagues at the Donnybrook practice. His favourite 'victim' was Dr Derek Carroll whom he regularly mimicked. Dr Carroll was 15 years older than Shipman. When head receptionist Vivien Langfield told Dr Carroll about Shipman's sneaky mocking of him, he told her not to make a fuss. 'It's better to let Fred have his own way,' the doctor told Langfield.

Some members of staff had already concluded it was better not to cross Fred Shipman. Miss Langfield later recalled an incident when Shipman was roasting yet another receptionist over some minor incident as one of the other doctors walked in and said, 'Hey, Fred ...'

Shipman turned on his colleague and snapped, 'This has nothing to do with you. I would appreciate you keeping out of it.' The doctor walked away without uttering another word.

But there were no complaints about Shipman's work and many of his patients adored him, so he must have been doing something right.

Undoubtedly, some doctors were scared of Fred Shipman. During the monthly practice meeting, Shipman put up many ideas for improving the surgery which were well received, but he'd get very annoyed if anyone didn't like what he was proposing. many saw him as a bully who demanded that people look up to him and have regard to his position. He'd often say, 'I am a good doctor. I have all the qualifications from Leeds Medical School' as if to say he should always be listened to.

But what really irritated Fred Shipman was if any female member of staff dared to challenge him when he was making rude and sarcastic comments. Answering back marked them down as targets for subsequent attacks. His favourite weapon was sarcasm; he rarely raised his voice. But as one former member of staff re-emphasised, 'That was far more chilling and sinister than shouting and screaming.'

Fred Shipman was such a control-freak that he ordered the surgery's hard-working cleaners to move his desk to clean under it. They couldn't get it out of the office so they left it in the doorway. Shipman returned the next morning and refused to put it back in its correct position until they came back and did it themselves.

Around this time, Fred Shipman got hold of his own medical records just before he became a patient of Hyde GP Dr Wally Ashworth. 'When I got them, it was clear that one of his previous doctors had given him access to his own notes,' Dr Ashworth later recalled.

At the back of the medical records were the scribbled words

'Query ... pethidine addiction?' but no other written material referring to Shipman's drug addiction and conviction in Todmorden. 'I don't know who wrote those words in his notes but obviously there should have been some paperwork and an explanation of the drug problems he'd experienced,' says Dr Ashworth. 'I didn't even realise the significance of the pethidine reference until years later. I'm conviced he'd tampered with his own medical notes.'

Fred Shipman was determined to erase those 'drug problems' from the doctors' grapevine in Hyde.

On 4 April 1982, Primrose gave birth to the couple's fourth child – Samuel. A few weeks later, Fred Shipman appeared on a national TV programme, when he enthused to the cameras about a new type of treatment for the mentally ill. He told British TV's *World in Action* documentary programme, 'If you can stay in the community, receive your treatment in the community with your family around you and your usual friends, then this all adds to the speed of recovery from the illness. ... 'In the past, if a patient has got a mental illness that required admission to hospital, the patient was formally admitted, undressed and placed in bed and was treated as though they had a physical illness. A consultant would come round – often in a white coat – and there was an invisible barrier between the patient and the doctor.'

Fred Shipman also gave interviews to journalists from two medical journals, *Medeconomics* and *General Practitioner*, about the problems of dealing with alcoholic and drug-addicted doctors but, in both cases, he made no mention of his own conviction. Shipman keenly advocated a much faster system of dealing with addiction and alcohol problems.

He happily pontificated to reporters about all aspects of his work as a GP, and was regularly quoted on a variety of issues. As a member of the local Medical Committee, Shipman appeared to thrive on his position of power and influence. Shipman clearly believed that others in the medical profession should be capable of his own high levels of knowledge. On one occasion he attacked a drugs company rep who addressed the local MC and got a small medical detail wrong in her speech. His old friend Dr Wally Ashworth later recalled, 'Fred tore this woman apart, viciously – he almost had to be hauled off. It was almost as though he had to prove himself superior, and she was not an easy target.'

And it wasn't just work colleagues who were reprimanded by Fred Shipman. One of the receptionists at Donnybrook never forgot how hard Fred Shipman was on his two older sons whenever they called at the surgery for a lift home from school. They'd sit down doing their homework in his surgery and then troop out, 'heads down, in tears' behind their father as he steered them towards his car outside. They were not even allowed to acknowledge the staff on their way out.

'They looked so miserable. I felt really sorry for them. He seemed to strike fear into them. It was really quite distressing,' recalled the former member of the Donnybrook staff.

Back at home, oldest child Sarah was the one who was confident enough to challenge her father's stern and ill-humoured mood swings. 'Sarah often laughed off her father's bad temper and that seemed to change his mood instantly,' recalls one neighbour in Mottram. Shipman was afraid of Sarah in some ways because she reminded him of his mother Vera.

Fred Shipman also found time to be a parent governor at her school, Longdendale High, and he even gave talks on family planning to some of the older students. School staff were naturally delighted to have such a distinguished member of the local community on the parent board.

Fred Shipman thoroughly enjoyed his positions of influence. He liked his children to know that he was always looking over their shoulder, ensuring they did well at school. That was how his own dearly beloved mother Vera had been and it had undoubtedly helped him to make a success of his life. Fred Shipman liked to remind his children that his childhood was a lot tougher than theirs and they should be grateful for what they had. Hard work was the key to success, he believed, and his children were all expected to live up to his expectations.

* * *

Fred Shipman welcomed in 1983 at a drunken gathering complete with party poppers draped around his neck and a balloon raised in salute. A harlequin mask replaced the mask of sincerity he so often used with his patients. Shipman surprised many by still seeming capable of letting his hair down occasionally. He consumed many pints of beer and was later remembered as the life and soul of the gathering.

At the time, Fred's star was still very much in the ascendancy. As one senior partner at the Donnybrook practice in Hyde later recalled, 'Fred had terrific potential.' He also had a chilling reputation as being 'wonderful at getting into veins'. This referred to his ability to administer injections with the least amount of pain – something that many of his patients truly appreciated.

The overriding impression from photos taken at the time was of a middle-aged doctor with a long, successful future ahead of him. There was no outward sign of the junkie who injected himself with pethidine. In the photos, Shipman even wore his favourite party outfit, an almost fashionable velvet jacket.

But not all his patients were impressed. Some of Shipman's younger ones began to despise the GP, who always seemed to have more time for his flock of over-60s than anyone else. Mother-of-two Lorraine Leighton was a nervous 17-year-old deeply embarrassed by her problem – a lump on the breast – when she made an appointment after ignoring the problem for months. She visited Shipman at a surgery where he was working as a locum.

As Lorraine shyly explained her problem, Shipman made an 'unsuitable comment' about the size of her breasts. Lorraine fled his surgery and left it many more months before returning to a different doctor who immediately removed the lump. Fortunately, it was a benign cyst.

'He was horrible. He gave me the creeps. I was so upset by the way he treated me,' said Lorraine, who never forgot the incident.

One of Lorraine's friends, a pretty young barmaid called Eve, also had a run-in with Shipman. When she visited him about problems with her nerves, he barked at her to pull herself together. 'Go home and look after your kids,' he snapped. When her husband went for the same reason a few weeks later, he got a two-week sick note. Eve believes to this day that Shipman has a severe 'problem with women'.

But behind Shipman's sometimes gruff manner lay a man in turmoil; he was fighting the demons that had first made their mark on him in Todmorden. He occasionally still used pethidine to try and kill the urges that led him to end the lives of a number of patients while he was in the small Yorkshire town. But he was losing the battle. It would only be a matter of time before the killing started again.

CHAPTER NINE

Private Grief, Public Saint

Fred Shipman's 70-year-old patient Winifred Arrowsmith lived in an apartment in a 15-storey tower block. The building had a warden to check on its elderly inhabitants, plus a social club for mealtimes. Winifred had only moved to the block on a temporary basis because her own home was being renovated. She was fit, active and fiercely independent. Her apartment was immaculate and she doted on her pet budgie. Winifred adored reading and always wore flowing floral dresses, whatever the weather and her friends considered her a sprightly lady for her age. Then, suddenly, she died.

Then Fred Shipman turned up at the office of the block warden Jenny Unsworth and asked if Mrs Arrowsmith was in, claiming he had knocked at the apartment door and there was no reply. Mrs Unsworth let him in with a master key. Inside, Winifred Arrowsmith was dead, sitting in an armchair as if she had fallen asleep.

Shipman previously visited Mrs Arrowsmith frequently at home to give her a repeat prescription of tablets for her arthritis. 'When they found her dead, she had just had her dinner,' recalled her daughter-in-law Maureen. 'The potato peelings were still on the worktop, and she'd had Fray Bentos steak pie, one of her favourites. I remember thinking that she couldn't have been gone long because she always used to tidy up straight after her meal. It was all so sudden, and we were all very distressed.'

But Winifred Arrowsmith's death seemed nothing more than the sad end to a happy, healthy life. There was no post mortem as the death was, according to Shipman, from perfectly natural causes. No one said a word about it back at the Donnybrook surgery. Why should they? Amongst the inhabitants of Hyde were a vast number of elderly pensioners. Deaths of this kind were to be expected.

* * *

The efficiency of Fred Shipman's medical career was in strange contrast to the appallingly run-down state of the family home on Roe Cross Green, in the village of Mottram, near Hyde. Bikes and children's toys lay scattered on the lawn outside the house. In the kitchen, the oven grill pan was thick with bacon fat from the thousands of rushed breakfasts for the six inhabitants of the property. The living room was scattered with colouring books and papers. Family life brought with it a measure of complete and utter chaos for the Shipmans.

Most mornings, neighbours were greeted with the sight of Primrose hurrying Sarah, Christopher, David and Samuel out to her battered Mini to ferry them to local schools. Fred Shipman usually left the house at about the same time, clutching his doctor's bag as he dashed to his own rusting Ford for the ten-minute drive to his surgery in Hyde. At that time, Primrose was still supplementing the family income by child-minding for villagers in Mottram but she was always careful not to let them into the house until after Shipman had left for work.

However, when it came to their own children's education, Fred Shipman remained in complete control. He offered little actual help with his children's homework but always insisted they show him their completed work before they could sit in front of the only TV set in the house.

At weekends, armed with a large bag, he would even knock on neighbours' doors collecting newspapers for the local scout group. He was trying his hardest to be a good father and husband. He so desperately craved a sense of normality, away from the drugs and death that seemed to haunt his professional life.

Fred Shipman considered himself an expert in wine and cuisine, although his taste wasn't exactly adventurous. On the rare occasions he did dine out, it was always at one of two local Italian restaurants, Ferrero's and Maestro's. Shipman loved flaunting his intellectual superiority to Primrose by making a big show of choosing the wine.

But Shipman found it difficult eating out because he often bumped into patients or relatives of patients and they always wanted a brief chat. He was a celebrity within a tightly-knit community. Shipman was far too polite to ignore any of these familiar faces, but he grew weary of the constant approaches in public places.

On family holidays to Brittany and Spain, Shipman adored playing the well-travelled European. During the summer of 1984, Fred and Primrose even accompanied Sarah on a school exchange visit to the Haute Marne area of France, parking their camper van opposite a house owned by Gilbert Thomas, also a doctor, and his wife Monique. They later remembered the couple largely because Shipman couldn't speak good French and because of his wife's tendency 'to be a bit fat'. They said 'please' and 'thank you' but that was about it, the Thomases said.

* * *

Something happened to Fred Shipman on 21 September 1984. Whatever it was, it rekindled those evil urges that drove him to kill again. That afternoon, Shipman claimed he found 76-year-old Mary Winterbottom 'dead in bed'. He recorded the cause of death as a coronary thrombosis. Later that same day, Shipman claimed a second victim, Elaine Cox, 72, who died at her home in Hunters Court, Dunkfield.

Then the killing ceased.

* * *

On 5 January 1985, Fred Shipman's 70-year-old father collapsed and died of a heart attack in the kitchen of the same council house in Longmead Drive, Nottingham, where he'd lived for 47 year. Fred's sister Pauline still lived with her father but was too upset to stay on in the house after his death. Father and daughter had even regularly gone to watch their local soccer team Notts County together and shared the cost of buying the house from the local council in the late 1970s for £5,500. It was now worth £30,000. Pauline worked as a secretary and also rose through the ranks to become one of the main organisers of the Nottingham Netball League.

Pauline sold the house and moved in with brother Clive in the nearby town of Long Eaton. Clive, three years younger than Fred, was a health inspector and father of two children. He lived in a semi-detached house, with a perfectly groomed yard, on a neat, modern estate and was, in many ways, the picture perfect image of middle-class respectability.

Fred Shipman was very confused about his father's death. He was still angry about old Harold Shipman's attitude towards his wedding to Primrose. Perhaps things would have been very different if his mother had still been alive? The death of Harold Shipman sent his older son close to a nervous breakdown because of the combination of guilt and anger he felt about his father. Some colleagues believed he was close to a nervous breakdown. He was clearly devastated.

Some believed the loss of his mother made Shipman very good at handling his women patients, although others heartily disagreed with that prognosis. Fred Shipman was upset that the family house had been left entirely to his sister Pauline, who then sank the proceeds from it into a granny flat attached to the large house bought with her other brother Clive. Fred Shipman had been completely cut out of his father's will and his affection.

When one receptionist at the Donnybrook practice in Hyde offered Fred Shipman her condolences, he turned towards her, grim-faced, and replied, 'Are you? I'm not.'

The death of his father and the continuing rift with Primrose's family certainly added to the couple's sense of isolation. That feeling of 'us against the world' was still growing by the day, sending Fred and Primrose spiralling into a hole of self-sufficiency. They lived in a world without any reference to the past. Fred to believed he was vastly superior to everyone else. Within the Shipman household, there were no challengers to that title, making Fred Shipman a very big fish in a very small tank.

Many who dealt with Shipman professionally say that around the time of the death of his father, the GP became a much more isolated figure within the practice set-up. 'He seemed more detached, less interested in the day-to-day workings of the surgery,' one member of staff later recalled.

In February 1985, just a few weeks after the death of Harold Shipman, the GP was making one of his routine home visits to patient May Brookes. He claimed he found her dead on arrival at her home in Hyde, but few doubt the fact that Shipman murdered her. Whether his father's death in some way sparked that killing we will probably never know, but it is recognised that something around this period forced Fred Shipman back into an even more vicious circle of killing from which he would never recover.

It may have been that he simply did not have enough money to go kerb crawling around the red-light district of Bradford. But the more likely scenario is that, by this time, Shipman derived more pleasure from the act of murder than sex. The thrill became the powerbase replacement for the lack of real excitement in his life. And he was always the one in control.

* * *

Occasional visitors to the Shipman household continued to notice the appalling state of the place and the strange way that Fred treated his children. The two older children had to share a cramped bedroom while the two younger boys were virtually penned into their bedroom like animals. If Fred was ever in the house during the day, he usually insisted that the younger boys were placed in their bedroom and only let out once he had departed.

Inside the chaotic and filthy home, the culinary skills that Primrose displayed at various public functions were not apparent. As another visitor later explained, 'The place was a tip. It was dirty and in some places downright unhygienic.'

One of the schoolfriends of the youngest Shipman, Sam, later recalled, 'There were clothes strewn all over and it was dirty and smelled a bit.' Primrose always kept up a happy mood inside the house but dropped that façade the moment Fred Shipman arrived home, tired and hungry after yet another gruelling day at work.

Wally Ashworth also had some interesting ideas about Fred and Primrose's relationship. 'He was a little man with a big woman. He was dominated at home; then he came to work. He was controlling and a perfectionist, a bloody hard worker but not very intelligent. I have seen other doctors with "God" complexes and I think that's what Shipman had.'

By this time, the Shipmans had a black-and-white tabby cat which added to the filthy state of the house by often urinating in the corners of rooms when it was unable to get out into the yard through the frequently jammed catflap in the back door. As one visitor to the house later recalled, 'Fred adored that cat. Sometimes, it seemed as if he gave it more love than his family.'

Shipman didn't like dogs. 'They are too needy. Cats always retain their sense of independence.' He made it sound as if he truly admired them.

In February 1985, Fred and Primrose actually entertained at their home, 15 Roe Cross Green for an eighteenth birthday party for daughter Sarah. The house was even unusually clean and tidy. But within days it was back to its old, familiar messy state.

* * *

In August 1985, a friend of one of Fred Shipman's male patients who had died of a rare disorder earlier that year made a complaint about the GP to the British General Medical Council. It concerned an alleged failure to treat the patient's condition and a breach of confidence about his condition. Neither allegation was ever substantiated and no one even bothered to see if Fred Shipman had been involved in any other 'problems' during his career as a doctor.

On 14 January 1986, Fred Shipman astutely invited some of his fellow doctors, including the bluff and popular Dr Smith, to his fortieth birthday party celebrations at York House. 'I had no problem with him then; he was a hard worker and the patients loved him,' explained John Smith. 'He had a lovely theatrical bedside manner that really worked with them.'

Those who attended the gathering said that Fred Shipman appeared totally relaxed and 'very full of himself'. Recalled one, 'Fred supped on a few pints of beer and then switched to red wine. He was extremely merry by the end of the day.'

So life wasn't all just work, work, work for Fred Shipman as he climbed the doctors' ladder in Hyde. He and Primrose even became regular fixtures at local cocktail parties and one extraordinary set of photos later released showed Fred Shipman clearly enjoying himself at a fancy dress party. He was dressed up as a Viking, much to the amusement of many of those present, and then proceeded to become so inebriated that he fell over.

At the same party, Primrose also wore a Viking hat made out of a colander and covered with silver paper. Alongside her, Fred looked resplendent in his toga. But the pictures show his eyes looking like huge black cesspits. The smile is there for all to see, but those eyes show none of his happiness. His pupils are so dilated he may well have been high on drugs at the time.

Fred Shipman was clearly trying to be more sociable in an effort to 'normalise' his life. He even hosted a couple of barbecues in the garden of his house, although those who attended later recalled that Shipman's favourite topic of conversation was his daffodils. To his neighbours and friends, he looked as if he hadn't got a care in the world. Yet Fred Shipman continued using pethidine. The drug was the only thing that truly enabled him to relax.

Fred Shipman tried to quit pethidine by using alcohol to help drown out the demons that filled his every waking hour, albeit temporarily. A few pints of home-brewed beer was tolerated with relief by Primrose, who'd harboured deep suspicions about her husband's continued use of drugs. She didn't believe his story about being allergic to bee stings, but never had the courage to challenge him about his claims.

Meanwhile, Fred Shipman's attitude towards the use of illicit drugs came to the surface in a bizarre manner. He was approached by two doctors in another practice who were very concerned that one of their partners was abusing drugs. Fred Shipman was extremely sympathetic towards the doctor in trouble. He even told the two partners that they should try and help the man. But they felt their primary duty was towards their patients.

'A drug addict is always a drug addict – they don't change,' one of the partners said to Shipman, not knowing anything about his background.

Shipman stared ahead thoughtfully before replying, 'Imagine, if you help him and it works, the satisfaction you will feel.' There was no doubt whose side he was on.

At home, Fred Shipman rarely had time to read for pleasure as he was always buried in paperwork from his surgery. But he did have a fascination with Britain's Victorian era, the 1800s. He enjoyed books like *The Adventures of Sherlock Holmes*. And he was also fascinated by a non-fiction book about a doctor in the mid-1800s who specialised in killing his patients.

Gambler Dr William Palmer was an arrogant and cavalier character, only ever charged with killing one patient but there were at least 13 others, including his own wife. When Palmer was only caught when he crudely forged the will of his final victim leaving him £4,000 (£240,000 by today's standards). He'd got away with killing so many because he prescribed the medicine and wrote out the death certificates. He had the utter trust of his patients and their families and would often go alone to their homes before lacing glasses of wine with strychnine.

On the final day of his Old Bailey trial, people queued from 5.00am for places in the public gallery and when he was hanged, the rope used was sold in small pieces to the crowd, desperate for souvenirs. But Palmer was a careless doctor compared with Fred Shipman; he killed people of all ages, not just elderly ones who lived alone and whose deaths, while lamented, would not be deemed suspicious. The Palmer case sparked a few uncomfortable thoughts inside the increasingly twisted mind of Fred Shipman.

* * *

Businesswoman Joan Dean – once an extra on the popular TV soap *Coronation Street* – died at her Hyde home in February 1988, just a few hours after a visit by Fred Shipman. Close family friend and *Coronation Street* star John Savident – who plays butcher Fred Elliot – read two Shakespeare poems at her funeral a few days later. But shortly afterwards, Joan's son Brian found that an 18-carat Omega watch and a £5,000 engagement ring were missing.

It seems that around this time Fred Shipman decided to start collecting trophies from his ever-increasing toll of murders. He began hoarding the jewellery in a cardbox box at home in Roe Cross Green. When Primrose came across the trophies, he calmy told his wife they were gifts left to him by his patients and that he was waiting for them to increase in value before he cashed them in. Primrose did not question her husband's explanation, but then she never did. In any case, Fred Shipman seemed so happy as he explained that the jewellery could end up providing them with a very healthy retirement 'bonus' when the time was right.

In November 1989, the General Medical Council received a letter of complaint from the Family Health Services Appeal Unit about an incident involving one of Shipman's epileptic patients called Derek Webb, who'd been prescribed a drug called Epilem to control his fits. Fred Shipman had changed his prescription, effectively doubling the dose. A month later, Webb was found in a dazed state at his home, unable to recognise his own sister, Jean Wood. He never recovered, having suffered irreversible brain damage.

His family sued Shipman, who fully acknowledged his mistake and was found in breach of his terms of service as a doctor. But despite this, the General Medical Council took no action against him. The case would continue to go through the courts for the following ten years and yet at no time was Shipman's previous record uncovered.

Meanwhile, the Shipmans became even more active in the parent–teacher association of their two eldest children's school. Fred Shipman had the perfect cover in many ways – the complete trust of his patients and the community in which he lived and worked. His psyche was, in everyone's terms, that of the Good Doctor; a man who could always be relied upon.

But the underlying urge to kill continued to grow within Fred Shipman. He tried hard to fight it off, but he soon kept finding himself trying to plan out more killings with careful precision. By 1990, staff at the Donnybrook clinic began to notice Fred Shipman was becoming increasingly withdrawn. And when he was away from the surgery, he became unsociable once again.

At home, he adored ambling through the long garden of the family home in Roe Cross Green and then sitting at the table outside writing a letter with his cherished tortoiseshell fountain pen – the very same pen he always had with him even when he was signing away death certificates. In many ways, that pen had a mind of its own, as far as Fred Shipman was concerned. He was proud of the pen and looked on it in many ways as a good luck charm. If he didn't have it on him at all times, then he became convinced something bad would happen to him.

The back garden of the family house was Fred Shipman's pride and joy. It featured in just about every photo taken of Shipman throughout the 1990s. Shipman found it to be the only place where he felt he could truly relax. He had lovingly built a rockery and garden wall, as well as planting numerous plants and flowers which sprang into full bloom early each summer.

Sometimes he'd spend hours in a white floppy sun hat, shorts and leather sandles, sitting quietly sipping wine, waiting for Primrose to join him on a warm summer's evening. But some photos of Shipman taken during this period show him squinting uncomfortably, looking as if he's feeling the strain of life … or death. Still only a relatively young man, his physique had become much bulkier and that once thick head of black hair had turned into an even more thinning grey thatch. Fred Shipman had the worries of the world on his shoulders. And his continued involvement with pethidine didn't help either.

CHAPTER TEN

Going Solo

Molly Dudley was a 69-year-old widow constantly beset with health problems. In the middle of 1990, she phoned her daughter-in-law to say she wasn't feeling very well and had called the doctor. But, she assured her relative, it wasn't anything too serious. She just wanted to be on the safe side.

Less than an hour later, Fred Shipman telephoned Molly Dudley's daughter-in-law from the elderly lady's house. 'I'm afraid your mother-in-law only has about half-an-hour left to live,' said Shipman in a cold, matter-of-fact voice.

Shipman also, bizarrely, insisted that she didn't have to rush round. 'I promptly went round, but by the time I got there she was already dead,' Mrs Dudley's daughter-in-law later recalled. Shipman told her that, when he'd arrived at the house, the old lady was 'cold, grey and sweaty and looked as if she was having a heart-attack'. Shipman then added, 'So I gave her a shot of morphine to kill the pain.' Shipman later claimed he couldn't have killed Molly Dudley because he never carried morphine. But the recollection of her daughter-in-law proved Shipman to be a liar.

Back at the Donnybrook practice, the other medical staff continued to be baffled by the hard-working but increasingly antisocial GP. Senior partner Dr Ian Napier insisted, 'Although he could be an excellent clinician, he could also be volatile and bombastic; but when he was nice, he was very nice. He was well read, but he liked people to know it. He was a funny sort of devil.'

Every few months, Shipman showed signs of violent and irrational mood swings, which he'd then take out on the staff. He was not violent in any physical sense, it was almost like a childlike temper tantrum. He didn't do it to any of the partners. He'd only talk like that to his subordinates. Fred had another side to him and, if crossed, he was capable of making people's lives a misery.

At one stage, Shipman even refused to speak directly to the practice manager. 'If he wanted to talk to her he would write her a letter,' explained Dr Napier. 'She was expected to do the same in response. Even though they worked in the same building and he had to walk past her every day, he would completely ignore her. It was totally ridiculous.'

Later in 1990, Fred and Primrose attended a close friend's wedding. Primrose had already ballooned up to a size 20 and she weighed well over 15 stone. Behind the façade of their apparently happy, contented home life, Primrose knew that her husband was hiding some dark secrets from her. She wondered if Fred was having an affair with another women. But such fears made Primrose become even more insular. Her increasing weight also made her reluctant to step out of the house, except to drive the family van around picking up the children. Primrose was using food as a replacement for a lack of true love and affection from Fred.

The couple's sex life had long since ground to a halt following the birth of youngest child Sam. Shipman refused to talk about their situation and Primrose was, in many ways, too afraid to ask. She believed that whatever problems were driving a wedge between them would eventually go away and they could get back to the way things were before.

Fred Shipman's mind was becoming increasingly obsessed by the sick and twisted killing fantasies that were fuelling his very existence. At that friend's wedding he attended with Primrose, Shipman looked tired and objected to having his picture taken by a photographer at the reception. 'He looked dreadful. His eyes were constantly staring at the ceiling even while I was talking to him. It was clear he had a lot of problems on his mind,' said one wedding guest later.

When Primrose's father George died in 1991, he left some money to his four grandchildren, but nothing to his youngest daughter. The majority of his estate went to her sister Mary. But her father's snub simply reinforced Primrose's unflinching devotion to Fred. Her mother Edna – still living in Wetherby – heard nothing from her wayward daughter, who didn't even bother to show up at the funeral. Edna hadn't spoken to her daughter for many years and she didn't know anything about her life, apart from the fact that she was still married to Fred Shipman.

Fred and Primrose Shipman remained completely cut off from their respective families. It was as if they didn't want anyone getting in the way of the life they were leading. Fred Shipman had taken complete control of his young family. Friends of the couple later recalled how Primrose would instantly respond to his every request. She was completely reliant on him, especially since she had no one else to turn to. That was the way Fred wanted it to be.

As one friend pointed out many years later, 'Primrose knew little about the outside world and her husband was all she'd got. In many ways, she was defined by him and, without him, it was difficult to imagine what she would do with her life.'

Primrose was never strong enough to challenge her husband's overriding control of the family. When Fred Shipman lost his temper with any of the children, she wouldn't dare tell him to stop shouting at them. Instead, she'd nod her head in agreement as Shipman exploded in a tirade of abuse. None of the Shipman children have ever admitted to being physically assaulted by their father, but neighbours in Mottram recall hearing screaming and crying coming from the Shipman house. On a couple of occasions, one of the children was seen rushing out of the front door crying hysterically. One child even spent hours cowering in the front garden until Fred Shipman appeared in the doorway and ordered the boy to come in.

The key question is whether Primrose actually knew that her husband had started systematically killing his patients and then putting their deaths down to 'natural causes'. 'If Primrose did not know anything and it's presumed she did not,' one neighbour later said, 'I feel very sad for her.'

* * *

A doctor who has criminal or evil intentions towards patients has unique opportunities to exploit, harm or even murder them. In the privacy of a consulting room, or on a home visit, the trust that patients invest in their doctors can provide the setting in which a special relationship can be cruelly abused. A consultation is similar to a confession in church. Anything said or done is supposed to remain within the walls of the consulting room. The surgery, sitting room or bedroom of a patient's home is considered to be a place of privacy. Patients expect confidentiality, and doctors normally provide it.

GPs feel this particularly strongly, because they often develop a deep and lengthy relationship with patients and their families. But in Fred Shipman's case, it simply provided the setting for him to be able to use his bedside manner to dispense not only care, but also death.

There are numerous patients who want to place their GPs on a Godlike pedestal. When illness strikes, it is a natural human desire to hand over to a doctor who can take responsibility, make decisions and, if possible, even make you better. Therefore, it is perhaps not that difficult to envisage a situation where a GP manages cleanly and quietly to commit mass murder. The opportunities were countless.

It was easy for Shipman to obtain the drugs he used as his weapon. Many chemists supply GPs with morphine and other drugs without batting an eyelid. Few would challenge the authority of a doctor. When a patient dies at home, the GP writes a death certificate indicating the cause of death. If that patient is elderly, everyone feels that it is far more sensitive to avoid the fuss of involving a coroner and a post-mortem examination.

Even coroners are reluctant to get involved in the deaths of elderly people, particularly if they can be reassured by a GP that death was explicable. All these factors conspired to make it possible for a much-loved doctor, Fred Shipman, to murder so many of his patients without anyone being alerted earlier.

Death wasn't something Fred Shipman could take or leave. It had become an overpowering, maniacal urge which took complete control of his mind and body. One minute he would be impressing himself with his ability to act out the role of the good doctor, the next he'd be in a cold sweat as he quietly rolled up a sleeve and injected his deadly medicine.

But in order to continue his evil work, he needed to strike out on his own so that he would then have complete control over his professional activities. By 1991, Shipman had been at the Donnybrook practice for almost 14 years and his hard work and popularity with patients remained evident throughout that period.

To satisfy those urges to kill then Fred Shipman needed to set up a practice on his own to be answerable to no one. Colleagues at the Donnybrook practice were getting in his way; they cramped his style. In public he had to show an assertive, caring manner, but on his own he would not have to pretend. That would take the pressure off him. It was a strain being so nice all the time.

Fred Shipman showed his true colours when he finally quit the Donnybrook practice to set up his own one-man operation at the end of 1991. In his original announcement about leaving the practice, Shipman claimed he was planning to move to Yorkshire, but had not yet found a suitable surgery.

Then a few days later, he told the partners in Hyde he was really leaving the Donnybrook surgery because he did not agree with GP fundholding and that, because of a loophole he had found in his contract, he was taking with him his list of 3,000 patients. 'It left a big hole in patient numbers and nearly decimated the practice,' one partner later recalled.

The other six doctors in the Donnybrook practice were stunned by Shipman's move because they now had no patient list to offer an incoming GP. This meant they'd lose his contribution to the running costs of the building and ancillary staff, about £20,000 a year. They would also have to buy out Shipman's share of the building for £23,000. They were connected to a bank loan, which they wouldn't finish paying off for many years. They'd also have to pay Shipman's tax bill of almost £30,000. In the days of 1992, tax was paid on the previous year's profits. When Shipman refused to pay his share, the others discussed suing him but they didn't have a cast-iron case, even though they were morally right. Shipman even took three receptionists and a district nurse from the Donnybrook staff after promising he wouldn't poach any of the employees.

Fred Shipman had planned his departure for many months with virtual military precision. He had not told anyone else in the practice because he felt he couldn't trust any of his colleagues. He wanted to be sure that nothing would prevent him from setting up on his own. Not for the first time, Fred Shipman was proving just how underhand and selfish he could be.

But throughout this period, only one thing was truly driving Fred Shipman forward in his ambitions; he wanted to be allowed to do *whatever* he wanted with his patients and the only way to achieve that was to ensure that no other doctors observed his work practices. Now the act of 'discovering' his victims shortly after he had killed them would be completely under Shipman's control. He even intended to get pre-printed sympathy cards made to send out to relatives after each death. It would also mean that he could choose his favourite time to watch those patients die – mid-afternoon. Admittedly, he did sometimes call on them on the way to work, just a few minutes after saying his goodbyes to Primrose and his four children.

Shipman even proved how much he cared about his patients by immediately holding an extra surgery session on Saturday mornings when Primrose would stand in as the receptionist to save him the cost of paying his regular staff any overtime. Everyone – patients and staff – had absolutely no doubt that he had his patients' well-being at heart. And Primrose relished playing a subservient role to her husband by addressing him formally as 'the doctor' in front of other staff.

One staff member later recalled, 'It was really weird. His own wife was calling him "Doctor" to his face.' In some ways, Fred Shipman's treatment of his wife summed up his role in the family and at work. He saw himself as the 'doctor' in every sense of the word. He needed that respect. He wanted to be looked up to.

Even erstwhile partner Dr John Smith – furious about Shipman's announcement that he was going solo – fell out with the GP. His fury was further compounded when he realised that Shipman had been lying about his reasons for leaving the practice. 'He told me he didn't like the way the group practice was modernising, getting in computers and that sort of thing,' recalled Dr Smith. 'What's the first thing he does? He gets in a computer.'

Fred Shipman soon put his own stamp on his new surgery by starting a special fund for medical equipment which eventually rose to £20,000. Shipman ran the fund with district nurse Gillian Morgan and his friend and patient Les Fallows, who organised raffles and social nights to try and raise cash. They eventually had enough to buy nebulisers, blood pressure monitors, even an electrocardiogram (ECG) machine and a sonic fetal heart detector.

Policeman Les Fallows was one of Fred Shipman's few friends at this time. The two men shared a love of rugby football. They often took Shipman's sons Sam and David to watch Sale Rugby Club on Fallows's season ticket. He also frequently gave Shipman's sons his tickets for the world-famous Manchester United soccer team if he was away.

Fallows felt sorry for the Shipman children because their

father worked such long hours. Fallows always felt that behind the friendly face lay a complex and intense individual. But Fred Shipman liked to use his 'gentle' bedside manner to hide a multitude of confused thoughts.

The closest Fallows ever came to seeing an emotional side to Fred Shipman was when they cheered on youngest son Sam, who'd followed in his father's footsteps by playing rugby football for his school. The youngster also played prop forward for the Ashton Rugby Club schoolboy team as well as Lancashire's youth team, alongside the son of Billy Beaumont, one of the most famous rugby players in England when he captained the national side in the early 1980s.

For the first few months following his split from the Donnybrook practice, Fred Shipman continued to work from the same building, which he part-owned, until the other partners could raise the finance to buy him out. Some of the other doctors warned Shipman that by working on his own he would be made an outcast. Fred Shipman didn't give a damn. This was what he had been working up to for many years.

It wasn't until after Fred Shipman had departed from the Donnybrook practice that one of the surgery managers pulled Shipman's CV up on the computer screen and realised that he had that drug conviction from Todmorden. So much time had elapsed since he'd first arrived in Hyde that virtually no one left on the staff had any idea about his past.

As one member of the practice later recalled, 'It's very odd, really, because the only reason anyone checked out Shipman's CV was because we were all so angry that he'd left so suddenly.'

But no one thought to inform the local health authority that a doctor with a serious drug conviction had set up as a sole practitioner.

Fred Shipman's one-man practice soon became renowned for his tireless effort and long hours. He gave people as much time as they needed and happily called at their homes after hours, even on non-emergencies. Few other doctors could match his style of personal touch. And Fred Shipman was pretty generous with medication as well; of the 104 registered doctors in the Tameside area, he was one of the top five highest prescribers.

When the West Pennine Health Authority's medical adviser called on the GP in 1992, she found him 'strong-minded' with a robust defence of his methods. He insisted he would control all his patients' needs and would treat them himself rather than refer them to hospital whenever possible. Shipman's words were like music to the authority's ears. The already severely over-stretched National Health Service needed more doctors like Fred Shipman if they were going to cut hospital waiting lists.

And Shipman always presented extremely rational arguments as to why he prescribed so many drugs and usually recommended the most expensive brands. This was simply further proof of his dedication to his job. No one doubted the word of hard-working Dr Fred Shipman. In any case, the West Pennine Health Authority had no idea about his previous drug conviction.

Fred Shipman set up his new surgery in a tatty-looking building compared with his previous workplace. But the location was good, just 100 yards away from Hyde's market square and the Town Hall, on the main street through the centre of Hyde. Number 21 Market Street was the second to the end of a terrace of shops, with a well-stocked pharmacy on one side, two Indian restaurants within a few yards, a used car lot and a pet-grooming parlour opposite.

Fred Shipman was running a practice virtually opposite the one he'd just abandoned. Between a tatty, old, grey bus station and an old bingo hall, where some of the good doctor's favourite elderly patients were regular visitors. Fred Shipman took out a 20-year lease on the property in Market Street, paying rent of £300 a week. Opposite his surgery was the charity shop Age Concern.

Fred Shipman stepped up the number of house calls to his elderly patients because he now had the freedom to do whatever he wanted. When one local bank shut down, Shipman began negotiating with a young woman doctor, Dr Lisa Gutteridge, to become his partner if he could expand into the larger property.

But after just one meeting, the scheme fell through and Dr Gutteridge never saw Dr Shipman again. Shipman dropped the idea because he was only too well aware of the difficulties of working in a shared practice.

* * *

In February 1992, an allegation was made to the General Medical Council that Shipman had failed to visit a female patient who'd suffered a stroke. Shipman disputed the facts, but the GMC's local medical service committee found him guilty of a breach of his contract and he was fined £800.

At no time was anyone at the GMC informed about Fred Shipman's drugs conviction while he was working in Todmorden. The GMC later claimed that the complaint it received did not suggest a pattern of performance sufficient to question Shipman's practice. 'However, even if they had suggested a pattern,' a GMC spokesman later recalled, 'we only had the power to look at isolated incidents of serious professional misconduct. We did not have the power to investigate potential patterns of poor performance.'

One of Fred Shipman's closest friends at this time was Dr David Walker, who'd first met him when he was GP to Walker's elderly mother. 'I also went to him a couple of times for an ear infection and once for insurance purposes on a medical,' Walker later recalled.

Shipman and Walker met up again when they found they were living in the same village – Mottram. Shipman's youngest son Sam was the same age as Walker's daughter Rebecca, and they both went to the village school together. 'Fred was active in the community and the parents' association and we were always bumping into him through those sort of things,' recalled Walker, who lived round the corner from the Shipman family, in Hall Drive.

About six months after crossing paths again, the two men began going out for an occasional drink at a real ale pub situated inside nearby Stalybridge Station. Shipman and Walker would 'sink five or six pints' on each occasion. Walker later recalled, 'We'd meet about once every six months. I'd ring up and say, "Do you fancy a drink?"' Among the others who met up with Shipman was John Davidson, a local police inspector whose own mother-in-law had recently died after a visit by Dr Shipman.

Walker and Shipman's conversations in the pub during these get-togethers were, on the surface, painfully ordinary. 'We would grumble about the health service but Fred seemed to prefer more relaxed conversations,' says Walker. Once, Shipman made a brief reference to the appallingly untidy state of his family home. Dr Walker recalled, 'Fred was laughing about how he had a bag of socks under the stairs. He said it was the only place he could keep them and be sure they'd be in the same place the next day. He made it clear his house was a chaotic place.'

Fred Shipman studiously made sure he always bought his fair share of pints of beer, says Dr Walker. 'He didn't need pushing. If six people went, there were six rounds. He was never mean.'

Shipman even admitted to Dr Walker that he particularly liked the pub inside Stalybridge Station because he was not as well known in that area. 'I think Fred didn't like to be seen out enjoying himself by his patients. He liked to leave that part of his life behind when he came out for a beer,' recalled Dr Walker.

But all the other men in the group noticed that Fred Shipman's character hardly altered even 'when he got a bit tipsy'. As Dr Walker recalled, 'The bar sold only real ale, which featured five good bitters. I think he tried them all, as we all did, but he certainly knew how to hold his ale.' The pub was located in the station's old waiting room area and people would walk through after getting off the trains.

And Fred Shipman showed absolutely no interest in other women, even if a pretty girl walked through the bar. 'Looking back, I suppose he was a bit guarded with his reactions. We'd all sit on the table at the back end of the bar well away from the main area.'

At the end of the evening, Shipman, Walker and their other drinking pals would walk the three-mile journey home because they all realised they were over the drink-driving limit. As Dr Walker later explained, 'Some of us would walk home faster than others. It was all uphill and took at least 40 minutes. Fred was a faster walker than me and he'd usually wander off ahead of the rest of us within the first mile. He seemed to prefer to be on his own.'

On the local middle-class cocktail party circuit, the Shipmans never looked entirely at home but they did turn up at a few gatherings after he opened his solo practice. Recalled Dr Walker, 'Primrose would often arrive first on her own, then Fred would arrive late and sit sullenly in the corner. He'd always have a drink at these parties but never as much as when we were out at the pub together. I think Fred liked to be in control when he was amongst a crowd of people.'

But Dr Walker noticed that Shipman rarely made any effort to circulate amongst people at these cocktail parties. 'He'd expect people to come to him and talk to him. Fred and Primrose usually stuck close together and they were never the last to leave.'

Primrose Shipman was virtually an enigma to neighbours and friends in Mottram. Said Dr Walker, 'I hardly knew Primrose at all. My daughter went to their house a few times but never stayed for longer than a few hours.' But Walker's daughter was never invited to stay overnight and, rather strangely, Shipman's son Sam was never allowed to go round to the Walker household. The two childhood friends drifted apart after they left junior school. Years later, Dr Walker asked his daughter what it was like inside the house and she simply replied, 'Nothing special.'

Once, Dr Walker did call round at the Shipman house unannounced. 'It was a Saturday morning and I needed to borrow a stethoscope because I was working as medical cover at a boxing match later that day. I got to the door, but Fred made a point of not letting me in. It was a bit strange.' Moments later, Shipman appeared with the stethoscope and gave it to Walker without saying another word. 'I couldn't see what was going on inside. The house was like a cocoon and few adults ever got in there.'

Dr Walker would often pull up outside the house when he was involved in a school run with the Shipmans. 'But Sam was always outside there waiting while Primrose was herding in a load of kids connected with her child-minding work.'

Behind Fred Shipman's attitude lay his bizarre relationship with the family house. 'That property represented a different section of his life,' says Dr Walker, 'and he clearly didn't want strangers in his home.'

But Dr Walker found it difficult to fault Fred Shipman's professionalism. Dr Walker recalled, 'When he did a life insurance health check-up on me, he was most efficient. When I said no to something, he immediately pointed out I'd had an operation ten years before. He'd bothered to read my notes very closely and was able to pick up on that. He actually made me feel bad because I was lying.'

Years later, Dr Walker found it difficult to believe that Fred Shipman was capable of breaking the law. 'I thought to myself if he is that honest ...'

But throughout the many years that David Walker and Fred Shipman were friends, he never talked about his marriage. 'I knew nothing about him and Primrose on a personal level,' recalled Dr Walker. The two men shared a similar background, grammar school boys from working-class backgrounds who'd worked their way into the medical profession, married young and even started a family while still at university. 'But we never really discussed any of this even though we had so much in common.'

However, Walker and the group of pub regulars were aware of Primrose's problems with her relatives – but only because she had mentioned it in passing to some of the other housewives in Mottram whose children she looked after. One of those women later recalled, 'Primrose's problems with her own family only came out because some of us were naturally curious about her background. But she didn't exactly expand on what had happened.'

One of the most memorable things about Primrose at this

time was her driving skills as she dropped and picked up her own children from friends' houses and, in some cases, dropped off children she had been minding during the day. 'She was a very tense driver, hands clutching the steering wheel. Sometimes she seemed to leave braking until the very last moment,' recalled one neighbour.

Occasionally, the Shipmans appeared at local functions, including a Mottram village hall show that featured a series of satirical sketches about local people based on the national TV news programme *News at Ten*. The Shipman's oldest child Sarah also appeared in the village hall in a local version of the musical *Grease*. Fred and Primrose Shipman were in the audience of at least 30 people. The show was hosted by the vicar of the village. Dr Walker recalled seeing the Shipmans applaud their daughter politely but 'it was clear they were simply going through the motions. I don't think either of them had a very good sense of humour, to put it mildly.'

Other Mottram village events summed up life in Middle England; church fêtes, gymkhanas, tombolas, even light-hearted local community association quiz nights. The Shipmans turned up to watch the local junior school's parents' sports day which featured events such as three-legged races and sack races. But neither of them took part. Dr Walker recalled, 'I particularly remember that Fred could often be found in the beer tent at these events. There's no doubt he liked a pint of ale.'

And the Shipman children were certainly a credit to the family. As well as going to nearby college, the two eldest – Sarah and Christopher – both worked part-time at the local pub, The Dog and Partridge. Those who knew them at this time say they were bright and mature with no qualms about hard work. Fred and Primrose occasionally turned up at the pub for Sunday lunch. The Shipmans adored the stodgy pub grub and regulars remember their favourite meal was roast beef and Yorkshire pudding.

Blonde, blue-eyed Sarah Shipman was immensely popular with the pupils at Tameside College where she was studying to go into the catering industry. She eventually went on to run a hotel in the south of England with her partner. Many of the family's friends and acquaintances insist Sarah takes after her mother, especially when it comes to her culinary skills. Primrose's skills in the kitchen were so renowned that she had often undertaken the catering for the practice's Christmas parties even though her cooking skills at home seemed non-existent.

Back at work as a GP, Fred Shipman took on a completely different persona as Dr Walker later discovered while visiting Shipman for a check-up shortly after the death of his elderly aunt, Edith Brady, who died in Shipman's surgery and was later counted amongst his victims.

'When I went for my medical, I said to Fred, "Am I lying on the same couch my aunt Edith died on?" Shipman replied very casually, "Yes, you probably are."'

As Dr Walker later pointed out, 'There was no wry smile on his face. He just said it flatly. I'll never forget it as long as I live. He seemed like a different person from the one I had enjoyed a few pints of beer with.'

Back in the tidy, leafy cul-de-sac of Roe Cross Green, in Mottram, Fred Shipman showed yet another side to his complex character. When one of his nearest neighbours fell seriously ill with lung cancer, Shipman became the doctor from heaven and showed extreme care and patience with the man's family. As another neighbour later explained, 'This man wasn't one of Fred's patients but he went out of his way to help the family. It was very touching and Fred seemed genuinely upset when the neighbour died.'

There is no doubt that Fred Shipman truly did love his job in a twisted way. He liked the feeling of responsibility which came with being a GP. Despite his shyness, he enjoyed being needed. The trouble was that some of his patients at his Market Street surgery were extremely demanding. They kept coming in for the pettiest of reasons and it was all becoming too much for him. They needed him desperately but all they were doing was pushing him to the edge.

Inside the sick and twisted mind of Fred Shipman, those omnipresent demons began once again surging to the surface. And that's when Shipman began showing a distinct lack of patience with some of his supposedly beloved 'flock'. When one regular female patient showed up at the surgery complaining of a vague illness, Shipman snapped at her, 'Stop disobeying me. There is nothing, I repeat, *nothing* wrong with you.' That same patient later recalled, 'He was so damn sure of his diagnosis but then that's why we trusted him so utterly. He controlled us all. I accepted his rudeness and left the surgery convinced he was right and there was nothing wrong with me.'

That need to control his patients was a crucial element of Fred Shipman's urge to kill. Escalating the risk factor added to the thrill of the entire evil scenario. Eventually, the perils of pretending that one of his patients had phoned and asked for a visit – something that a technocrat such as Shipman would know was easily checkable – added even more to the thrill of killing. Then he'd call at their homes and administer a lethal injection. But each time he felt the need to replace that level of risk with something even more hazardous.

On the morning of 17 April 1993, Fred Shipman obtained by prescription in the name of Mrs Sarah Ashworth 30mg of diamorphine. A few hours later, he was calmly and coolly filling a syringe with the morphine before squirting it gently into the air to make sure there were no blockages. Then Shipman leaned down and pulled up Mrs Ashworth's sleeve. 'You won't feel a thing, my dear' – he'd uttered those words hundreds, if not thousands of times, over the previous 20 years.

As he pressed the needle into her vein, she thanked him. He felt no pangs of emotion, no guilt. It was all so familiar, he performed his duties virtually on automatic pilot. After all, he was just another doctor treating just another patient. Those feelings helped him block out the reality of the situation. Fred Shipman saw himself as merely treating a needy patient. But he was putting that patient into an irreversible spiral towards death. Soon after that injection, Mrs Ashworth's body went limp. Her breathing became stilted.

The GP felt Mrs Ashworth's pulse. It was getting weaker virtually by the second. She was fading into oblivion before his very eyes. Soon she would be nothing more than a corpse. The very thought sent a shiver of satisfaction through Fred Shipman. Her skin colour began to change to a slight grey.

He still wasn't absolutely certain how he should feel at the moment he inflicted death. But he knew he never wanted her to awaken from her unconscious state. Shipman knew precisely what he had just done; he'd injected Mrs Sarah Ashworth with morphine and then watched the life drain out of her body.

Dr Shipman leaned down once more and checked Mrs Ashworth's pulse. She'd gone. Shipman dropped his patient's limp wrist on her lap and stared into oblivion for a few moments. He kept telling himself he was only trying to help her. Then he snapped out of his dreamlike mode, and tried to compose himself after the excitement of yet another 'kill'. It was a weird, floating feeling, as if the entire episode had been a dream and he would wake up to find that the devil hadn't infiltrated his mind after all. But then he looked at the corpse and the reality was there for him to see, still sitting in her favourite armchair.

Shipman knew he couldn't turn the clock back. In any case, he felt strangely satisfied; like a cat who'd got the cream. There was no grim reality to face; his patient had died of natural causes and there was no question of him being held responsible for her death.

Not long afterwards, Shipman signed a death certificate for Mrs Ashworth stating that she'd died of 'heart failure/natural causes'. Shipman even phoned her family on the morning of her death to tell them the sad news. He told them Mrs Ashworth had called him out to her home after suffering breathing difficulties. Shipman said Mrs Ashworth had 'gone out like a light' as he treated her. He even claimed he'd tried to save her with an injection, but he never said what was in his syringe.

The truth was that Mrs Ashworth had telephoned Shipman but she certainly never then answered the door to him, as he later claimed. Shipman said he'd earlier talked to her on the phone and told her to leave the back door open and she had happily obliged. Later, tests on Mrs Ashworth's body showed there were significant traces of morphine in her bloodstream.

Fred Shipman was in a permanent state of denial. He simply did not consider himself a killer.

CHAPTER ELEVEN

The Angel of Death

I n Hyde, gossip had started circulating about Dr Shipman's habit of 'losing' so many of his older female patients. Some even called him 'Dr Death' behind his back. But no one ever considered the nickname to be anything more than a light-hearted jibe.

One of those who heard the rumours was district nurse Katie McGraw who encountered Shipman through her work at an old people's hall opened through the efforts of former Hyde mayoress Kathleen Grundy. Little did she know that when she introduced Mrs Grundy to Shipman, their paths would cross some years later.

McGraw had been a ward sister at the nearby Tameside General Hospital and had also met Shipman when they both sat on the area health authority. McGraw was the nurse's representative. Often, Shipman and McGraw would share a cup of coffee before or after the AHA meetings, usually held in the hospital boardroom.

Recalled Katie McGraw, 'Fred was quite open to me about certain things. We even discussed some very personal matters.

He'd come out with the odd thing which surprised me at first. He was intense. Looking back, he wanted to tell me more than he actually did but I didn't push him for more information.'

Shipman even broke his own golden rule and talked about his family during conversations with McGraw. 'He mentioned rugby and stuff like that and kept referring to "his boys". He was obviously very proud of them. But he seemed a complicated man. Sometimes when you met with him he seemed very thoughtful, then at other times he could be extremely arrogant. He didn't suffer fools gladly, particularly colleagues, whereas I frequently saw him put on a very understanding look for his patients.'

Although Katie McGraw never saw any evidence that Shipman was using drugs on himself at the time, she did later concede, 'There certainly was a darkness about him. But in many ways, Fred was a highly moral person so I can't imagine him being involved with drugs.' And Katie McGraw still believes to this day, 'Fred was into preventative medicine in his own mind.'

Shipman made a point of telling Katie McGraw he was extremely worried about his children taking drugs. 'He was really worried about that. He seemed to view the outside world as an evil, nasty place full of obstacles for his children.'

Katie McGraw frequently saw Shipman out in Hyde's busy town centre at lunchtimes going from one shop to another. 'He was always in a bit of rush, but still noticed me straight away and said, "Good morning". But I did used to wonder why he was out busily shopping during his lunch break.'

Rumours circulated at the time that Primrose Shipman had suffered some kind of nervous breakdown because she was hardly ever seen out in the town and she'd suddenly given up her child-minding business without explanation. Katie McGraw recalled, 'I knew Primrose by sight and these rumours were very strong at one time but I never got to the bottom of it. I met Primrose a couple of times at drinks parties connected with the area health authority. She seemed a bit of a simple soul, education-wise. I expected Fred Shipman to have been married to a more dynamic lady and they did make a strange couple.'

But Katie McGraw had no doubts that Primrose was 'blindly loyal to Fred. He was her whole life. If Fred said the moon is blue, she'd say, "Yes, Fred."'

Katie McGraw concluded that Fred Shipman was 'such a hard worker that he seemed to get angry with people who didn't put 100 per cent into his practice like him'. She added, 'On the surface, Fred might have appeared to be an open person but he wasn't really. I don't think anyone ever really got to know him properly.'

* * *

Fred Shipman stuck to a rigid routine at the end of each day, especially after he had set up in practice alone. He'd leave his surgery in Market Street at 6.00pm on the dot and then drive to the family home in nearby Mottram. Primrose would always be in the kitchen preparing the evening meal as he walked in. But Fred Shipman never kissed his wife – instead, he'd take off his jacket and say, 'Good evening, what time is dinner?'

Then he'd carefully wash his hands and sit down in his favourite armchair while Primrose carried on cooking. Shipman would barely utter a word other than to complain about the patients who'd annoyed him that day. 'They're wasting my time. The surgery is so busy. I've got too many patients to look after,' was Fred Shipman's favourite moan.

Then, with the family gathered around him at the dinner table, Shipman would bark out orders to his two youngest sons. 'Samuel, serve the potatoes. David, the carrots.' They never dared answer back and there was no conversation until they had finished eating.

Says one of the children's friends who attended one such meal, 'It was very uncomfortable. None of the kids were allowed to speak unless spoken to by Dr Shipman. It was easier just not to say a word. And neither of them asked me one question about myself.'

And the food wasn't all that pleasant, either. 'The sausages were undercooked and still a bit pink. The potatoes were hard and not completely baked and there was some tinned corn. I didn't rush back there in a hurry,' recalled the friend.

Most evenings after dinner, Fred Shipman would slope into the sitting room and bury his head in the business pages of a newspaper, checking the prices of a few stocks and shares he'd invested in over the years. He harboured a dream that he'd get lucky and find that they had gone up massively in value. Fred Shipman hoped that one day he'd get his hands on enough money to leave England and retire to a pretty cottage in somewhere like France.

By this time, the once pristine white interior walls of the Shipman house on Roe Cross Green were faded yellow. Three-foot-high piles of unwashed clothes were left downstairs in the kitchen area near a run-down, rusting washing machine with shoes, newspapers and magazines cluttering the floors. In the kitchen, dirty saucepans and plates lay untouched for days.

Then Primrose gave up her job as a registered child-minder with Tameside Council and began running a sandwich shop in the nearby village of Hollingworth. 'I think she grew tired of looking after other people's children. It was an exhausting job and it caused even more chaos in an already chaotic household,' explained one friend.

Shipman's oldest son Christopher was definitely more like his father and went on to university. The two youngest – David and Sam – were still at West Hill High School. Both were known locally as responsible, polite teenagers and both went on to captain the school.

While Fred Shipman was undoubtedly quite a stern father, he was not opinionated in the obsessive sense. He craved to be regarded with respect and admiration, and this dominated everything he did. Evidence of domestic violence inside the home suggests that he was prepared to hand out severe punishments to those who disobeyed him. 'Dr Shipman certainly wasn't afraid to hand out physical punishment to his children,' says one of his son's childhood friends. 'The boys especially seemed afraid of him and hardly dared speak unless he spoke to them.'

And periodically, his frustration pushed him towards another kill. Whether murdering another human being was an attempt to assert what he was capable of, or whether it was some strange, sadistic compulsion that crept over him with certain people, we will probably never know. The only thing that seems certain is that the killings were connected with the need to be something more than he was.

Shipman felt his daily life was a sort of contemptuous lethargy, devoid of virtues or vices. He often simply did not feel as if he was part of the world he inhabited, but an amused and sometimes disgusted spectator to it. Shipman detested the human race and its pretences. To him, life was a fine art and he was completely devoid of the ultimate values or distinctions of right and wrong.

* * *

A Tameside Health Authority audit was carried out at Fred Shipman's one-man practice in the middle of 1993. A full computer system was to be installed within the following few months and the premises were being improved to provide new facilities – a staff room, computer room and a midwife's consulting room. The local authority report at the time concluded, 'An enthusiastic practice where we were warmly received and an audit is clearly an integral part of the work.'

That same year, Fred Shipman asked the Tameside authorities if they would award him £200 to support a survey of 16-year-olds in his practice. The aim of the project was to identify health problems and provide appropriate advice. Twenty-three of the thirty-two patients invited to take part were given advice about lifestyle and also provided with facts and figures about cholesterol levels.

A second health authority visit to the Shipman practice in February 1994 was sparked by a much more serious situation. Officials were concerned about the amount of a drug called benzodiazepine which was being prescribed by Shipman to his patients. It was supposed to be used for congestive cardiac failure. Health authority officials urged their superiors to agree to a fresh audit on the Shipman practice, but the surgery was judged by officials to be 'highly motivated' and the Shipman surgery was given the benefit of any doubt because it seemed to be such a popular practice.

Yet again, Shipman's previous involvement with drugs did not come to light.

The only other real criticism of the one-man operation was that Shipman did not have a district nurse on call for patients to consult on the premises. Shipman told health authority officials he held open access consultation sessions and dealt personally with patients who might otherwise consult a district nurse. He made it clear he did not need any help.

In 1994–95, Fred Shipman completed a questionnaire to assess the practice's all-round performance. Shipman referred to the problem of epilepsy in patients, the needs of those 16-year-olds and the repeat appointment situation.

On a more practical level, Fred Shipman's skills as a doctor had clearly deteriorated. When one patient bumped into a surgery nurse called Jill, she told them, 'I'm not in tomorrow. You'll have to see Dr Shipman for your next jab.' She then paused before adding, 'He's not very good at injections, mind, so you'll probably have a huge bruise for the next week.' In fact, Fred Shipman – once renowned as a gentle doctor who could give an injection without the patient even noticing – had become much clumsier. Or was it that he simply didn't care any more?

Fred Shipman and his syringe were a popular subject of conversation amongst his patients and staff. Yet despite this, he continued to show great interest in his new patients. He always sat them down and explained the workings of his surgery. He made a point of mentioning that he was a 'prescribing doctor' who kept abreast of new pharmaceutical developments and didn't hesitate to use them. He was also proud that the practice had access to its own counselling service.

At least on the surface, Fred Shipman continued to appear avuncular, reliable, friendly and knowledgeable. Most new patients were very impressed. Shipman's Market Street practice seemed no different to any other surgery; a waiting room filled with piles of dog-eared women's magazines, ranks of senior citizens and subdued kids. The surgery was never quiet, but it always seemed to be efficiently run.

Fred Shipman – not an ostentatious man by any means – continued to drive a modest car and still live in that smallish semi-detached house in the village of Mottram, a ten-minute drive from his surgery. Money for the practice remained tight, and Primrose still helped out in the reception at weekends when she could. Fred Shipman gave the impression that all his patients' problems were his own. He was revered by many for his meticulous attention to detail. 'He never forgot anyone's name. It was remarkable and it made his patients feel so reassured,' one former member of staff remembered.

Fred Shipman even had a plaque on the desk of his consulting rooms which read, 'Every day's a bonus.' And he remained a generous prescriber of medicine. 'He always said cheap medicine was not the best. That was why his surgery was one of the most expensive in the country,' recalled Brian Dean, whose mother died while under the care of the GP.

All this made Fred Shipman as popular as ever. It also made his name very familiar with the West Pennine Health Authority, since he steadfastly refused to be constrained by the National Health Service underfunding other GPs had learned to live with. Of West Pennine's 230 GPs, Shipman continued to be among the top five prescribers, exceeding his budget for seven years. Jan Foster, the area's directory of primary care, remembered Shipman as 'always defensive, but he had rational arguments for his prescribing'. And he usually won his argument because he was an excellent GP. He performed high numbers of immunisations, had a good postgraduate education record and there had been few complaints from the public about him. He had 3,100 patients, well above the national average.

But there was another side to Fred Shipman's care and attention – whenever he came across a patient who wasn't completely forthcoming, he would place a tick alongside their name. He knew that such patients had to be treated with care. They might be on the look-out for any mistake he made and that could prove very costly. For Fred Shipman was still stockpiling morphine by making out prescriptions to patients who did not need it or who had died and it was imperative that those 'more difficult' patients did not have any suspicions about his 'habits'.

Fred Shipman falsely prescribed 14 lots of 30mg doses of morphine in 1993. The following year, he prescribed even bigger amounts. On one occasion, he prescribed ten 100mg ampoules for a woman patient the day before she died (her records later revealed she did not need it). Another 20 ampoules of 500mg doses prescribed for a male patient on the day he died. It was more than Shipman would have needed to feed a morphine addiction, if, indeed, he had one. Shipman would go on to procure a total of 22,000mg of morphine – the equivalent of 1,466 fatal doses – during his six years running a solo practice.

On a more practical level, Fred Shipman saw computers and cutting-edge technology as the way forward in medicine. He could be irascible and even bad tempered with those who did not share his enthusiasm. But it was his willingness to embrace the new that provided him with the confidence to drive forward in his quest to commit murder on a horrific scale.

Shipman had been a disciple of computer records from the moment he'd entered into general practice in Todmorden in 1974. At his one-man practice, he worked late into the night transferring records of patients from old buff folders into computer files. One member of the Market Street surgery staff later recalled, 'Dr Shipman was very meticulous and had a computer system which he used all the time. He was very proud of what he could do with patients' notes in terms of auditing and things. In fact, he could be quite a bore about computers.'

Yet for a man who prided himself on having the most up-to-date computer equipment, his sheer arrogance led him to completely ignore the safeguards that were built into modern hardware. He just couldn't come to terms with the fact that every single time he opened up the computer it recorded the exact time and date. That meant that every time he put in new information on his MicroDoc software, a specialist program for GPs, he left a 'shadow' on the hard disk.

The system at his one-man practice was even upgraded to allow for such an audit trail to be retrieved. Shipman was unaware of the facility, but anyone with a basic knowledge of computers could easily throw up a wealth of information on how Fred Shipman was tampering with the files of some of his patients in an attempt to make sure that their deaths seemed entirely 'natural'.

And Shipman's treatment of subordinates within his surgery remained extremely inconsistent. One teenage medical student who joined the practice for one day was traumatised when a patient died in the surgery and Fred Shipman treated the incident as an irritation. 'The body was left in the treatment room for all to see and this poor girl was asked by Shipman to get a folder from right next to the body,' explained one member of staff. The girl later told another doctor friend that she had been so upset by working at the Shipman surgery that day that she had been put off practising medicine for life.

* * *

Then Fred Shipman deliberately upped the stakes by risking killing a patient while a friend of the victim was in the next room. He'd already got away with murdering a patient in his consulting room. The boundaries had all but disappeared and now there was no stopping him.

Fred Shipman's patient Renate Overton had always lived life

to the full, working as a nurse at the Redferns rubber factor in Hyde. Even when she was made redundant, she refused to feel down as her world revolved around her family and friends. Then on a February night in 1994, Renate, aged 44, returned to her neat terraced house after a night out with friends when she suffered a minor asthma attack. Her 20-year-old daughter Sharon was concerned, but not overly worried as the attacks happened two or three times a year. She phoned Fred Shipman and he arrived at the house within 15 minutes. Sharon immediately took him through to her mother in the sitting room who was having trouble breathing.

'I'll leave you to it, then, doctor,' Sharon told Shipman before going up to her bedroom.

Five minutes later, Sharon heard Fred Shipman yelling for her and she rushed down the stairs. When she walked into the sitting room her mother was laid out on the floor unconscious. Shipman immediately instructed Sharon to give her mother mouth-to-mouth resuscitation while he massaged her heart. 'We tried it but it didn't work,' Sharon later recalled.

Then, without uttering a word, Fred Shipman reached inside his medical bag and brought out a syringe. 'He sucked in liquid from a little bottle and shot a small squirt into the air just like doctors do on the television,' Sharon later recalled. 'Then he rolled up the sleeve on her left arm and injected the fluid into her.'

'What is that?' asked Sharon.

To this day she cannot remember if he said 'morphine' or 'adrenalin'. But he then told Sharon to call for an ambulance after saying her mother was in a serious condition. 'It arrived quickly,' she later recalled, 'and the paramedics got out a defibrillator. After three goes they got a pulse and put her into the ambulance to rush her to the hospital.'

Shipman said little to Sharon and didn't accompany them in the ambulance. Moments later, he left the house.

Within minutes of arriving at hospital, Renate Overton was put on a life-support machine. One doctor even pointed out that

Renate appeared to have been injected with morphine. 'At the time, it did not mean anything to me,' Sharon later recalled. 'All that was on my mind was my mother and her health. It never occurred to me that this was the reason that she was in this state.'

For the following 14 months, Sharon Overton visited her mother in hospital virtually every day and watched her steadily deteriorate. Sharon recalled, 'She had asthma problems and also suffered from epilepsy. But it was not serious and neither condition had prevented her from living a normal life. She was full of life before all this.'

In April 1995, Renate fell into what doctors called a 'persistent vegetative state' and died. When Sharon next visited Shipman as a patient, she hoped he might be able to offer her some kind of explanation. 'But he didn't even ask me about her,' Sharon later recalled. 'I just didn't know what to say. I couldn't understand why he wasn't interested.'

In fact, Fred Shipman knew only too well about Renate's fate. As far as he was concerned, she was just another notch on his belt. All that mattered was that he'd once again got away with murder.

It wasn't until many years later that Sharon Overton discovered that morphine should never be given to people with respiratory problems.

* * *

Fred Shipman had an undoubted passion for order and neatness in his professional life even though the family home remained in a constant state of untidiness. And his compulsive list-making knew no boundaries. Not only did he assemble more than twice the number of patients any GP would consider sufficient, he knew exactly how many there were – 3,200 at one point, 3,100 at another.

He'd even volunteered to work as secretary of the local Medical Council, a job of such overwhelming tedium that doctors normally did all they could to avoid it, in order to monitor his own performance as a GP. His love of lists meant he could control without fear of intrusion or dispute. But sometimes he got angry that people seemed to fail to appreciate the accuracy of his skills.

In Shipman's mind, it was all a question of efficiency – the cold, authoritative pride of a thing done well. Shipman relished issuing death certificates. They really were proof of his brilliance. But between the killings, Fred Shipman slipped back into deep, dark moods; an overwhelming emotion of helplessness like the feelings sparked by the loss of his mother. Taking pethidine had only been a brief respite. But killing had eased the pain.

His mother's death had left Fred Shipman with a sense of self-preservation; he knew how to look after himself. But as a loner – despite his large immediate family – he tended only to do things for others that were convenient to him or to his benefit. He wasn't a 'giver' or a 'taker'. He just didn't trust people much. After all, most of them had betrayed him at some time in his life. To the outside world, he remained the perfect picture of respectability, but he was never content and this made him moody and unpredictable. Shipman also suffered a serious degree of nervous irritation, due to the secrets he was holding inside himself. That further diminished his willpower.

Fred Shipman lost his integrity after his mother died. He wasn't really interested in conforming to the legal or moral ways of life even though he wanted his family to grow up as 'normal' as possible. He wanted his children to be a success in an honest, straightforward manner. A bit like a criminal who wants his children not to make the same mistakes.

Meanwhile, Shipman was prepared to continue to deceive other people to get his way. He liked acting out the impression of being open and honest, whereas in reality he refused to take any responsibility for his own actions. His arrogance would not allow him to look ahead as far as his medical work was concerned, unless of course he was covering his own tracks. However, Fred Shipman had been clever enough to conceal the truth for many, many years. He was a smooth and effective liar, leaving out essential parts of any story, even inventing facts or simply not telling the truth as it should be. He had the insight and the intelligence to spot opportunities and the ability to turn them to his own advantage without caring about the dishonesty of his decision. He also loved to find excuses for his bizarre behaviour and then blame others for his predicament.

Fred Shipman still believed that the killing only started when his first victim-to-be was slipping towards death and he simply gave her a helping hand. But that had been exciting because it gave him a role in life, as a ministering angel of mercy. He'd then wanted to try it again, and when he got away with it for a second time, he began to believe it was his God-given right to continue doing it. Not surprisingly, it soon became a casual, even habitual, regular event.

By the mid-1990s, he saw his mission of mercy as an open-ended culling of the geriatric population of Hyde. And Fred Shipman certainly couldn't imagine anyone being clever enough to stop him. He had the perfect cover and he was convinced no one would ever dare question him; he was the good doctor, the life-saver, the man who *really* cared. He reckoned he was doing them a favour by killing them. Killing was something else again. Doctor or not, he would have gone there all the same. But then his victims meant nothing to him because he meant nothing to himself.

Fred Shipman so enjoyed the thrill of being there at the moment his patients died that his compulsion did lead him to kill one patient in her home unaware that her best friend stood in the kitchen waiting for his visit to end. Shipman was visibly shocked when he found Marion Hadfield in Marie West's kitchen minutes after she died in her living room on 6 March 1995.

Shipman immediately said, 'She's collapsed on me.' Then he leaned down to his patient and tried to open her eyes. 'Look, there's no life there.'

Then Mrs Hadfield asked, 'What can you do? Can't you do something?'

'No, she's gone.'

At no time did Fred Shipman try to resuscitate Mrs West or contact the emergency services. Her collapse had been caused entirely by a phial of morphine provided by Dr Shipman.

* * *

Primrose Shipman was never more proud than in January 1996, when Fred gathered his family and 60 friends, many of them patients, at Maestro's Restaurant, in Hyde, to celebrate his fiftieth birthday. He chose a menu of insalata di pollo, polla alla provinciale, salmone belladonna and bistecca alla boscaiola and the finest wines. Each guest was given a menu card reading: 'Happy Birthday 14.01.46. HF Shipman 14.01.96'.

But one who was present at the gathering later recalled, 'Fred seemed strangely subdued although he still enjoyed ordering a pricey bottle or two of wine. But some of us did wonder if running his own practice was putting him under a lot of strain.'

It was just three days after he'd claimed the life of two victims within eight days of each other – 79-year-old pensioner Erla Copeland (11 January) and 81-year-old Hilda Hibbert (2 January).

But Shipman's addiction to killing became even more insatiable when he murdered five patients over a seven-week period between April and June of 1996. Only he knows what drove him to such intense depravity over such a small period of time.

On 11 July 1996, Shipman visited an elderly patient called Mrs Irene Turner at her bungalow in St Paul's Hill Road, Godley, near Hyde. Neighbour Sheila Ward later recalled how Fred Shipman called her outside, asked her to wait five minutes then go to the bungalow to pack a bag for Mrs Turner, as she may have to go to hospital while he did some tests. When Mrs Ward went into the house, she found the 67-year-old widow dead in bed. 'She looked beautiful,' she later recalled.

Mrs Ward then ran to the house of Mrs Turner's friend Michael Woodruff and, when he wasn't in, went home to find a telephone number for him. She then noticed that Fred Shipman had returned and gone back into Mrs Turner's bungalow.

'Was it cancer?' Mrs Ward asked the GP as she walked back in.

'No, diabetes,' replied Shipman almost casually.

Yet when Mrs Turner's son-in-law Alfred Ishwerwood saw Shipman the following day, he said she had died of ischaemic heart disease. Isherwood was baffled but was too polite to question the doctor's verdict. Shipman even said he'd advised Mrs Turner to go into hospital, but she'd refused because she thought she was not ill enough. Isherwood immediately pointed out that she would have happily accepted any treatment recommended by a doctor. He later recalled, 'He was very matter-of-fact, very businesslike. No compassion.'

Mr Isherwood went on, 'She took Dr Shipman's word. She thought he was a great doctor. She really liked Dr Shipman. She took every pill he prescribed to her because she trusted her doctor.'

Alfred Isherwood never forgot how Shipman explained to him that the veins in Irene Turner's arms and legs had collapsed and blood had rushed to the centre of her body, putting too much pressure on her heart. Shipman assured Isherwood that Mrs Turner would have fallen asleep before she died. But a post mortem examination more than two years later showed that Mrs Turner died from morphine poisoning.

* * *

On 30 August 1996, Fred Shipman paid a visit to the home of a patient called Sid Smith after he'd complained of feeling unwell. Moments after arriving at the house, in Garden Street, Hyde, Sid's brother Ken went into the kitchen to make them both of them a cup of tea.

Minutes later, Fred Shipman strolled into the kitchen to tell Ken that his brother had died. When the two men walked back into the sitting room, Sid Smith was still sitting in his favourite chair. 'When the undertakers arrived 20 minutes later, they started talking to Sid, thinking he was asleep,' Irene's daughter Sheila Marshall later recalled. 'They were disgusted he had been left that way.'

And from that moment on, Ken Smith began referring to Fred Shipman as 'the Angel of Death'. His niece Sheila Marshall later recalled, 'He did not like his arrogant and overbearing attitude and said he was uncaring, the way he left the body just sitting in a chair.'

Three months later, in December 1996, 78-year-old neighbour Thomas Cheetham died during a visit by Shipman while his wife Elsie was out shopping. Two weeks later, Ken Smith was also found dead, sitting in the same chair as his brother. A window cleaner had spotted him sitting motionless and asked a neighbour to see if he was all right. She walked in through the back door, which was unlocked as usual, and was unable to revive him.

Four months after that, Elsie Cheetham, 76, who had been fit and lively, went the same way – on the same day as Shipman murdered another patient.

But there was a twisted logic behind Fred Shipman's decision to wipe out these residents of Garden Street, in Hyde. He saw them all as potential witness to the first murder in the street of Sidney Smith, and he knew they had been voicing criticism of his methods as a doctor. Shipman was undoubtedly in control of his killing because he was quite prepared to obliterate anyone who threatened his ability to murder without detection.

* * *

Fred Shipman had got into the habit of standing by the side of many of his patients and watching them die. Lizzie Adams, 77, was so active and in good health that up until six months before her seventy-seventh birthday, she'd been a dance teacher and danced regularly with her partner, William Catlow. But that didn't stop Fred Shipman deciding her time had come on the afternoon of 28 February 1997.

Shipman later claimed that Lizzie Adams died while he was

in the next room looking for a telephone to tell her daughter she needed hospital treatment for bronchial pneumonia. It was at this point that he was disturbed by Mrs Adams's dance partner Bill Catlow. Shipman said, 'I listened to the chest. There were no heart signs. Mr Catlow said he felt something on her wrist and I told him it was his own pulse.'

But Mr Catlow later insisted he called at the house that afternoon and let himself in with his own key to find Shipman standing in the lounge looking at Mrs Adams's collection of Royal Dalton figurines. In fact, Fred Shipman had been waiting for her to die when he was most rudely interrupted by Mr Catlow.

Shipman turned to Mr Catlow and asked, 'Are you Bill?'

'Yes, that's right,' he replied.

'Betty is very, very ill.'

Shipman said he'd called for an ambulance and Mr Catlow rushed past him into the living room to find Mrs Adams. Shipman followed him in and immediately pronounced her dead.

'She's gone. I'd better cancel the ambulance,' Shipman told Catlow.

'Are you sure?' Mr Catlow asked the GP. 'She looks as if she's asleep.'

'I'm afraid so,' came Fred Shipman's reply.

Catlow later recalled that the GP then made a telephone call. He assumed it was to cancel the ambulance. But no telephone call was made or received that day requesting or cancelling any ambulance. It was merely a charade performed by Shipman to help conceal further the murder of Lizzie Adams at his hands.

CHAPTER TWELVE

Dangerous Liaisons

It would be a gross over-simplification to say that Fred Shipman's frustration was the result of an unsatisfied lust for power. But he certainly considered himself to be brilliant at his job. Members of staff at his one-man surgery often spoke of his fanatical attention to detail. As William Blake once wrote, 'When thought is closed in caves, Then love shall show its root in deepest hell.'

No doubt, Fred Shipman found being a doctor a very numbing experience. He couldn't afford to care too much if he was to remain good at his job. When he'd first started, he'd found it difficult when patients died unexpectedly, but that feeling passed quickly. Fred Shipman could face death as long as he was in control of it.

In many ways, Shipman didn't consider his victims to be human beings. He'd become completely desensitised. His version of caring for his patients was to want them all to die happily and peacefully without ever realising that death was about to occur. So, as the number of victims had increased, Fred Shipman felt a physical dependence on the act of killing. His addiction had turned into a physical dependency on watching people die.

The first few deaths had probably been unplanned. Opportunities arose and he couldn't resist the temptation. But now he felt a rush of adrenalin every time he had an opportunity to kill again. And, crucially, he still believed he was cleverer than everyone else around him.

Fred Shipman – on the surface a friendly, if reserved, local GP – felt completely alienated from society. He found it virtually impossible to function in normal situations. That's why he needed the outlet of death. His so-called normal life with a wife and four children helped overshadow his innermost fears. Now the strain of keeping those evil thoughts and deeds to himself was taking a punishing toll on his psyche.

But it was the Godlike regard in which most of his patients held him that was the biggest clue to the warped and twisted mind that had already turned Fred Shipman into a serial killer. For he continued to harbour grandiose ideas about himself. He saw most other people as 'stupid' and believed he was on another, higher plain to them all. This arrogance made him believe he was above the law. And his aloofness made him fixate on things that were not always the most intelligent choice. Morphine was a classic example of that. It could be traced in the body. Yet morphine had become the thread which ran through his life. He didn't seem to care that it would inevitably one day lead to his downfall.

* * *

Hyde really was an unlikely setting for mass murder. There was little to divert motorists as they hammered past on the nearby M67 motorway. It remained a distinctly low-key type of place. Even the biggest local supermarket boasted that it was a 'No-Nonsense Foodstore'. Entertainment for the residents of Hyde still only consisted of the Bingo hall near Fred Shipman's less-than-impressive surgery and a few pubs. And two grim, concrete tower blocks cast a shadow over the main shopping arcade. Shipman hadn't even bothered putting a brass plate up announcing his name and title, but it didn't seem to put off his vast list of patients.

Some years after starting his one-man practice, Fred Shipman became heavily involved with an attractive middle-aged female patient called Bianka Pomfret who had recently divorced her husband and was suffering from a wide range of psychiatric disorders. Her ex-husband Adrian later recalled, 'Fred Shipman seemed to really care about Bianka. She was a very warm person underneath her very mixed-up exterior and she desperately needed guidance.

'She had a tendency to buy people, even to buy friends, in a sense. She'd shower them with gifts but she was extremely confused and terribly over-sensitive.'

German-born-and-raised, Bianka's life was filled with contradictions; she drove, but she didn't own a car; she rarely went out, but she was very outgoing when she talked to people. As Mr Pomfret explained, 'It was all a form of self-punishment. She even chopped all her hair off at one stage. She had a lovely head of strawberry, reddy-blonde hair, but it was typical of Bianka to get rid of it – she was always trying to make a statement about her life.'

It had all been very different when Adrian and the 26-year-old Bianka married more than 15 years earlier. Adrian, aged 30, was stationed with the British Army in the German town of Munster. Bianka was unable to have children and that had deeply affected the Pomfrets' marriage, so they adopted a baby boy and called him William. Bianka Pomfret knew she was highly strung, even during her marriage, and her ex-husband believes to this day that she had a deep-set fear of passing on that mental illness to any of her children.

Bianka's mental problems – manic depression – eventually cost her her marriage to Adrian Pomfret. Her condition would also cause a deep rift with their son William.

Just before Adrian Pomfret ended the marriage, he went to see family GP Fred Shipman to warn him that she might 'go a little crazy' once he broke the news to her. Adrian had first encountered Shipman when he had had problems with high cholesterol and had to get his blood checked regularly. 'He seemed extremely good and trustworthy and we felt very safe in his hands,' he later recalled.

That day, Mr Pomfret told Shipman, 'I've made this decision and I'm going to leave home. The situation is such that I can no longer live with her and I've made the decision to move out in a month. The reason I've come to see you is to give you fair warning and make sure that she is looked after.'

Fred Shipman responded by nodding his head thoughtfully. Adrian Pomfret later recalled, 'He seemed genuinely concerned about Bianka's well being and I felt secure in the knowledge that he would keep an eye on her after I left home.'

Shipman even made a point of telling Adrian Pomfret, 'I think you're making the right decision.'

Fred Shipman was even adamant that Bianka Pomfret was not as crazy as everyone else thought she was. 'She is not mentally ill. It's just the way she is. She's a highly intelligent person,' he told Mr Pomfret.

But Mr Pomfret never forgot something else about Fred Shipman that day. 'He didn't look me directly in the eye. He had the strangest stare. He never once blinked. It was quite the reverse. I'll never forget that stare.'

Soon afterwards, Adrian Pomfret left the family home and set up with another younger woman. But he so trusted Fred Shipman that, a few months later, he returned to the surgery in Market Street to give him an update about his marital situation. Shipman was already monitoring the pregnancy of the new woman in Adrian Pomfret's life.

That's when Shipman said to him, 'Do you think Bianka will stay in the UK after the divorce or go back to Germany?'

Adrian later recalled, 'At the time I didn't see the significance, but it was a very personal approach and Shipman seemed to be crossing the line between patient and friend in his attitude.'

Adrian Pomfret replied at the time, 'Well, my honest opinion is that she prefers it here.'

Fred Shipman asked, 'What d'you mean by that?'

'I'm going to give her 60 per cent of my assets to ensure that she is OK,' replied Mr Pomfret.

'How d'you mean?' asked Shipman again.

'Well, she'll own her own property, her own home and she will have money besides ...'

All of a sudden, Fred Shipman jumped in and said, 'I don't want to know about that.'

As Adrian Pomfret later recalled, 'I remember thinking, What d'you mean by that? If you care about somebody and, as a GP, you would have thought one of the things that was important was that a woman with a serious mental illness was not going to be penniless.'

After the shock of her marriage break-up, Bianka Pomfret tried to mend her relationship with her son William. But her mental health was fast deteriorating. Eventually she agreed to visit the local community mental health centre for more intense treatment.

Dr Alan Tate, consultant psychiatrist at Tameside General Hospital, treated Bianka for manic depression. He'd encountered her some years earlier when – during her marriage – Bianka had asked Dr Tate to commit her to hospital because she was feeling suicidal and her husband was telling her to pull herself together. But, as Dr Tate later explained, Bianka's condition was one in which 'patients think about their death and about taking their life but do not necessarily intend to do it'. She was released within days.

But just after the marriage break-up, Fred Shipman contacted Dr Tate and asked him to see Bianka once again because she had been suffering a 'recurring depressive disorder'. She was admitted to hospital as a 'crisis case' and stayed over Christmas and New Year. By 1995, Bianka Pomfret's illness had become psychotic. She was hearing voices and believing her thoughts could be read by other people. She was rapidly 'moving towards a high risk of completing her suicidal thoughts', according to one specialist.

It was then Fred Shipman decided to take a much closer interest in Bianka Pomfret's life. Adrian Pomfret later explained, 'Some time later, Shipman sent for me and said that Bianka's grandmother had suffered mental illness as well and he was convinced Bianka needed to be hospitalised once again. They were obliged to get her treated.'

Mr Pomfret continued, 'You have to appreciate that most people just gave Bianka a wide berth. They all acted as if she had something catching, but these sorts of mental problems lurk in everyone. We all should be aware of that. And Fred Shipman seemed to really care about her.'

Shipman told Mr Pomfret he was going to personally handle Bianka Pomfret's case from now on. 'I never thought twice about it at the time. I thought he was a caring GP so I went along with him. We all trusted him implicitly. And for some time, Shipman's decision seemed to help. He even gave her intensive counselling and prescribed her anti-depressants. She seemed to get better.'

Adrian Pomfret's relationship with Fred Shipman was then further cemented when his baby son Nathaniel by his new wife suffered severe liver problems – septicaemia – and almost died at six months of age. 'He was marvellous over that and his quick thinking almost certainly helped save Nat's life. We both thought he was a fantastic man.'

When Adrian Pomfret visited his former wife – now back at home after her spell in mental hospital – he made a point of singing the praises of Fred Shipman. He soon noticed that Bianka was becoming more and more dependent on Shipman. Sometimes she'd visit his surgery three or four times a week for 'counselling'.

To begin with, Mr Pomfret was relieved that his deeply troubled ex-wife seemed to have found someone she trusted to treat her and listen to her. 'At that time, she definitely improved,' he later recalled. Shipman put Bianka on a course of lithium to try and end the extreme mood swings she was suffering from.

Bianka – a highly religious woman who attended Catholic church every Sunday – was deeply confused about the existence of God. 'That used to get a grip of her sometimes, she found it difficult to handle,' recalled Adrian Pomfret.

But Fred Shipman's propensity for prescribing drugs was not the main reason why Bianka Pomfret became so dependent on her GP. Shipman's 'counselling' of Bianka was becoming increasingly personal. He found he could relate to Bianka's problems because she seemed to be coming from a similar direction to him. After some months, she began turning up at Shipman's Market Street practice just as he was completing surgery. Then she would enter his office, sit herself down and pour everything out to him.

Eventually, Shipman found himself revealing things about his own life to Bianka that he had never ever discussed with anyone else before. A close bond was forged between them. They shared a mental telepathy about certain sensitive subjects and Fred Shipman had formed an emotional attachment to Bianka Pomfret.

In the middle of all this, Adrian Pomfret managed to sit down and have some reasonable conversations with his ex-wife. 'But I learnt to be very careful not to criticise her. She didn't want her views questioned.' Mr Pomfret noticed Bianka was receiving a large number of house visits from Fred Shipman. 'There aren't many GPs who'd do the number of house calls he did,' he later recalled.

Shipman even, on occasions, visited Bianka Pomfret when she was in hospital drying out from the high dosages of lithium that he'd prescribed for her. Lithium was known to damage the liver, so she had to go into hospital to wash it out of her system on a regular basis.

Then, one day, Bianka Pomfret made a bizarre comment to her former husband: 'Isn't it strange that Dr Shipman is married to someone who looks so odd?'

Mr Pomfret later recalled, 'Looking back on it, that was a very strange thing to say. It made me wonder how close Bianka was to Shipman.' But he added, 'I do know that Bianka was the last person who could have coped with a sexual relationship with a man. You have to remember that her illness made her incredibly intense; she used to think about things far too much. The other side is that it can also make you bond with people who seem to understand where you are coming from. Shipman definitely came into that category.'

But was Bianka Pomfret in love with Fred Shipman? 'It's possible,' Adrian Pomfret says today. 'She needed him and he seemed to provide her with some kind of security. He was always there for her. I still wonder about their relationship to this day. But remember she had very high morals so she would not have entered into a relationship without a lot of thought and consideration.'

And local district nurse Kate McGraw insists, 'She clearly adored him. She had a lot of problems. I think Fred Shipman took advantage of her in many ways.'

But did Bianka Pomfret and Fred Shipman really have a proper relationship? 'Something happened between them. It was definitely on a mental level and might well have been something more. It was a cat and mouse game. One side of her tried to ignore it, but the other side of her would kick in and enjoy the attention. Bianka had this ability to look inside people's minds and she could see what Shipman was up to. She probably knew the truth behind what he was up to and it must have frightened and depressed her.'

Adrian Pomfret believes that his ex-wife confided about the true extent of her relationship with Shipman to the people she met while attending counselling at the local health centre. Mr Pomfret later recalled, 'Bianka got herself into situations where she had no other contact, no other friends apart from those people at Brindle House [the health centre]. She spoke to them at some stage.

'She may have fallen in love. I'll never forget how she'd come home from seeing her proper psychiatrist who'd put her on a particular line of therapy, then one week later she'd go back and see Shipman and she'd come back with him pushing a completely different line. I thought that was baffling at the time, but it shows how much control Shipman had over her.'

'I believed Shipman was after something. As a GP, he could get away with all sorts of things. I have no doubt you can be in love with someone mentally and you don't even have to go out with them. Certain people attract certain other people. Bianka needed feeding mentally and Shipman did that to perfection. I think he tried to make Bianka feel she was right about everything, but occasionally he did disagree with her and that wound her up completely. Bianka respected and needed Shipman so much and he played that role so well for so long, but then the goalposts changed.'

At one stage, Shipman even told Bianka Pomfret, 'Don't worry about it [the illness]. We can't cure it, but at least we know what it is and we can treat it.'

In early 1997, Adrian Pomfret went to see Fred Shipman about his ever-increasing cholesterol levels but ended up discussing his ex-wife. 'He brought up her name first,' recalled Mr Pomfret.

'She's doing OK,' Fred Shipman told his patient. 'Don't worry about her. She is a very strong person and she will dance on your grave.'

'I'm glad about that,' replied Adrian Pomfret. He later recalled, 'I thought that's a strange thing to say.'

After approximately two years of intensive contact between Shipman and Bianka, it was inevitable that someone as mentally ill as her would want more from such a relationship. That was when Fred Shipman pulled the shutters down – leaving Bianka devastated. As Adrian Pomfret later explained, 'She dived into a really deep depression suddenly. She was in such a terrible state that I advised her to start seeing a psychiatrist yet again. Something weird was going on.'

Mr Pomfret believes that Fred Shipman had so much control over his former wife that at first he urged her not to see a psychiatrist. 'I took her twice to see a woman doctor and she refused to go back on each occasion. I know Shipman was urging her not to see this other doctor. He wanted to retain control over her.'

He finally relented and Bianka went back to seeing Dr Tate at the local hospital. Then another man came into Bianka's life whom she met during counselling sessions. Adrian Pomfret recalled, 'I knew him as Czech Andy. He spoke fluent English and German. And he took a lot of Bianka's attention away from Shipman.'

Fred Shipman was deeply offended when this other man came on the scene. He seemed almost jealous. As Mr Pomfret explained, 'You have to remember that Bianka was a highly intelligent person. In some ways, she was flattered by the attention of these two men. She needed to feel she was in control sometimes because of her own fears and her actual inhibitions about herself.'

But it was Fred Shipman who really had the control.

CHAPTER THIRTEEN

A Model Family

Most of Fred Shipman's patients smiled and thanked their trusted doctor as he injected them with a fatal dose of morphine. He always felt better about killing them when they looked so happy to be on their way.

Fred Shipman's life revolved around being a doctor – nothing else mattered. His profession enabled him to exercise the power to bring about a sudden and complete cure of patients' illnesses. But that lust for power was no longer a benign one. As a relatively lowly general practitioner, the scope for being a real life-saver was limited. So, with this absence of an opportunity to bring about such dramatic changes to people's lives, Fred Shipman had resolved to bring about their deaths.

To adapt the words of Richard III slightly, since he could not prove a healer, he was determined to prove a killer. Each time Shipman's patients exasperated him, he concluded that wreaking vengeance upon them was what they truly deserved. Sensitised by the death of his own beloved mother, he was more inclined to rage against his elderly female patients. They were the lucky ones who had managed to live to old age. His mother had never had the choice, and here they were complaining and moaning about their lives. They didn't know how lucky they were. In any case, Fred Shipman thought to himself, I'd be doing most of those old women a big favour, since no doubt many believed their lives were not worth living.

By the mid-1990s, Fred Shipman had been a GP for almost 25 years. Death had become a routine part of his job and it was easier to resolve certain 'problems' by murdering his patients than dealing with them when they became difficult. The act of killing had become a release for Shipman from the irritations, frustrations and angers of his life. He found a strange sense of peace from taking someone else's life.

Fred Shipman might not have been regarded as the most charismatic of characters, but he had an ability to plug away at things and that gave him his sense of achievement. Yet by this time he had become increasingly socially and psychologically isolated. His relations with his work partners had been far from successful. Beneath the surface, Fred Shipman was deeply afraid of what the future held for him. He wanted to believe he could do anything, just as his dearly beloved mother had predicted. But she was wrong, and coming to terms with that was eating away at his self-esteem.

Fred Shipman's low threshold for irritation and anger came to the surface when he publicly tried to prove he was superior to other people. He desperately craved recognition and the outside world was failing to acknowledge and reward his brilliance. Shipman had allowed himself to develop into a man who derived twisted relief from killing old and helpless people – it helped alleviate the frustrations of his life, albeit on a purely temporary basis.

Shipman believed the killings were further evidence that he'd been in control of his entire life ever since the day his mother died and that extended to all those around him. He needed that charge of having the ultimate power of life and death. But, like any addiction, each 'hit' lasted less and less time and he needed even more regular 'fixes'.

Another victim around this time in late 1996 was widow Irene Heathcote, aged 76. She told her relatives and friends she wanted to change her GP – Fred Shipman. Mrs Heathcote had been upset with Shipman for cancelling one of her hospital appointments. 'She felt he was giving her the wrong treatment,' her daughter later recalled. 'She said she was going to see him to "have it out" with him.'

A few days later, Mrs Heathcote was found dead in a chair at her home in Coronation Avenue, Hyde. Her neighbours alerted police when they couldn't get any answer from the house. Retired policeman William Trattles, who helped break into the house, later recalled what happened when Fred Shipman appeared at the house.

'He arrived, examined the body and said she'd died the previous evening,' said Mr Trattles. 'He said she had suffered a stroke and that he could issue a death certificate because he'd seen her the previous day. There didn't seem to be anything suspicious. He seemed a quiet, unassuming man and professional.'

But there was no evidence that Mrs Heathcote had died naturally. The way Mrs Heathcote was found sitting 'peacefully' in her chair was inconsistent with someone who'd died of a stroke. Mrs Heathcote had been murdered by Fred Shipman.

* * *

Pensioner Charles Killan's wife had died in 1984 and he'd planted a rose bush in his back garden in her memory and tended it each day. During the Killans' long marriage, the pair had enjoyed holidays away in north Wales and rides out on Charlie's motorcycle. In one treasured family photo, he could be seen standing next to his beloved Bond three-wheeler car.

But on 3 February 1997, Fred Shipman proved that it wasn't just elderly female patients who helped feed his addiction to death. For 90-year-old Mr Killan died at the hands of Fred Shipman who then called on a next-door neighbour to tell him that Mr Killan 'wasn't very well' and asked the neighbour to wait for the ambulance he claimed he had called. That neighbour then walked into Mr Killan's house in Bagshaw Street, Hyde, and found the retired bus driver already dead. Moments later, he watched as Fred Shipman put his hand round Mr Killan's throat and said curtly, 'You're right, he's dead.'

Shipman even signed a death certificate saying Mr Killan had died of heart failure and heart disease.

* * *

On 25 April 1997, Shipman visited 58-year-old Mrs Jean Lilley at her flat in Jackson Street, Hyde, after she complained of chest pains. It was his first ever home visit to her. He later claimed, 'She was a very interesting patient and when she came to the surgery I listened to her chest because I had never come across the condition before. When I visited her this time, there were far more noises, squeaky noises, harsh noises. I would say she had severe arthritis.'

Shipman said he then decided she needed to be admitted to hospital. He explained, 'She was not very happy. She said, "Couldn't I just have some antibiotics and see you tomorrow?"'

Shipman claimed he then persuaded Mrs Lilley to discuss going into hospital with her family, including her husband, long-distance lorry driver Albert Lilley. He said he left her sitting comfortably in a chair that afternoon.

Shipman said he was at the flat for 15 to 20 minutes, not 40 minutes as later claimed by Mrs Lilley's neighbour, Elizabeth Hunter. He said he saw no one and spoke to no one as he left. Mrs Hunter found Mrs Lilley collapsed and rushed after the doctor as Shipman was driving off, but he completely ignored her.

Another neighbour, Janet Aldred, was looking out of her window at the very same moment. She later explained, 'I saw Liz on the path shouting and waving and trying to attract his attention. He must have seen Liz. His head was out of the car window turned towards where Liz was coming down the path but he just drove off.'

Paramedics later told Mrs Hunter her friend had been dead 'for some time'. One expert – Dr John Grenville – later explained it was 'inconceivable' that Mrs Lilley could have been other than 'in extremis' or dead when Shipman left her.

While the ambulance crew was at Mrs Lilley's flat in Jackson Street, Hyde, Shipman even returned clutching his dead patient's 4in-thick medical file. Paramedic Sandra Smith later recalled that she thought it unusual that a doctor would bring a patient's medical file and then go over it in great detail.

Smith also noticed that Shipman became agitated and kept saying that Mrs Lilley's pregnant daughter Odette was due to arrive. She later explained, 'He did not want to be there when Odette turned up. You'd have thought a doctor would have wanted to be there to sympathise and help, especially as Odette was pregnant.'

And during his return to the flat, Shipman hadn't even gone into the bedroom to examine Mrs Lilley. Neighbour Mrs Hunter later recalled that Shipman gave the impression that the death did not matter, 'that it was irrelevant'. A later examination of Mrs Lilley's body revealed that, despite suffering from serious lung and heart problems, it was morphine that actually caused her death.

* * *

At 7.30am on 29 May 1997, one of Fred Shipman's elderly female patients died inside his own treatment room. Less than an hour later, he told the daughter of Mrs Ivy Lomas that she had died of a 'massive coronary'. Mrs Lomas did suffer from emphysema and narrowing of the coronary arteries – one by 70 per cent, another by 50 per cent and a third by 10 per cent – but this did not kill her. Once again, it was morphine administered by the good doctor which sent her into another world.

Shipman had continued seeing other patients in his

consulting room, even though the body of Ivy Lomas lay in his treatment room. Shipman later claimed that, after Mrs Lomas's collapse, he immediately started heart massage and mouth-to-mouth resuscitation, but after what seemed like 15 minutes or longer, he stopped because there was no response.

Shipman then went into the reception area and told receptionist Carol Chapman that he had a 'little problem' with the ECG machine 'but would see the next patient'.

He later said he did not immediately tell Mrs Chapman that Mrs Lomas had died because 'to do it in front of three other patients I thought was inappropriate'.

Ivy Lomas's daughter, Carol Dalpiaz, had spoken to her mother on the phone a few hours before she died because she was worried about her mentally ill son Jackie. She later recalled that her mother had never even mentioned she had any heart problems. Shortly after Ivy Lomas's death, Fred Shipman met Mrs Dalpiaz at her mother's home in Thornley Street, Hyde. He explained how he'd left her in his treatment room to tend to other patients then returned to find her collapsed. He insisted he'd tried to revive her.

Later, under police interrogation, Shipman changed his story and said that he had not, in fact, tried to revive Mrs Lomas.

But what Carol Delpiaz did not realise was that Shipman had labelled Ivy Lomas one of his 'nuisance' patients to other members of staff at his surgery. Shipman even later joked that within a few hours of Ivy Lomas's death, he'd considered putting up a plaque in the seating area saying 'seat permanently reserved for Ivy Lomas'.

PC Phillip Reade, who went to the surgery, explained, 'This lady had been left for a brief period of time and Dr Shipman was telling me that she could have taken her last breath as he left the room and been dead for 15 minutes, or she could have just taken her last breath as he went in. I was amazed, to be quite honest.'

During 1997, another round of gossip circulated in Hyde that Fred Shipman's patients didn't always live to a ripe old age. A few patients took the rumour and gossip seriously and moved away from his one-man practice but most simply laughed and shrugged their shoulders. The local health authority heard that some patients were quitting the practice so they sent questionnaires to them to find out why. But they never followed up their own enquiries.

Meanwhile, Fred Shipman's need for a 'fix of death' continued. During one visit to the home of a patient he'd just killed, Shipman told the daughter that 'morphine is a nice way to go'. His words implied that he believed he was relieving them of their lives of misery and pain. It was important to Fred Shipman that his victims didn't feel the anguish of death creeping up on them. Vast doses of morphine meant they'd drift off into a happy oblivion called death. There was no struggle. There was no pain. Just a never-ending sleep.

* * *

Despite his preference for quiet evenings in with Primrose, Fred Shipman did attend class reunions involving his fellow students at the Leeds University Medical School. The get-togethers were organised by Dr Colin Wilkinson and held at the Bramcote Trust House in Leeds. For Fred Shipman, it was a relatively easy journey 40 miles up the M63 freeway from Hyde. He even brought Primrose with him on two occasions. The reunions were amusing, gossipy affairs and Fred fitted in well. His dark sense of humour only came to the surface when talking about other people. And he seemed very passionate about his work. Shipman also breathlessly told other guests of his ambitious plans for the Market Street practice.

One other GP he met at the reunions later recalled, 'Fred obviously deeply loved it in Hyde; he was very caring. He wanted to give a better service to his patients, do things his way, which he couldn't do before.'

Shipman underlined that attitude by taking on even more work when he became the treasurer for the Small Practices

Association, a support group for medical practices of three or fewer. His fellow graduates from Leeds were impressed, 'and he was running an appeal for new equipment on top of that. He worked his socks off.'

Primrose just about held her own at these reunions. On one occasion, the couple even brought two of their children. One partygoer invited the Shipmans to his hotel room, as their children were of a similar age. 'Fred spoke most, took the lead, because it was his reunion, but Primrose seemed pleasant and amiable. The children were very polite, too, well brought up,' the doctor later explained.

Fred Shipman was a considerable social success at these gatherings. Even the fact that the GP looked older than his years now seemed to work to his advantage. 'While everybody else had aged, Fred always looked middle-aged. I suppose it's partly because he got married so young,' said one old colleague.

* * *

When Muriel Grimshaw, 76, died unexpectedly at her home in Berkeley Crescent, Hyde, on 15 July 1997, her daughter Mrs Ann Brown noticed that Fred Shipman didn't even bother to examine her mother's body before pronouncing her dead. 'He just gave her a cursory glance,' Mrs Brown later said.

She'd found her mother fully clothed on the bed with the television on after being alerted by a neighbour, and then she phoned Shipman's surgery. He arrived at her flat within 20 minutes. But Shipman didn't reveal to Mrs Brown that he'd visited her mother the previous day. It was then that Shipman had shaken with excitement as he arranged her clothes so that she would look almost as if she was asleep. This method of 'dressing' the death scene had become an important part of Shipman's routine after he'd administered a fatal injection. Later, he even recorded in Mrs Grimshaw's computerised medical record that she had died of a stroke, even though she had, like so many before her, died of morphine poisoning.

Shipman recorded the time and date of Mrs Grimshaw's death as 6.00pm on 14 July. He also recorded on her death certificate that the last time he'd seen her was on 2 July 1997, when he had actually called on the day that she had died – 14 July.

'That was an error on my part,' he later admitted.

Four years earlier, Fred Shipman had taken a supply of heroin from the home of Mrs Grimshaw's daughter whose husband had just died. The GP removed it on the day that 54-year-old cancer sufferer Raymond Jones died. Following Mrs Grimshaw's death, local undertaker Alan Massey tackled Fred Shipman after noticing how frequently he was being called out to deal with the sudden death of Shipman's patients. Usually, there was little evidence that they'd been seriously ill in the first place.

Alan Massey explained, 'Anybody can die in a chair or drop down dead in the street, but Dr Shipman's patients always seemed to be in the same or very similar positions. They'd be sitting dead in the chair or on a settee and 90 per cent were always fully clothed. There was never anything in the house that indicated the person had been ill. Clearly something was not quite right.'

When Massey asked Fred Shipman if there was 'any cause for concern', the GP responded, 'No, there certainly isn't.' Shipman then produced his death certificate record book and said, 'There's nothing to worry about.'

Alan Massey's daughter, Deborah Bambroffe, later recalled, 'It was as if you were going and asking for a prescription for a cold or something. He just got up, got his register out where he gets his death certificates from, opened it up at different pages and his exact words were, "Anybody can inspect this book, there's nothing to worry about ..." Shipman was calm and not in the least defensive. He invited Dad to look through the case notes of every death in his filing cabinet and said he had nothing to hide. That was good enough for Dad; he came back telling me there was nothing to worry about.'

Mr Massey added, 'Dr Shipman's attitude was very friendly considering what I was suggesting. I thought he'd hit the roof, but then I wasn't making a specific accusation. We were just concerned about the actual number of deaths and that was what we were really pointing out.'

But Mr Massey decided not to pursue the matter.

CHAPTER FOURTEEN

Unhinged Minds

In mid-1997, Fred Shipman's close relationship with patient Bianka Pomfret crossed all sorts of boundaries when she suddenly decided to make him the main beneficiary of her will. Mrs Pomfret told her ex-husband Adrian Pomfret about her decision when he called round on one of his twice-monthly visits to her home. 'There was about £100,000 in property and cash. She told me she'd discussed it with Shipman and how he could use it all to help improve his surgery,' Adrian Pomfret later explained. 'She just sat there and calmly explained to me that she'd made the decision to leave her estate to Shipman. I was so stunned I said, "Suit yourself."'

Two weeks later, Mr Pomfret went to see his ex-wife again. 'She was still going on about it. She asked me my opinion, especially in relation to our son William and the grandchildren. I told her I thought it was out of order.'

Then Mr Pomfret added, 'Bianka putting Shipman in her will proved just how close he had become to her. You leave money to the ones you love and adore. There must have been a very intense relationship between them. I'd just like to know how he found the time to get so close to her.'

The rest of the Pomfret family were stunned to discover she was leaving her estate to her GP. Bianka even wrote a letter to her own mother back in Germany telling her about her decision. As Adrian Pomfret pointed out, 'Bianka was a manic depressive and part of her illness was that she needed attention all the time and that was what she was doing by changing her will. She thought he would give her even more attention by leaving the money to him.'

Then, one day during this period, Shipman turned up unannounced at Bianka's house and found her in the company of her friend known only as 'Czech Andy'. He was a fellow patient from the local mental health clinic. Shipman was still unhappy that someone else might be trying to influence the woman he controlled. Adrian Pomfret explained, 'There was some kind of confrontation.'

It was initially caused by Bianka Pomfret's terrier dog Sam attacking Shipman as he let himself into the back door of her home. Shipman – who'd often advised her to get rid of the dog and get a cat instead – was furious that it had not been kept locked in a room when he called. Then he encountered 'the Czech', a huge, lumbering giant of a man who stood at least 6ft 4in tall.

Within minutes of the departure of Czech Andy from Bianka Pomfret's house, Shipman and Bianka had another argument. This time, Bianka screamed at him that she was no longer going to leave him her estate. Fred Shipman's temper boiled over. Meanwhile, Bianka Pomfret became so distraught that Shipman tried to force her to let him inject her with drugs 'to calm her down'. Bianka Pomfret refused to allow Shipman to inject her with anything and he stormed out of the house. He'd failed to kill her before she could change her will.

Mr Pomfret has long since concluded that what happened during that encounter made Bianka no longer trust Fred Shipman. 'It's such a shame because, for the first time in years,

Bianka seemed to be on the mend. The medication had been reduced. It must have dawned on her that Shipman was not to be trusted. He was losing his power over her. She was getting out more and even became friendly with another woman from the clinic called Mary.'

Shortly afterwards, Adrian Pomfret made another of his regular visits to his ex-wife's home and Bianka Pomfret immediately informed him, 'Dr Shipman is a horrible person.' She refused to explain the reasons behind her outburst but she asked him about the will.

'She asked me what she should do,' Mr Pomfret later recalled. 'She no longer wanted to leave all the money to Shipman. The way I put it across to her was that, at the end of the day, the only lifeline she had left were the two grandchildren, no matter what the situation was between us. I said you have to think deeply and sensibly and leave it to the grandchildren.'

A few days later, Bianka Pomfret saw her attorney and amended the will so that everything was left to her son and grandchildren. 'Shipman had lost his power over her,' recalled Mr Pomfret. 'Something had come between them but I never got to the bottom of it.'

* * *

Sixty-seven-year-old Marie Quinn, a regular at St Luke's Roman Catholic Church in Hyde, had become a local celebrity overnight when she was seen by millions of television viewers talking about the rising problem of crime in the community. 'Every day in our area, you will hear of a murder being committed ... We are just getting worse all the time. It's been forecast in the Apocalypse; there will be a cleansing.'

The BBC TV programme *Everyman* filmed the widow sipping tea in the kitchen of her terraced home in Hyde, before she set off on a pilgrimage to a Catholic shrine in Medjugorje, Bosnia, where the Virgin Mary was reputed to appear.

At 6.30pm on 24 November 1997 – a year to the day after the

programme's transmission – Fred Shipman arrived at Mrs Quinn's house to find her 'breathing her last breath'. Yet earlier in the day, she'd telephoned her son John and, as he later explained, she'd sounded 'in very good spirits'.

Shipman later claimed that Mrs Quinn had called him at his surgery and said she was 'feeling poorly'. He said he then went round to her house where he found she'd apparently suffered a stroke and was partially paralysed. Later investigations showed that there was no phone record of a call from her home to the surgery that day. Fred Shipman's lies were all part of his deadly addiction.

Shipman then called Mrs Quinn's friend Ellen Hanratty to tell her Mrs Quinn had died. He said that when he'd called round he found Mrs Quinn had suffered a stroke. That same day, Mrs Quinn's son John phoned Shipman from Japan. The doctor told him that his mother had tried to call him a few hours earlier to say she thought she'd suffered a stroke.

By this stage in his murderous career, Fred Shipman had become so confident, and reckless, that he thought no one would notice that he hadn't bothered calling the emergency services when he first found Mrs Quinn. Also, Mrs Quinn was found in the kitchen at the back of the house, even though the only telephone from which she was supposed to have called him was in the living room. Shipman immediately issued a death certificate, stating the cause of death as a stroke, narrowing of the arteries, hypertension and secondary scleroderma.

The following day, her son rang Shipman from Japan once again and suggested that he might have come quicker or sent his mother to hospital. But Fred Shipman calmly assured him nothing more could have been done and had she survived she would have been paralysed with no quality of life, waiting for an inevitable second fatal stroke.

In fact, Mrs Quinn had no heart abnormality and her coronary arteries were virtually free of any narrowing. She had died from a massive injection of morphine.

* * *

At 1.45pm on 9 December 1997, Fred Shipman left an ante-natal clinic at his practice without explanation. Surgery staff only knew where he'd gone when he called them 45 minutes later to say that patient Mrs Kathleen Wagstaff had died. Receptionist Carol Chapman later recalled, 'He telephoned me and said Mrs Wagstaff was dead. Her name had not featured in any other phone call or conversation that day.'

Gardener Andrew Hallas had seen Mrs Wagtsaff earlier that same morning when she offered him a cup of tea outside her home in Rock Gardens, Roe Cross Green, near Hyde. Hallas later said that the widow had gone into Hyde to do some shopping and Shipman arrived at the house when she returned after lunchtime. He saw Shipman knock on the front door and then let in by Mrs Wagstaff. Thirty minutes later, Shipman was spotted by Hallas in a nearby car park. Fred Shipman told relatives that he'd called an ambulance from her home but there was no record of either a request for a home visit or any calls for an ambulance.

Shipman later claimed he was just around the corner when a call from Mrs Wagstaff came in and he went straight to her house. Shipman said he found Mrs Wagstaff looking very grey and sweating profusely. He then escorted her upstairs before taking her pulse. Realising she was in a bad state, he immediately phoned for an ambulance and went downstairs for his bag. But, he later claimed, she died soon afterwards so he cancelled the ambulance. 'We were relieved it had been a relatively easy death. It seemed right that she was with the family doctor we trusted and believed in,' said her son Peter Wagstaff.

Fred Shipman had looked after three generations of the Wagstaff family of Hyde and they thought the world of him. 'We had a lot of respect for him,' said Peter Wagstaff. 'He was a gentlemen and seemed to do more than the normal doctor. Nothing seemed too much trouble for him. We often said we wished we had been younger than we were because we would have loved him to be our GP when we were old.'

The Wagstaff family were so grateful to their trusted GP that they sent a donation for £217 towards his surgery fund.

The cheque was accompanied by a letter from the family to Fred Shipman:

> Dear Dr Shipman,
> Just a few lines to thank you for all your care and attention for my mother as your patient. It was comforting to know that you were with her during her last moments. We greatly appreciate how you look after us as a family and we couldn't ask for a finer, more caring doctor.

The day after Fred Shipman murdered Kathleen Wagstaff, he drove across Hyde to see the very demanding Bianka Pomfret who'd already upset him by deciding not to leave him all her estate after all. No one will ever know if she was pleased to see her GP walk into her house that lunchtime. But Fred Shipman already knew he was going to be the last person to see her alive.

With Christmas 1997 approaching, Bianka Pomfret had struggled to come to terms with spending yet another holiday period away from her family. Adrian Pomfret explained, 'She was so worried she even managed to get on speaking terms with her son William, by popping into the corner shop he owned just around the corner from her home.'

Bianka also made an effort to stay on good terms with neighbours Paul Graham and Jeanette Millward, who later remembered how kind and generous she was towards their young sons. 'She was a nice person, very quiet, you didn't know she was there,' Mr Graham later recalled. 'She was always talking to the kids; they thought she was lovely. Once she brought them a stick of rock back from a day trip to Blackpool, to thank them for looking after her dog.'

And during the last few months of 1997, Bianka, still in her forties, began to age with alarming speed. 'She suddenly completely let go of herself. She looked about 20 years older than her age. It was really disturbing to see the change in her,' one neighbour later recalled.

In December 1997, Bianka Pomfret became so distressed by her problems with Fred Shipman that she went to see her psychiatrist Dr Alan Tate again. She told him she was feeling extremely depressed and lonely. She told Tate she was still dreading being alone on Christmas Day, watching TV and smoking. She didn't go into any details about her clashes with Fred Shipman, but Dr Tate was convinced that something specific had deeply disturbed her.

Over the next few days, Bianka Pomfret called Fred Shipman at his surgery on a number of occasions but he refused to come to the phone. The GP was playing cat and mouse with a deeply disturbed middle-aged woman who was close to a major nervous breakdown. Then Bianka Pomfret made a very serious error; she left a message for Fred Shipman telling him she was no longer leaving her estate to him.

Shipman was so furious, he decided then and there that the blonde housewife would soon become just another statistic in his computerised medical records.

On the second Sunday in December 1997, Bianka Pomfret went to Mass at her local Catholic Church. Parish priest Father Denis Maher has never forgotten that day. 'Throughout the service, she was following my every movement with her eyes; her eyes were pleading with me constantly. Outside after the service, she waited for me and asked me to visit her again. She wanted to have a long chat and I told her I could see her the following Wednesday or Thursday.'

The other person who saw Bianka Pomfret on that Sunday was her ex-husband Adrian Pomfret. 'She wanted me to take her out for a meal, which was unusual for her. It was as if she wanted to confide something to me. But, instead, I gave her some money and said that she and her social worker – who was in the house that day – should treat themselves to a Chinese meal.'

Then Bianka Pomfret mentioned Fred Shipman once again:

'He's a horrible man. Not a nice person.' She repeated the words over and over again.

'She also made a point of saying she was going to see Dr Tate the following day, so something was obviously bothering her deeply,' Mr Pomfret later explained.

Then Bianka Pomfret admitted to her ex-husband that she'd had a dose of 'flu earlier that week and Shipman had visited her home to treat her and she'd also been to his surgery.

'She hadn't actually dropped him. It was almost as if she couldn't let go of him,' Mr Pomfret later explained.

That Sunday evening, Bianka Pomfret also told her former husband that she was going to see Shipman again within the next few days to tell him she wanted to join the list of another GP.

'She clearly didn't like him any more. She'd gone from singing his praises to hating him,' Mr Pomfret pointed out. 'But then manic depressives are like that, although I still think her attitude was significant.'

That evening, as Mr Pomfret got up to leave, his ex-wife turned to him and said, 'I realise you were right and I want to be with normal people.'

'Everyone's normal. What is normal?' pointed out Mr Pomfret.

'No, what I mean is I want to be with normal people like I used to do with you.'

Adrian Pomfret believes to this day that his ex-wife was trying to escape the influence of Fred Shipman when she uttered those words. 'I regret it now but I had to leave that night because I was going to see our son and grandchildren to give them their Christmas presents. I just wish I'd stayed longer.'

The following day – 10 December 1997 – neighbour Paul Graham noticed Bianka sitting in her chair in the front room, gazing out of the window. He thought she was watching him as he worked on his van in the front yard. It was only later that he realised she was waiting for someone.

Mrs Pomfret received a visit from Fred Shipman later that day. 'I was allowed into her house and I asked what had happened to make me come and visit,' Shipman later claimed.

'She said she had not felt very well and that she had chest pains which went right up to her jaw and into her left arm. She couldn't go anywhere fast; she had a small dog and she said the dog ran while she walked. She recognised there was a limitation to her physical activity.'

Shipman said he and Mrs Pomfret then discussed her history of chest pains. He suggested an ECG at his surgery that Friday and also suggested she could take some tablets.

He said later, 'She pointed to the multiplicity of bottles of tablets on her table and said she was taking a lot of tablets and didn't want to take any more. She was not happy about a referral to another hospital.'

Fred Shipman later claimed that Bianka Pomfret had not taken her pain seriously because it came and went. Shipman claimed he visited her home between 1.30pm and 2.00pm on Monday, 10 December, and said, 'I was upset by Bianka because she hadn't trusted me enough to tell me about the pain earlier.'

Shipman also later pointed out that Mrs Pomfret smoked around 30 cigarettes a day. He said, 'Any patient who has heart disease and who smokes is silly and looking to die.'

But the Pomphret case further revealed that Shipman was stealing trophies from his vicitims. Jewellery from Adrian Pomfret to his ex-wife, plus gifts and keepsakes from her family in Germany, were taken.

Shipman had also stolen jewellery from Winifred Mellor, as well as more than £60 in pension money. A distinctive Irish designer ring was later found when the police searched his surgery where he kept a few trophies, although most were kept in that cardboard box at home.

Four hours after leaving Bianka Pomfret's side, she was found dead by her adult son and a social worker. As her former husband Adrian Pomfret later explained: 'She was found in a casual position … half a cigarette burning in the ashtray, half a cup of coffee and the TV switched on.'

According to other eye-witnesses, Bianka Pomfret's body 'looked relaxed' – she had her arms and legs folded. Parish priest

Denis Maher was one of the first people to arrive at the house after the discovery of her body. 'I was terribly upset,' he later recalled. 'She did suffer from depression, but I thought she was coming out of it.'

That day, Father Maher took an instant dislike to Fred Shipman. 'I opened the door to him and he just rushed in and almost knocked me over. I was a rival in a sense because I was on his level as a priest. He seemed very cold, arrogant and uncaring. There was no sensitivity in his voice. Nothing. He didn't expect to find me there and was probably a bit annoyed.'

Fred Shipman simply walked in and immediately asked, 'Where is she?' before going to examine Bianka Pomfret's body sitting in her armchair. Shipman hardly looked at her and then said to her son William, 'You know your mother had a heart condition, don't you? She wouldn't take the treatment and she wouldn't go to the hospital. She's only got herself to blame.'

Father Maher stood by getting increasingly angry. Then Shipman said, 'Have you got an undertaker?'

Maher responded, 'If you don't mind, doctor, I'll help the family with that.'

Shipman then snapped back, 'Don't worry, there won't be an inquest. Just come down to my office in the morning and I'll sign off a death certificate.' William Pomfret later insisted he had no idea about his mother's health problems but accepted the doctor at his word.

When Adrian Pomfret arrived at his ex-wife's house he bumped straight into Fred Shipman walking out. 'I was in such a state I didn't even remember to ask him about an autopsy,' recalled Mr Pomfret.

Minutes later, Adrian Pomfret concluded that perhaps Bianka had committed suicide. 'There is a strong possibility that your mother took her own life …' he told their son William, '… and if she has, it's down to me, not you. I was the one who walked out on her, not you.'

Close to tears, Adrian Pomfret later recalled, 'I told William to go and see Shipman to ask him if there was any possibility she killed herself.'

When Adrian Pomfret later heard that Shipman was insisting that it was death by natural causes, he concluded that the GP was being extremely humane by hiding the fact that she may have committed suicide.

'I thought to myself, 'He's playing the game here'. When the truth finally came out years later, I felt relief. That may sound odd but I felt better about it because I didn't kill her. I thought I had killed her up until then.'

Fred Shipman signed Bianka Pomfret's death certificate, giving the cause as a clot in the heart and heart disease, with secondary causes being smoking and manic depression. When Bianka's psychiatrist Dr Alan Tate telephoned Shipman after he heard the news, the GP reiterated that there was no need for a post mortem examination. Shipman also informed Tate that he'd tried to save Bianka's life. 'He said she had been resuscitated and defibrillated and then had died,' Mr Pomfret later recalled.

That day, Shipman then went back to his surgery and made three entries in the records of Bianka Pomfret. He later claimed they would then provide a better picture of her medical history, including the angina he recorded on her death certificate.

He explained, 'I back-dated the entries because they showed the progression of an illness – because it showed something going back six to eight months. My practice was proactive. I went out looking for illnesses rather than patients having to come in to see me.'

But over at the Hyde medical centre where Bianka Pomfret had received regular psychiatric counselling, Dr Alan Tate was mystified by her death. He even called Shipman at his surgery to ask why there was not going to be an autopsy on Bianka. Shipman insisted it was not neccessary. Dr Tate was so concerned by the circumstances underlying Bianka Pomfret's death that he wrote down everything that Shipman said to him.

* * *

Bianka Pomfret's funeral was a grim affair, held in pouring rain with a small number of people in attendance. One of her friends from the clinic, the tall, dark-haired Czech who'd earlier upset Fred Shipman, unintentionally caused some of the family distress by taking photographs of the coffin as it was laid to rest in the cemetery.

But as Adrian Pomfret later explained, 'I told the priest not to worry about it as it was quite common on the eastern side of Germany. They photograph the bodies quite often and I have been in Polish and Czech homes where you walk in and there's the grandad laid out in a coffin.'

Bianka Pomfret was buried on a rain-sodden day at Hyde Cemetery, her plot marked with a black marble gravestone, inscribed 'She will be loved and missed forever'.

Adrian Pomfret was so concerned about Shipman's role in his wife's last years that he went to see her psychiatrist Dr Alan Tate and mentioned his concerns. Then, a few months later, Pomfret visited Fred Shipman in his surgery to pick up some blood test results. 'Shipman said Dr Tate had spoken to him and that Bianka obviously was still suffering from mental illness. I couldn't understand why he was saying this since before he'd been saying the exact opposite.'

Adrian Pomfret found the 12 months following Bianka Pomfret's death 'probably the worst twelve months of my life. I was still wracked with guilt. I had something worse than even depression. Even her family in Germany believed she'd killed herself. The only thing that stopped me accepting that she'd done it was that she was very strong morally. She had no time for people who took their own life. She thought they were weak and I couldn't quite believe she would do it.'

Bianka Pomfret's neighbour Paul Graham and his family have kept Bianka's Bible, which they found in her back yard after the house was cleared following her death. It was inscribed, 'God loveth a cheerful giver – Corinthians II'.

The church had meant everything to Bianka. When she was feeling at her lowest, Bianka had even considered throwing herself from the motorway bridge as she walked to St Paul's Church. But she always insisted to her psychiatrist Dr Alan Tate, 'I don't want to die.'

Then she'd upset Fred Shipman.

CHAPTER FIFTEEN

Covering the Tracks

At 1.00pm on Christmas Eve 1997, 83-year-old Hyde pensioner Jim King was so ill from 'flu and an ear infection that he called up Fred Shipman and asked him if he'd call round at his sheltered apartment. He was found dead in the chair of his front room just a few hours later.

The death of Jim King bore all the hallmarks of a Fred Shipman killing. As his son Jim King Jr later explained, 'A healthy person dies suddenly. Found in a chair as if asleep shortly after a visit from Shipman. The only difference was that he was an old man not an old lady.'

Jim King's son Jim had recently married his wife Debbie and his father had even escorted his son down the aisle. 'He was a quiet man and a gentlemen. The week before he died, we did a five-mile walk along the side of the canal together. He was so fit he gave me a run for my money.'

It was only years later that Jim King and the rest of his family realised that Shipman had also killed his 69-year-old aunt Molly Dudley back in 1990. She had had 'flu as well and was visited by Shipman. 'He called her daughter to say he had given her an injection of morphine because she was in pain and seemed to be going into cardiac arrest,' Jim King later recalled. 'By the time they arrived, she was dead – he said she had died in his arms.'

Not long after Jim King Sr's death, his son's aunt Irene Berry called Shipman complaining about a severe case of shingles. She was found dead a few hours later. As Jim King later explained, 'Death was completely out of the blue. She only ever suffered from shingles. She was in pain so she called Shipman.'

That day, Fred Shipman coolly telephoned Mrs Berry's relatives with the news. When asked how sick Irene was after he'd been in to examine her, the GP replied, 'Well, how bad d'you think it can get?'

'Has she passed away?'

'Yes,' Shipman replied without a hint of emotion.

When Mrs Berry's daughter Jean Darlington and her husband arrived at the house, Shipman was still there. He then told them, 'She's very comfortable, cup of tea, the fire on. And she was just sat in the chair where she would normally sit with her book and half a cup of tea. She just looked as though she was asleep.'

Jean Darlington's training as an accident and emergency nurse left her far from happy with what Shipman was saying. Shipman then claimed that Irene Berry called him out because she had chest pains. He didn't mention shingles. 'I immediately wondered why he didn't do something about it,' recalled Jean Darlington. 'He said he gave her a GCM spray, but that didn't work so he said he'd decided to go back and see how she was later. He'd brought the ECG machine with him which seemed odd to me, but he said that when he got back she was dead and he didn't think it was a cardiac problem. But then why did he go for an ECG machine – why didn't he just get an ambulance? I felt concerned about my mother, but I wondered how could he have done this, but I didn't think he did it on purpose. I just thought he'd been negligent.'

But, as Mrs Berry's nephew Jim King later recalled, 'The strangest thing is that my father dies and then my aunt dies in the same circumstances with Shipman in attendance.' However, Jim King resisted the temptation to go to the police about the 'strange coincidence'. He recalled, 'Basically, I trusted the doctor. I couldn't even consider he was guilty of anything.'

But Jim King believed he was already indebted to Fred Shipman since his own brush with death.

Jim King had returned to Britain from the USA in 1996 before marrying his wife Debra, 45, in Hyde. A week later, he began getting backache and noticed blood in his urine. Fred Shipman immediately referred him to hospital where cancer was diagnosed in his bladder, urethra and prostate.

'Dr Shipman started prescribing me morphine and told me I had only 18 months to live,' he later recalled.

What Jim King didn't realise was that the hospital consultant knew Mr King had been misdiagnosed and had immediately written to Fred Shipman to say a mistake had been made. But Shipman did not pass that vital information on to Jim King and continued to tell him he was terminally ill because he was using his prescriptions to help increase his stockpile of morphine.

Jim King – once a highly successful engineer in Texas – recalled, 'By having a patient like me on his books, he was able to draw Class A drugs for pain relief. He fed me massive doses of morphine – enough to kill me – but I don't know how much more he obtained in my name for use on other people. I was on as much as 360mg a day – the normal dose for pain is 30mg – and he was prescribing as much as 24,000mg at a time. I became addicted to morphine. It was terrible, what he did to me. I didn't know what was happening for 12 months. I lost my job with an engineering firm and the mortgage on our £56,000 home in Denton was withdrawn. I lost my company car and we had to sell the Jaguar I had bought Debbie. We ended up here in a council house. Yet he seemed to be my saviour in many ways. He was prepared to give me as much morphine as I wanted to help kill the pain.'

But then Fred Shipman knew what a joy it was to have morphine running through your veins. But, of course, there was another motive – he needed the drugs to keep killing his patients and he was more than happy to let an innocent man believe he had a fatal disease in order to feed his killing habit. Recalled Jim King, 'I thought I was dying anyway so I kept taking it and he kept prescribing vast amounts.'

Just before Christmas 1996, Jim King took a serious turn for the worse. As his American wife Debbie later explained, 'Jim was in a bad way so I rang Dr Shipman to have him come round and check him over.'

Jim King takes up the story. 'He tested my chest and said I had a bad dose of pneumonia and I'd got liquid on the lungs.'

Then Shipman hesitated for a moment before saying, 'I need to give you an injection to help all this.'

Jim King looked over at his wife and noticed that she seemed concerned by the GP's suggestion. Mrs King later recalled, 'For some reason, I don't really know why, I said, "No," and said, "Can't you just write out a prescription for him?"'

But Fred Shipman was insistent that Jim King needed the injection. 'I kept telling him, "No". I didn't like the way he was being so arrogant about it. He had a real snotty attitude towards me,' recalled Mrs King.

Jim King believes at that moment his life was saved by his wife, who had worked with doctors when they'd lived in the United States. Debbie believed Shipman should be using antibiotics instead of morphine if his claims about pneumonia were correct. At that moment, alarm bells went off in Shipman's twisted mind and he resisted the temptation to finish off Jim King because he knew there could be repercussions.

'I honestly believe that if I had had that injection it would have killed me. He would have said it was cancer, Debbie would have gone back to the States and no one would have known any different.'

Fred Shipman had wanted to kill off Jim King because then he could go to his house after his death and offer to dispose of any excess medicines in the house. Shipman already had a huge stockpile of diamorphine in his office and even kept some at

A killer in the making.

Top: Fred Shipman aged five (back row, third from right), and (*below*) aged six at Burford Infants' School, complete with a bow tie his mother insisted he wear (*middle*).

Top: The house at Longmead Drive in Nottingham where he was born and brought up with his sister and brother.

Bottom: Shipman (second from left on middle row) in the High Pavement rugby team when he was fifteen years old.

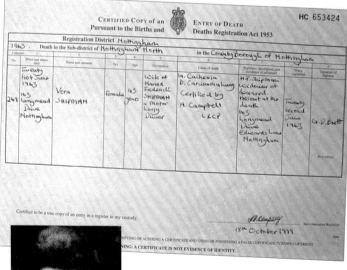

Top: Shipman (centre with bright waistcoat) during a High Pavement rugby tour in the north-east of England.

Above: Shipman's mother's death certificate.

Left: Fred Shipman, aged 17, just after his mother's death.

Left: The death certificate of baby Christian Orlinski, who died just one day after birth following a visit from Fred Shipman.

Right: Ruth Highley, aged 72, was Shipman's first known victim. She died on May 10th, 1974 in Todmorden.

Top: The house in Todmorden where Shipman first began his reign of terror in the mid-1970s.

Bottom: The Shipmans' family home in Mottram.

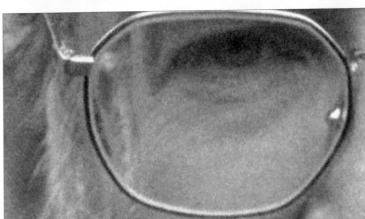

The good doctor and eight of his hundreds of victims.

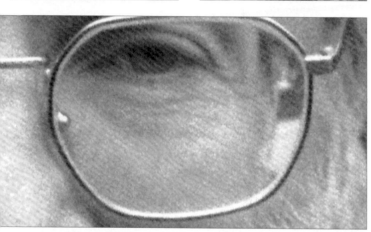

Top: District nurse Kate McGraw had many 'highly personal' conversations with Dr Shipman.

Left: Victim Bianka Pomfret with whom Fred Shipman formed a close and disturbing relationship.

The destruction of a family.

Top: Primrose Shipman and son David shortly after the doctor's arrest.

Bottom: Shipman's eldest son Christopher.

CJ8198   10·11·98
SHIPMAN·H·F· R·X

home 'for emergencies'. But he believed he could never have too much of a good thing.

Shortly afterwards, Jim King discovered he did not have cancer when he went to see a urologist about another matter. 'He read my reports and said they did not make sense. I told him I was dying and he replied, "Oh no, you're not."'

A month later, Shipman confirmed the news without even bothering to elaborate. Jim King immediately moved to another GP, but it took him eight months to wean himself off morphine.

Mr King also suspects that Fred Shipman killed his 80-year-old mother Elizabeth who died suddenly in hospital in 1994 after a visit from the GP. 'The hospital rang to say she was having heart palpitations but, by the time we got there, she was dead. There was no post mortem.'

Jim King added, 'I can never forgive him. What blows my mind is that all this could have been stopped. I want my mum and dad back. My life has been destroyed and I want it back.'

* * *

Undertaker Debbie Bambroffe had spent all her life in Hyde and even went to school with Fred Shipman's son Christopher. Part of her job was to visit local GPs so she often talked to Primrose Shipman about Christopher's progress as an engineer when she went into Shipman's surgery.

Her entire family were on Fred Shipman's books. But by the start of 1998, Debbie felt a growing sense of unease about Shipman, who'd earlier convinced her father that the high number of deaths was of no importance. 'We would go to the home of the deceased and it had got to the point where we could tell by the scenario that greeted us whether that person had been a patient of Dr Shipman. It just didn't add up.'

Off her own back, Debbie began comparing Shipman's death rate with those of the three other surgeries in Hyde. His numbers were significantly higher. At first, she convinced herself more people were dying at home because Shipman didn't like to send people to hospital to die. 'It was easier to think that than to contemplate that he was killing these women off.'

Debbie Bambroffe noticed that many of the deaths handled by Fred Shipman were elderly women, but they had not been ill just before they died. There were no pills at their bedside, no oxygen tanks, no district nurse notes. They often had not been in bed; usually they were dressed and sitting up in a chair with a cup of tea at their side.

Debbie Bambroffe knew what she suspected could wreck Shipman's career and, if she was wrong, it also could destroy hers. She had no real proof, just a gut instinct. She knew that if she was wrong and he sued, the family business would be financially ruined. Then, one evening in the early weeks of 1998, Shipman rang Debbie to ask her to attend the death of a woman who lived alone. 'The woman had died suddenly, alone, and yet the coroner was not involved. And I found myself wondering how come Dr Shipman had the key to the house?'

Debbie mentioned her fears to another GP, Dr Susan Booth, as she visited the undertaker's chapel of rest to countersign a cremation certificate for the victim.

'Here I am again to do one of Fred's,' said Dr Booth on seeing Debbie Bambroffe.

'I think you're coming here too often. His death rates are very high, and they're nearly all women,' responded Debbie Bambroffe.

Dr Booth promised to mention it to her colleagues.

Another Hyde GP also harboured deep suspicions about the activities of Fred Shipman. Dr Linda Reynolds was already haunted by the memory of another GP, Dr Soe Myint, who had sexually assaulted his patients. For years, she'd known of his attacks on women patients, who went to her for treatment to get away from him. She'd tried to persuade them to tell the police, even offering to go with them, but they'd refused until Dr Myint finally came to court and was imprisoned in 1997.

'I swore never again,' she later recalled, shuddering at the recollection. 'And this time it was more serious. Those other women could do something, but Dr Shipman's patients couldn't. He had killed them.'

Fred Shipman's one-man practice was just across the street from the Brooke Surgery where GPs were often asked to countersign cremation forms after Shipman's patients had died. These forms always had to be signed by doctors in another practice as a matter of procedure. That other doctor was also obliged by law to ask about the patients' medical history and view the body.

Dr Booth mentioned her suspicions and they struck a chord with Dr Reynolds, who'd already noticed the number of cremation certificates Shipman had asked her to countersign – almost always, it seemed, for elderly women.

Across the street at his practice, Fred Shipman – first alerted by Paul Massey's initial approach a few months earlier – was already mounting a damage limitation exercise, by rotating his requests for death certificate co-signatures between the Brooke practice's five GPs but nothing could hide the fact that his one-man surgery had completed 41 certificates in 1997 compared with Brooke's 14.

Dr Linda Reynolds then alerted the South Manchester coroner Dr John Pollard, who immediately called in Greater Manchester Police. A detective inspector, acting as an agent for Dr Pollard, began looking into the claims about Shipman. Dr Reynolds later insisted that she had specifically told the police that she suspected Shipman of killing his patients. Yet a combination of oversight and Shipman's deceit conspired to limit the evidence at the police's disposal at that time. In any case, who would seriously believe that a doctor would commit mass murder on such a vast scale?

But for the moment, Dr Reynolds was relieved by Dr Pollard's receptive attitude. 'Afterwards, I felt very encouraged because he was taking me seriously.' Dr Pollard also gave Dr Reynolds a personal promise of complete confidentiality. He told her, 'As far as I am concerned, if nothing comes of this, we have never spoken.'

A detective was dispatched to interview Dr Reynolds at her surgery that same day. Dr Reynolds told the investigator she'd concluded he was a killer by referring to the death rate. She also gave the detective the Brooke Group's cremation records book going back to 1993.

Dr Reynolds also told the same officer that the bodies of two of Shipman's most recent victims still lay at Massey's funeral parlour and suggested that he ask for a post mortem on them, but the detective insisted he did not have enough evidence to do that.

She also warned him that Fred Shipman seemed to have been tipped off about enquiries into his activities.

The detective insisted that was highly unlikely and he left Dr Reynolds's surgery saying he'd investigate the claims very thoroughly. But that officer had no back-up team, no incident room. Just columns of complicated figures that could have simply meant that death rates went up for a period.

Dr Reynolds later recalled how she felt powerless to do anything more, but remained convinced that Shipman was a mass murderer. 'I felt quite bad. I had accused another doctor – albeit old-fashioned but concerned for the community – of killing his patients. I was dragging this man's reputation through the mud.'

Shortly after that, two more cremation forms arrived at the Brooke Surgery. Dr Reynolds noted them, then went off for a long holiday to America with her husband and children. Ironically, those two deaths both seemed to be genuinely terminally ill patients. She even hoped that he'd stop the killings because he knew that an investigation was under way.

'I was convinced he knew,' Dr Reynolds later explained. 'I hoped that, because he had this shot across his bows, he had got the message and stopped. It was the best hope I had in the circumstances.'

Hyde taxi driver John Shaw was already convinced of Shipman's guilt because he'd lost an incredible 24 customers to Fred Shipman. He later recalled, 'I knew for at least a year that something was wrong with Shipman. I kept losing my customers and it was always him who was the doctor. At first, I thought he was unlucky or incompetent, then I realised it was something more sinister. I felt guilty, like an accomplice. I could have saved them. But I couldn't tell anyone. Who would have believed me?'

Manchester Police investigated these initial claims by visiting Manchester's Registrar of Births, Marriages and Deaths. They were asked to provide details of those Shipman patients who had died over the previous six months. There had been 30 but only 19 death certificates were provided – 11 others were completely overlooked due to a clerical oversight.

Investigators even asked Dr Alan Banks, 49, a medical adviser to the authority who paid Shipman's salary, to examine the files of 14 Shipman patients who had died. He told detectives he could find nothing wrong with the deaths. By pure luck and inefficiency, Fred Shipman was slipping through the net.

The other five deaths were dated from a time when GPs were entitled to store records of dead patients so detectives could not get the details without first visiting Fred Shipman. They knew they'd need a High Court warrant to seize Shipman's computerised medical records so they relied on Dr Banks from the local Family Practitioner's Committee to cross-reference death certificates with the medical records. The records seemed consistent with the cause of death on the certificates – but that was only because Fred Shipman had fabricated them in the first place.

Fred Shipman was never directly contacted by police investigators. Detectives believed they had 'insufficient' evidence to win any legal argument to search his premises. And the surgery death rate statistics were not even available at that time. But Greater Manchester Police did interview undertaker Alan Massey three times while carrying out their initial enquiries.

After six weeks of probing, the force informed South Manchester Coroner Dr Pollard that they had drawn a blank and they did not believe that Fred Shipman was a killer in any shape or form. The investigation was dropped.

Detective Chief Inspector Mike Williams later admitted, 'Dr Shipman quite successfully covered his tracks. As soon as we started interviewing doctors, it became public. We didn't have that sort of enormous piece of information which would justify us making that step and putting a slur on his character.'

The force's Assistant Chief Constable Vincent Sweeney later insisted, 'Relatives of Dr Shipman were not interviewed because approaching them about the paperwork would have been tantamount to accusing Dr Shipman of wrongdoing and would have breached the confidentiality of the inquiry. The system of justice in this country requires police officers to clarify facts and establish whether there is evidence to support accusations.'

Yet a simple check on Fred Shipman's criminal record would have shown his conviction for that drugs offence back in 1976. The police later insisted that even this would have been an insufficient basis on which to interview him.

But the fact remains that they failed to make that check in the first place.

And it meant that Fred Shipman's addiction to killing was far from over.

* * *

In the middle of the police inquiry – on 9 February 1998 – the daughter of Fred Shipman's elderly patient Pamela Hillier called her mother at 4.30pm but there was no reply. Jacqueline Gee then phoned her mother's neighbours Mr and Mrs Ellwood and asked them to check on her. Mr Ellwood found Mrs Hillier lying on her back on the bedroom floor at the foot of the bed. A packet of tablets lay on the bed. Mr Ellwood and his wife tried to resuscitate Mrs Hillier and called an ambulance.

Paramedic Stephen Morris then arrived and carried out a cardio-pulmonary resuscitation and even used a defibrillator. But she was already dead, although her body was still without rigor mortis which indicated that death had occurred very recently. Fred Shipman telephoned the house in the middle of all this. He asked Mr Morris the circumstances and promised to get round to the house as quickly as possible.

Mrs Gee then arrived, followed by Shipman, who was overheard by Mr Ellwood telling the paramedics that it was not necessary to call out the police as they had suggested. That was when Mrs Gee and her husband asked about a post mortem. Shipman replied, 'Let's put it down to a stroke,' and said there was no point.

Shipman later insisted he'd left Mrs Hillier alive after a home visit on the day she died. Shipman said that Pamela Hillier's blood pressure was 'high and very worrying' so he told her to increase the dose of drugs. Then he left her Stalybridge Road town house, which was close to his own home in Mottram.

Shipman claimed he'd called to see the 67-year-old widow because she'd tripped over a carpet and fallen down. He said she had told him she had felt restless and tired on two previous occasions on 6 January and 5 February. After her death, he returned to the surgery and put those incidents into his computerised medical records, including blood pressure readings taken by practice nurse Gillian Morgan. However, Shipman made a mistake by first entering them on 5 January and 6 February 'because five comes before six'.

It proved a costly mistake.

Just after the police dropped their enquiries, Fred Shipman was visited at his surgery by another elderly patient called Maureen Ward. Practice receptionist Carol Chapman later explained, 'Dr Shipman came out with her after her appointment and told us she was going on a cruise.'

'I joked, "I'll carry your bags for you." She was fine. We had a little conversation and a few pleasantries.'

The following day, Fred Shipman informed the warden at Mrs Ward's sheltered housing complex at Ogden Court, in Frank Street, Hyde, that he'd called to give her a letter about a hospital referral and found her dead. Shipman later changed his story further by telling his receptionist Carol Chapman that he'd called at Mrs Ward's apartment after seeing an ambulance on the street corner outside her home. Then Carol Chapman noticed Fred Shipman changing his story again by telling other receptionists that he'd gone to give Mrs Ward the letter. Fred Shipman was breaking the golden rule by forgetting his own lies.

As Mrs Chapman later recalled, 'Dr Shipman came back into the surgery in the afternoon and said Mrs Ward had died. I said, "Which? Maureen?"'

'He said, "Yes". I was very shocked and a little bit angry, I think, probably a little snappy. I said she was in here yesterday and she was fine.'

Christine Simpson – the warden at the complex where Mrs Ward lived – was also shocked to hear that Mrs Ward had died as she'd seemed so well earlier that day. Shipman even asked her to go with him to Mrs Ward's first-floor flat after he'd found her dead. 'I was very, very surprised, very shocked,' Christine Simpson later said. 'I said I couldn't believe it. He said to me, "Well, she did have a brain tumour, you know." I said I didn't know, I had no idea, I was very surprised.'

Other neighbours were equally stunned by the news. Mary France and Mrs Ward had been excited by the prospect of going on a cruise together and they'd even arranged to have a cup of tea later on the very day she died. 'I put the kettle on,' she said, 'but she never came round.'

There was also a chilling link between the death of Mrs Ward and five other Shipman victims; they all lived at Ogden Court, just a few hundred yards from Shipman's surgery in Market Street. Resident Alice Prestwick, 69, was the first one to go. She died in October 1988, followed by 81-year-old John Charlton 12 months later. Alice Kennedy, 88, died in January 1995, and then 87-year-old Muriel Ward died in October of that year. Gladys Saunders died in June 1996 and James King, 83, on Christmas Eve 1997.

Another of Fred Shipman's patients – Winifred Mellor – felt as if she had had a new lease of life in May 1998. As her Catholic parish priest Father Denis Maher explained, 'We'd organised a trip to the Holy Land and Winifred was the first person to put her name down for that trip. She was like a child looking forward to Christmas. She even said to me, "All my life, I've wanted to go to the Holy Land and now I am going."'

Then 73-year-old Mrs Mellor went to Fred Shipman's surgery complaining that she felt weary and unwell. The GP diagnosed pneumonia and pleurisy and prescribed her antibiotics and told her to go home. Several hours later, she was found dead at her flat in Commercial Street, Hyde. Shipman had even helped nurse her husband before he died in 1989.

Some hours afterwards, Shipman knocked on the door of one of Mrs Mellor's neighbours and claimed he'd come to see Mrs Mellor and he could see her sitting on her chair through the front window and he thought she was dead. He never mentioned his earlier visit.

Shipman and the neighbour then managed to get into the house where they found Mrs Mellor dead in the chair. Shipman used the phone in the house to call Mrs Mellor's daughter.

The first thing he said was, 'Did you realise that your mother had been suffering from back pains?'

Her daughter had no idea. Shipman then admitted he'd been to see Mrs Mellor earlier that afternoon and she'd needed hospital treatment. Mrs Mellor's daughter offered to come round to the house.

'Oh, there's no need for that,' replied Shipman. 'There's no point in sending her to hospital.'

It was only then that it dawned on Mrs Mellor's daughter that her mother might be dead.

'D'you mean my mother's dead?' she asked.

'Now you understand,' responded the GP.

As Mrs Mellor's daughter said later, 'He'd made me guess that my mother was dead.'

Father Denis Maher hadn't liked Fred Shipman from the moment they'd first met. He found the GP 'insensitive and unsympathetic' following the death of Bianka Pomfret. Now he had a similar reaction to the way Shipman had handled Mrs Mellor.

He never forgot how he'd been comforting Mrs Mellor's family and had just given her the last rites when Shipman 'breezed into her home, ignoring us completely'. But then death was the norm for Fred Shipman. He'd long since dropped any emotional response to the occurrence.

In June 1998, Fred Shipman was called out to the home of Mrs Joan Melia after one of her neighbours and closest friends found her dead in a chair. Derek Steele immediately noticed that Shipman seemed 'nonchalant' about her death and he left her flat within minutes saying he would issue a death certificate citing pneumonia as a cause of death. He insisted there was no need for a post mortem.

Derek Steele was heartbroken by the loss of his close friend. 'We were companions and buddies. She had no close family and we spent a lot of time together. She walked everywhere and hardly ever visited her GP,' recalled Mr Steele. He'd lived a few doors away from Mrs Melia and had called at her house only to go upstairs and find her in a chair.

'Shipman seemed very blasé, nonchalant. I said, "It's Joan." Then he said the tablets haven't had time to take effect. He didn't do anything. He never touched her. I was quite surprised. Then he said to me, "You'll have no problem with a death certificate. I'll make one out and you can tell the undertaker to get in touch with me."'

Fred Shipman later wrote in Mrs Melia's medical notes that she'd been to the surgery and he'd diagnosed a chest infection and prescribed antibiotics. He clearly implied that she had nothing more than a mild infection. So why didn't Shipman insist on a post mortem when she'd died suddenly the next day?

It was only when Mrs Melia's body was later exhumed that toxicology tests showed she had died from morphine poisoning. Mrs Melia's niece Jean Pinder remembered her aunt as always being a very fit lady so she confronted Dr Shipman shortly after her death. Shipman immediately responded by insisting her aunt had been in very poor health. 'She died from pneumonia aggravated by emphysema,' he told her.

'Did you tell Auntie Joan how ill she was?' she asked.

'I told her to go to bed,' replied the GP.

'If she was so ill, why didn't you contact the hospital?'

'I'm afraid it was just one of those things. She could have just as easily died on the way to hospital.'

On 18 June 1998, Joan Melia was buried at St Mary's Parish Church, Newton, Hyde.

* * *

Few of of the streets in Hyde and few of the town's families had escaped Shipman's attentions. He'd returned time and time again to particular streets, sometimes even to the same house, in search of fresh victims. Shipman even killed twice at the same house – Number 2, Leigh Fold, in Hyde. Alice Gorton, 76, had died there on 10 August 1979. Nine years afterwards, on 15 February 1988, a later resident of the same house, Jane Jones, 83, was also found dead after a Shipman visit. But it was Joel Lane, a long street that rises through one of the most affluent parts of Gee Cross, near Hyde, that was his favourite place of all. Over a period of four years, he killed six in that street alone.

His addiction didn't distinguish between areas. Whenever he needed a fix, he went out in search of a vulnerable person to prey upon.

CHAPTER SIXTEEN

The Net Closes In

The Shipman house still resembled a rubbish tip, with clothes, books and plates scattered across the floor, dirty dishes shoulder-high in the sink, the carpets thick with grime. One villager described 15 Roe Cross Green as the sort of place where you would wipe your feet on the way out.

The Shipman house represented a deep-seated rebellion against life by both Fred and Primrose. Primrose had given up on certain aspects of their life together. She knew her husband was secretive. She even picked up clues about what he'd been doing, but she never once confronted him about it.

But the stress it was putting her under was almost unbearable. Primrose just battled on with her own demons, afraid even to question her husband's activities. Primrose knew of her husband's obsession with his work, the long hours he put in, the contempt in which he held almost everyone else. Not helped by the fact the Shipmans lived in a state of semi-isolation, cut off from both their respective families Primrose couldn't work out what it was. At first, she thought he had another woman, but soon dismissed that idea as her husband simply wasn't that sort of man. But soon she could no longer be bothered to even run the home along reasonably organised lines. Primrose was gradually becoming yet another of Fred Shipman's victims.

Despite all this, the bond between Fred and Primrose remained as strong as ever, although the Shipman children were frequently caught in the middle of this bizarre marriage. At Shipman's Market Street surgery, the staff whispered amongst themselves that Fred was something of a tyrant at home who made impossible demands on his family.

'Nobody eats until I get home,' he would bark down the telephone at Primrose most afternoons from the practice. Primrose and the children would be waiting stiffly at the dinner table staring at their plates until the patriarch marched through the door, sometimes as late as 10.00pm. Primrose's stubborn devotion to her husband was remarkable.

It was always Fred and Primrose against the world, so they had to stick together. Even when Primrose suffered a mini-nervous breakdown around this time, she managed to keep it to herself so that it didn't upset Fred. Her illness made her far more isolated within the family home, but she knew that she would have to get over it all by herself because Fred had a lot of other things on his mind.

'Primrose refused to discuss Fred or her breakdown, yet it was clear she was really suffering at the time,' recalled one neighbour. 'But she was too scared to admit anything to anyone. It was so tragic. She desperately needed someone to turn to.'

* * *

'This lady's gone,' was one of Fred Shipman's favourite remarks when he was flicking the eyelid of a victim. Another phrase, usually as he was pronouncing dead a patient who was in her own bed or armchair, was, 'That's a nice way to go.' So different from the convulsive tears, the desolation and final exhaustion of his own mother's tragic death.

Most of Fred Shipman's victims died within minutes of the moment he injected them with a lethal dose of drugs. Injecting the drug into a vein would instantly lead to a slowing of breathing and loss of consciousness before breathing would stop altogether. Diamorphine – the clinical name for heroin – and morphine were commonly used as painkillers. But there was always a danger they could suppress breathing, particularly if injected into a person who was not ill. And by injecting into a vein rather than a muscle, Shipman could provoke rapid death. Diamorphine is twice as strong as morphine. Just 30mg is enough to kill a human being.

Fred Shipman was lost in a kind of labyrinth of death. The early killings had been carefully carried out; the women were primed for murder and there was no evidence left behind. Then Shipman had so enjoyed the quiet, peaceful thrill of a kill. He had no regrets. It had been as deliberate as a fox stealing a chicken.

But during the most recent killings, Shipman had become less calculated and in the aftermath he had made certain errors. If he stuck to certain patients and continued to go about his job as usual, his chances of escaping detection would have remained high. However, Fred Shipman was running completely out of control. Killing had become necessary and he had already had one close shave. Shipman's addiction left him no time to run the rest of his life efficiently. For years, he'd managed to hold it all together, but now it was starting to fall apart. Why?

The net was closing and he was getting sloppy. He was completely losing touch with reality. There had been the warning signs like Jim King and then that approach by funeral director Alan Massey. For the moment, that first police investigation had been shelved, allowing him to carry on feeding his addiction to kill. But Fred Shipman knew in his heart that it would only be a matter of time before it would have to end.

* * *

Fred Shipman used a computer to store most of his patients' medical records in his one-man practice. But he also made handwritten records to detail particularly confidential information that he didn't want patients to see. He knew that some patients could see computer entries during their consultations. Shipman wrote notes on so-called 'Lloyd George' cards when he made home visits. Information about those home visits was also recorded on a standard form which was attached to the notes whenever he visited a patient. That information would then be transferred on to the computer when he got back to the surgery.

These forms were supposed to be filed away once the details had been entered on to the computer. Years later, investigators failed to locate many of them. The few that were found contained only the information noted by the practice receptionist at the time a visit was requested. Fred Shipman knew it was important to get rid of all written 'evidence' of those visits.

By this time, Shipman's handwriting had virtually become illegible and he recorded few current details about patients. His own clinical management of their illnesses was equally disorganised. All information about prescriptions of drugs was usually brief and vague. The quantity of medicine was often not even mentioned, and the batch numbers of injected drugs were never recorded.

And when it came to 'signing off' cremation forms, Fred Shipman was fond of using certain phrases and additional details about the circumstances of deaths. They included the following:

seen by self 11:30; neighbour saw patient at 13.00; found at 15.00 by self and neighbour

seen 2 hours before death with ct, atrial fibrillation & PND; found in chair by neighbour

own, seen at 15.00; found by relative about 16.00

saw patient at home, diagnosis made, arranged admission

ambulance, patient dead when went back, all within 10 mins.

On the cremation forms, Shipman made other comments in response to the question about persons present at death. Examples include:

no one, seen at 15.30; found at 16.00
no one other than self
no one, seen by me 13.00; found by relative 14.30

Those cremation forms all featured the time and place of death, suddenness of death and whether Shipman was present or had seen the patient shortly before death.

Around this time, Fred Shipman went to the Dutch city of Amsterdam for a weekend medical conference and made a lasting impression on one female colleague. Dr Amy Cumming explained, 'He was a patronising man – rather like a Dutch uncle. I'm a little older than him and yet he had this ability to make me feel small and inexperienced. We spent a weekend in Amsterdam for a conference. I had to keep reminding myself that I was older and more experienced than he was.'

It was Shipman's confidence which put Dr Cumming in a state of awe. She understood why so many of his patients were deceived by his veneer of compassion and authority. 'He was very keen to explain to me all about the wonderful things he was doing in his practice. I was left thinking, How does he do it? He must have 36 hours in the day!'

Dr Cumming went on, 'He talked a lot about the "latest" methods, the "latest" drugs and their benefits to his patients, how the drugs worked. It seemed to me he gave his patients a vast amount of time. I was filled with admiration. He was some kind of Super Doc.'

And Fred Shipman never once behaved in an improper way towards Amy Cumming.

Back in Hyde, it certainly seemed at this time as if Fred

Shipman's deathly secrets would never be uncovered. Not only had the police dropped their investigation into his activities, but the General Medical Council continued to sit on at least two disturbing psychiatric reports about Shipman that were produced after his 1976 drugs conviction. They also hadn't been asked anything in relation to the complaints of three other incidents between 1985 and 1994. The GMC believed, in their own words, that 'these did not suggest a fundamental problem'. Yet those complaints definitely suggested a pattern of poor work performance sufficient to question Shipman's practice. The GMC later claimed, 'Had Greater Manchester Police asked us if we had any information regarding Dr Shipman, we would have co-operated with them fully.'

Yet, since setting up his solo practice at the end of 1991, at least 100 of Shipman's patients had died under circumstances that would later lead investigators to conclude that he had killed them deliberately. Other clues to this extraordinary death toll came from the number of death certificates Shipman had been signing.

For most doctors, the numbers remained pretty constant and low, normally 6–10 in a year in a community such as Hyde. In 1992, when Shipman first set up his solo practice, he issued just 7 certificates. But then in 1993 it jumped to 28 before dropping to 16 in 1994. Then in 1995 it leapt up to 38 and then 42 in 1996, followed by 47 in 1997. In the first half of 1998 it was 24. The 1997 figure of 47 was five times more than would be expected in a community such as Hyde.

The ease with which Fred Shipman was killing his patients threw the GP into a permanent state of over-anxiety. In some ways, he hoped against hope that his latest victim would prove unkillable. But Shipman's addiction to death meant his mind had become completely stagnant. If he'd become as deeply interested in something else then perhaps this deadly obsession might have passed away. Shipman was as preoccupied with death as most people are with hanging a picture on a certain place on a wall; there was nothing else to look at. This state of purposelessness and boredom produced what Sartre has described as 'the vertigo of freedom'.

Shipman also suffered from severe bouts of insomnia as well. His mind sometimes seemed like a light, a balloon. He lacked inner strength and felt he was at the mercy of the environment around him so that everything that happened blew him off course. Depression, misery, boredom, nausea were all suffered by Fred Shipman in the second half of 1998.

That was why he needed the adrenalin rush that came with each killing. It was the only time when he became truly excited, happy, driven by a strong sense of purpose and expectancy. Then Shipman's mind became like a sledge-hammer, smashing through his dark and sombre mood swings. Murder gave him a sense of being real, solid, Godlike.

In Fred Shipman's mind, there was little else to live for. What was the use of having all this power if he couldn't exert it? His mind was like a car engine, tearing itself to pieces because it was not properly connected to the chassis.

* * *

On 9 June 1998, Fred Shipman took blood samples from an elderly patient called Mrs Kathleen Grundy which he told her were part of a government health survey. Former mayoress of Hyde, Kathleen Grundy, regularly told friends of her admiration for the GP. She'd even considered donating part of her own charity fund to his practice appeal but then decided it was an 'inappropriate cause' and gave it to the new Tameside Hospice instead. Mrs Grundy had been introduced to Shipman many years earlier when they both belonged to a local medical committee.

'She thought he was a good doctor,' her friend Mary Clarke later explained. 'She thought he was good for the practice and the people of Hyde. She admired his work. But then all the people of Hyde thought highly of Dr Shipman, not just Mrs Grundy.'

The morning Mrs Grundy visited Fred Shipman's surgery, she also agreed to 'sign some papers' for Shipman which he said related to the blood test he'd just given her. Moments later, Fred Shipman called in his next, younger, patient at the surgery and asked him to sign a document. The piece of paper was folded over so patient Paul Spencer could not tell what it was, but he assumed it was a medical document.

'Dr Shipman asked me if I wouldn't mind writing my name and address and putting my signature and occupation on the piece of paper,' Spencer later recalled.

Spencer did notice the signature 'K Grundy' on the far right-hand side and put his own signature on the far left. 'Then I was told, "Thank you very much, and you can leave the room,"' Spencer later explained. He noticed that the patient who followed him was then told to do the same thing. Spencer has always insisted he had no idea that the paperwork was Kathleen Grundy's will.

That same day, Mrs Grundy also met Linda Skelton, a part-time clerical assistant who knew Mrs Grundy from the luncheon club they all attended. Mrs Grundy mentioned she'd been at the doctor's 'to sign some papers'. Mrs Skelton later recalled, 'She said there was nothing wrong with her and there were people waiting and she felt guilty because they were obviously people who were ill and waiting to see the doctor.'

Back at his surgery, Fred Shipman was typing out the following on a standard last will and testament form he'd bought at his local stationery supplier: 'I give all my estate, money and house to my doctor. My family are not in need and I want to reward him for all the care he has given to me and the people of Hyde.' Shipman left behind one fingerprint which was later to prove crucial in bringing him to justice.

The entire note had been written in the upper case, with missing letters where the typewriter had failed to keep up with his greedy fingers. Those who later saw the document described it as a 'cack-handed attempt at forgery'.

Was Fred Shipman deliberately setting himself up for a fall?

Was he trying to end his murderous reign by pointing the finger of suspicion squarely at himself? That will purported to leave the GP an estate worth £386,402, including Kathleen Grundy's home and a house she owned in Stockport.

When later asked by investigators if he knew anything about Mrs Grundy's will, Shipman replied, 'I have no knowledge of Mrs Grundy's will. Is that the answer you were wanting?' Shipman later insisted Mrs Grundy had asked him to witness her will but he'd requested two patients to do it instead. He even added chillingly, 'Mrs Grundy had used my pen, something I am never happy about people doing.'

Although there seems little doubt that Fred Shipman killed his victims in secret and alone there has been growing evidence that someone else knew of his murderous spree. When Shipman's fingerprints were later found on Kathleen Grundy's will, there was also another set of prints that have never been accounted for. It must have been someone close to Shipman.

'It seems likely that, at some stage, Shipman must have revealed his crimes to someone close to him,' says one criminal psychologist. 'To keep such dark and terrifying secrets to oneself is far beyond the realms of normal behaviour.'

Whoever Fred Shipman poured out his problems to was surely burdened with the most ghastly secrets anyone could ever have. As one police investigator later surmised, 'Somewhere out there is a person who knew what Shipman was up to. I'd hate to be in their shoes.'

Kathleen Grundy's neighbour, Audrey Adshead, had lived next door to the former Hyde mayoress for 20 years and in all that time Mrs Grundy had only ever been in hospital once. One day, in June 1998, she saw Mrs Grundy cutting bushes in her garden. They later chatted for over an hour and she seemed very excited about a trip she was about to take.

A few days later – on 23 June – Kathleen Grundy visited another friend. She appeared fit and well and, as usual, talked with pride about her family. 'She was very, very fond of her family,' her friend later explained. 'She never stopped talking about her grandsons and her daughter and her son-in-law. They were a very, very close, happy family.'

Mrs Grundy even mentioned that Dr Shipman was due to call on her the next day to do some more blood tests. 'She thought it was very good of him to visit her house to save her going to the surgery.'

At 8.30am on 24 June 1998, Fred Shipman called at Mrs Grundy's house to take another blood test. Shipman later claimed he left the house soon afterwards. Within minutes Mrs Grundy's breathing slowed down to a rate of two to three breaths a minute. Within another few minutes it stopped altogether. She appeared to be asleep but her lips, fingers and toes were turning a blue tinge. Her brain was no longer getting any oxygen. Shipman had injected a dose of morphine into Kathleen Grundy.

At 11.55am that day – 24 June 1998 – Mrs Grundy was found dead by her friends John Green and Ronald Pickford, who'd called round when she failed to turn up to serve lunches at the local old people's club. They found the front door closed but not locked and then walked in to discover Mrs Grundy's body, fully dressed as if she was about to go out. They both knew that Mrs Grundy was very security conscious with two mortice locks on her main door which she always locked even if she was in the garden.

Shipman was immediately informed and contacted local police constable John Fitzgerald to explain that he'd visited Mrs Grundy earlier that day and she had been complaining of feeling unwell. 'He said he'd liaised with the coroner's officer. As a result of the conversation he had with the coroner's officer, he was going to issue a death certificate claiming death from natural causes.'

On 25 June 1998 – the day after Mrs Grundy's death – Shipman made four computer entries about her within six minutes of each other, even though they referred to visits made up to a year previously. He'd certified death as old age and would later make outrageous claims that she had been a heroin addict.

He planted three specific references to Mrs Grundy's supposed drug addiction in her medical notes.

The first, dated 12 October 1996, noted: *'Pupils small (?) constipated – query drug abuse – at her age (?) wait and see.'*

Another, dated 15 July 1997, says: *'Had every (?) drug possible. Pupils small, dry mouth, possible drug abuse again (?). Denies taking any drugs other than for irritable bowel syndrome.'*

The third, for 26 November 1997, notes: *'Denies everything. Still clinically nothing of note to confirm my suspicions.'*

Fred Shipman seemed in a very good mood to his staff in the days following Mrs Grundy's death. He even told one GP he knew in Hyde that he was planning to move to France to retire 'very soon'.

* * *

Solicitors Hamilton Ward received Fred Shipman's version of Kathleen Grundy's will in the post on 24 June 1998, the day she died. Kathleen Grundy's estate came to more than £380,000. The will was accompanied by a letter which Shipman wrote on the same typewriter he had used for the will. He dated it 9 June and signed it 'K Grundy'.

It read:

> *'Dear Sir, I enclose a copy of my will. I think it is clear in intent. I wish Dr Shipman to benefit by having my estate but if he dies or cannot accept it, then the estate goes to my daughter. I would like you to be the executor of the will. I intend to make an appointment to discuss this and my will in the near future.'*

Staff at the offices of solicitors Hamilton Ward were puzzled. They had never acted for Mrs Grundy. They filed the will and awaited developments.

On 30 June they received a letter, without an address, dated 28 June and typed on the same Brother typewriter as the earlier correspondence.

'Dear Sir, I regret to inform you that Mrs K Grundy of 79 Joel Lane, Hyde, died last week. I understand that she lodged a will with you, as I, a friend, typed it out for her. Her daughter is at the address and you can contact her there.'

The letter had been signed S or F Smith.

Fred Shipman had ticked the 'cremation' box on the will form. But Mrs Grundy was not cremated, she was buried at Hyde Chapel on 1 July after a funeral service attended by hundreds of friends. Shipman was not among them.

A couple of weeks later, staff at Hamilton Ward managed to contact Mrs Grundy's daughter Angela Woodruff, herself a solicitor living in Leamington Spa, Warwickshire, in the centre of England. She was surprised to hear about the will because she had one signed by her mother leaving the estate to her. When she saw it, she at once suspected it was a forgery. 'The whole thing was just unbelievable,' Mrs Woodruff later recalled. 'The thought of Mum signing a document so badly typed leaving everything to her doctor just didn't make any sense. It was inconceivable.'

Mrs Woodruff began her own enquiries; contacting the will's supposed witnesses and comparing the signatures. It took time to accept the 'credibility gap' in order to come to her own conclusions. 'For us to believe that the doctor had possibly forged a will, and had possibly killed my mother, was a huge gap to cross,' she later recalled.

On 24 July 1998, Mrs Woodruff told police of her concerns and re-instigated one of the biggest murder investigations in British criminal history.

But why did Fred Shipman decide to try and make a financial profit from his killings? His first attempt at being left an estate had gone wrong when earlier victim Bianka Pomfret had re-amended her will back to leave everything to her family at the last minute. Did Fred Shipman believe Kathleen Grundy's estate might give him enough money to quit his job and get away from Hyde? Or did he believe the killings would stop if he inherited some money and then ran away?

No doubt, greed played a significant role in Shipman's decision. Just a few days after killing Kathleen Grundy, he took Primrose to a kitchen and bathroom store and told her to choose some new items for their run-down house. He even told staff at the store, 'I am coming into a large amount of money soon from a will, so money is no object.' Shipman specified to the store that he wanted to order a new fitted kitchen which included a double sink, waste disposal, an oven, hob, extractor fan and ten cupboards.

Fred Shipman reckoned he was about to strike it rich.

CHAPTER SEVENTEEN

Caught in a Web of Deceit

Detectives believed that Fred Shipman was unlikely to confess to his crimes, so they knew the case against him would have to be carefully constructed on a foundation of circumstantial and scientific evidence. In a unique move for the force, Detective Chief Inspector Mike Williams and Detective Chief Superintendent Bernard Postles, an officer with 27 years' experience, sought permission from Tameside coroner Dr John Pollard to have the body of Kathleen Grundy exhumed from Hyde Cemetery for a post mortem examination on 1 August 1998.

The pathologist could not find any immediate cause of Mrs Grundy's sudden death, as the secret of how she came to die was hidden in the tissue samples sent away for forensic examination.

Shipman's mystery informant told him investigators were carrying out toxicology tests on Mrs Grundy's body. Shipman knew they would uncover evidence of morphine, so he began busily smearing Mrs Grundy's good name by adding even more written claims about her 'drug addiction' to her computerised medical records at his practice. Subsequent enquiries have revealed the likely identity of Shipman's 'deep throat'. He was a onetime health authority official who also had contacts inside the local police. The informant was also, like so many in Hyde, convinced that Shipman was the victim of a vicious slur sparked by rival doctors in Hyde. Shipman's informant even accepted the GP's claims that he had legitimately been named as the main benefactor of Kathleen Grundy's will.

There was gossip about detectives looking into the activities of highly respected Dr Fred Shipman. There was mention of a body being exhumed and Shipman seemed to know a lot about it. When one patient asked Shipman what was happening, he shrugged his shoulders and commented calmly that it would be a while before the results were known, because the pathology labs were overloaded with work from the Omagh bombing in Northern Ireland that week.

When another patient gave Shipman's loyal receptionist Carol Chapman a ride home and asked her what she thought about the police enquiries, she replied, albeit crudely, 'It's a crock of shite.'

On 12 August 1998, Fred Shipman spoke to district nurse Marion Gilchrist in what would later be described as 'a rehearsal of his later police interviews'. Shipman told the nurse how Mrs Grundy had changed her will on the day of her death. He even admitted to Gilchrist, 'I read thriller books and I would have me guilty on the evidence.' Then he broke down and wept, saying how unfair it was, that he should become embroiled in a nasty row over a will. Then his voice lowered as he added with a burst of black humour, 'The only thing I did wrong was not having her cremated. If I had had her cremated, I wouldn't be having all this trouble.'

Two days later, the tests came back with confirmation that a huge dose of morphine had killed Kathleen Grundy. That discovery triggered a wide-ranging investigation into the sudden deaths of numerous other Shipman patients. Detectives immediately checked telephone and pager records for the surgery, the women's homes and Greater Manchester Ambulance Service. They soon uncovered more trickery with Shipman falsely claiming his victims had called him out or he had cancelled ambulances or that his surgery staff had paged him.

'That's when we first started realising the enormity of it,' senior investigator Bernard Postles later recalled. 'My people at HQ reckoned that we had a tiger by the tail. My response to this was, "We have got a pride of tigers by the tail." It wasn't just the enormity of the deaths but the enormity of what we were accusing somebody of, given their position in the community. What we did was constantly question each other, "Have we got this wrong? Are we missing something here? Are we dealing with something so out-of-character for a doctor that there is something wrong with us rather than him?"'

Meanwhile, the remains of Kathleen Grundy were reburied just over two weeks after they'd been removed from her grave. Investigator Bernie Postles decided that, from then on, any other exhumed bodies would have to be re-interred within 24 hours to minimise the distress to relatives.

On 14 August 1998, investigators searched Fred Shipman's surgery in Market Street as the GP and his still loyal staff stood by. Inside the surgery, Shipman – still acting the complete innocent – handed detectives his typewriter. 'I believe this is what you are looking for,' he said with a hint of condescension. The officers thanked him and took it away for forensic examination. Fred Shipman later claimed he lent Mrs Grundy the Brother typewriter, but fingerprint experts eventually confirmed that there was no sign whatsoever of Mrs Grundy's prints on the machine.

A thorough examination of Shipman's medical notes was also carried out. There were paper documents bound in the traditional light-brown 'Lloyd George' envelopes. The passage Shipman had written claiming that Mrs Grundy was a drug addict immediately caught the attention of investigators. The entry for 12 October 1996 read: 'IBS [irritable bowel syndrome] again. Odd. Pupils small. Constipated. Query drug abuse? Query at her age? Query codeine? Wait and see.' Two more entries, dated 15 July and 26 November 1997, suggested the same thing.

That day, police made an arrangement with Shipman for him to visit Ashton-under-Lyne Police Station on Tuesday, 7 September. They were piling on the pressure but were happy to let him 'sweat it out' for a few weeks.

Some days later, Fred Shipman had a beer with his old friend Dr David Walker, who later recalled, 'He didn't seem to have any worries in the world and he didn't seem concerned about what would happen. He was able to talk on all sorts of levels.'

Walker and some of Shipman's other drinking pals had decided to take the GP out to 'help him keep his spirits up'. He explained, 'We all thought he was innocent. It was all a terrible mistake and it would soon all be cleared up. We didn't discuss it much.'

Fred Shipman briefly mentioned that he was due to visit the police station the following Tuesday. 'He said he'd sort it all out then.' Walker and Shipman's other friends decided not to push the matter any further. Dr Walker later recalled, 'There was never a time when I didn't think he was anything but a decent guy. A dedicated doctor. He said he couldn't be doing with drug addicts and he wouldn't have them in his practice. He always seemed open. He talked about other things away from medicine, like his lad playing rugby. Most conversations were very normal. We enjoyed the real ale and the atmosphere. It was as simple as that.'

Despite the obviously serious nature of the police's investigation, the GP was determined to continue practising. The waiting room remained as hectic as ever. Patients queued beneath a huge array of good luck cards pinned to the wall. The receptionists had put them up with pride – there was no question of him being guilty. Most believed it was all a 'terrible misunderstanding'.

A siege mentality began to develop at the Market Street surgery. Fred and Primrose now had his patients and staff on their side against the rest of the world. 'He's a marvellous doctor, why don't you leave him alone?' was one of the most popular slants on the situation.

All around the town, Fred Shipman's friends lined up to

defend him. Shipman was overwhelmed by the support and chose to make some statements to certain, carefully chosen patients and associates. Shipman told one patient he would scold Kathleen Grundy if she came back from the dead for all the trouble she had caused him. Lesley Pullford described how Shipman told her he and the staff had a meeting and made plans of what to do with the money to be left by Mrs Grundy should they get it. Shipman then said, 'We will all have a week off each and, on the anniversary of her death, give so much to old people's homes and, if anyone had a baby that day, give the money to a charity of their choice.'

He also added that it would not be over quickly. 'The next thing she is going to accuse me of is forging her will.' Mrs Pullford later claimed she took this to be a reference to Mrs Grundy's daughter. He broke down as he also told Lesley Pullford how he'd like to scold Mrs Grundy, if she came back from the dead. 'If I could bring her back and sit her in that chair, I would say, "Look at all the trouble it has caused." I was going to say I did not want the money but, because of all this trouble, I will have it,' he railed.

But when Shipman bumped into a medical colleague out on the streets of Hyde, he seemed in an altogether different frame of mind. Shipman's associate later recalled, 'I saw him Wednesday afternoon and spent about two hours talking to him. It was a moving conversation. He was very distressed and on a couple of occasions came close to tears. He actually told me about the Grundy will and by the end I was utterly convinced this was a man who had for whatever reason been unjustly and wrongfully accused of trying to gain by ending a patient's life.'

During those early days of the police investigation into Fred Shipman's activities, detectives were intrigued by the relationship between the GP and his wife. Primrose Shipman had long since happily settled into the role of doctor's wife, believing it gave her real status – something that had undoubtedly attracted her to Fred Shipman in the first place. But as she and her husband began to grow into their roles as pillars of the community, they'd become quite aloof from their neighbours. Primrose unintentionally gave the impression that they were invisible. In the middle of all this killing, she still encouraged Fred Shipman to join the board of the junior committee of the Ashton Rugby Club where youngest son Sam played. 'It was a baffling relationship,' said one investigator.

Meanwhile, relatives of some of Fred Shipman's deceased patients were waking up to news of the Shipman investigation in the *Manchester Evening News*, which was the first newspaper to reveal the Shipman story to the world.

Bianka Pomfret's ex-husband Adrian contacted the police within hours of the first article appearing about Shipman. Many of his friends and relatives refused to believe that Fred Shipman was guilty of anything. 'They said I had no right to condemn an innocent man,' Mr Pomfret later explained. 'I told my mother-in-law she was probably on the list, yet she sat there and said I should take people as I find them and, as far as she was concerned, he wasn't guilty until they found him so.'

Adrian Pomfret became even more convinced of Fred Shipman's guilt when the police rang back and said Shipman had claimed there were no witnesses who saw him at Bianka's house the day she died. 'You'll have no problems with that because he told me he was round there when I saw him later that night to view the body.' The police also asked Mr Pomfret if he knew that Shipman had been treating his former wife for angina for two years. 'Straight away I remembered how he'd said she was going to dance on my grave because she was so healthy. There was no mention of angina.'

Police soon established that Bianka had been on the verge of leaving her entire estate to Shipman which further fuelled their belief in his guilt. However, Adrian Pomfret was banned from discussing this until after Shipman's trial in case it was deemed to influence the jury.

Outside the Shipman home, an army of journalists were soon camped day and night. At one stage, a local TV crew snatched some footage of Fred Shipman getting out of his Renault Espace people carrier. He looked harassed and weary but still managed to give off the air of a friendly country doctor. Was this really the man suspected of murdering countless elderly patients? That footage was sent around the world and was run over and over again because it was one of only two pieces of footage ever filmed of Shipman.

Inside the Shipman home, the family spent most nights gathered round their TV set watching the investigation unfold through the local and national news programmes. One of youngest son Sam's friends who visited the Shipman house at the time later recalled, 'Dr Shipman would look at the screen but not say a word. Nobody said anything or even commented on it. It was as if it was nothing to do with the family. I don't think any of them believed it.'

But Sam's friend revealed that Fred Shipman continued to be a strict disciplinarian at home. 'Sam had a 100 per cent attendance record at West Hill School in Stalybridge that year. His father was very strict about that. He used to say just because you had a cold didn't mean you could stay at home. He was determined for his sons to do well at school.'

Many of the families of Shipman's victims still refused to believe that he had killed their loved ones. 'When this first broke about the will it was like going into the surgery on Christmas Day where people festoon walls with Christmas cards,' recalled Peter Wagstaff, son of Shipman victim Kathleen Wagstaff. 'There were literally hundreds of cards from people wishing him well and hoping the matter would soon be sorted out. No one believed it.'

Peter and Angela Wagstaff rallied behind their doctor. 'We sent a letter of support to him. We didn't believe anything. It was beyond the realms of belief that this well-respected GP could do anything like that.'

But then Peter Wagstaff decided to check out for himself what the doctor had said about how his mother had died. 'I checked the phone bill from her home to see if she had phoned for Dr Shipman and also to see if Shipman phoned for the ambulance.'

Peter Wagstaff immediately discovered that no phone calls had been made that day and contacted investigators.

Fred Shipman knew that the police net was closing in on him, but he refused to believe detectives would uncover the full enormity of his crimes. He even bragged to one patient, whose mother later turned out to be yet another victim, that he'd be out of jail within six years at the most.

Margaret Williams had visited Shipman's surgery unaware that 13 years earlier he had murdered her mother May, 74. Mrs Williams later recalled, 'I said to him one day that I'd heard about the Mrs Grundy case and that everyone in the town supported him in his troubles. He replied, "I've discussed it with my wife and we think I'll get 12 years. I'll probably serve six years and when I come out I'll retire and we'll move away."'

* * *

At 8.30am on 7 September 1998, Fred Shipman arrived with his solicitor Anne Ball in her car at Ashton-under-Lyne Police Station. An old-fashioned blue police light embellished the modern structure and there were a few sparse trees dividing the car park from the constant queue of traffic on Manchester Road. Shipman greeted the *Manchester Evening News* photographer Chris Gleave with a shrug of the shoulders. As Gleave snapped shot after shot, his film whirring through his camera, the GP faced him up, stared intently and held out his hands, saying dryly, 'Sure you got enough?'

Fred Shipman and Anne Ball then took a sudden detour away from the entrance to the police station after he told her he wasn't ready to go in. They took a 20-minute walk away through the terraced streets that ran behind the building. They walked past the local primary school where kids were playing in the playground. Then they moved alongside a builder's yard which was slowly stirring to life. There were also long rows of red-brick houses where families were rousing themselves for work.

Photographer Gleave and reporter Mikaela Sitford then appeared again alongside Shipman asking for a comment. Solicitor Anne Ball was angry with the journalists. 'He has nothing to say. Leave us alone.' Shipman, hands jammed in his pockets, looked serious. He knew it would soon be over.

Finally, at 9.00am, Shipman and his solicitor walked into the police station. He was immediately arrested for the murder of 81-year-old former mayoress Kathleen Grundy. Despite his bravado, Fred Shipman was mightily shocked by his arrest, especially when he was then handed over to be questioned by two more junior officers, Detective Sergeant John Walker and Detective Constable Mark Denham.

Fred Shipman's first recorded response to detectives was, 'You're stupid.' Detective Chief Inspector Mike Williams, 50, later recalled, 'I think we wrong-footed him. It was a deliberate ploy. I believe he felt he was important enough to warrant an officer of my ranking. It immediately showed in the inflection in his voice. I think he would have liked the Chief Constable to have interviewed him.'

Detective Chief Superintendent Bernard Postles also noticed Fred Shipman seemed contemptuous of the low rank of the officers questioning him. 'He tried to confuse them by saying, "You don't understand medical matters. You are only plods,"' Postles later recalled. 'He thought he had the upper hand because he had the superior intellect.'

As Fred Shipman's fingers were pressed on to a moist, inky fingerprint pad, he joked with one investigator to be careful with his little finger, in which he suffered RSI. 'Repetitive strain injury,' he explained. Fred Shipman later claimed it was all as a result of his busy hours at the computer keyboard.

Outside the modern, low-rise police building, Primrose and Sam waited patiently after showing up in the family's big red Renault people carrier, ready to take him home after 'he'd helped police with their enquiries'. Within half-an-hour, they'd been advised to go home.

Shipman told Detective Sergeant Walker and Detective

Constable Denham about the running of his surgery. When asked about his methods of record-keeping, he said, 'I am a firm believer in the concept of general practice and computerisation being held back by the underdeveloped finance and political decisions by the Government. It doesn't stop me from computerising my practice.'

Ten miles away, police searched the Shipman family home. They quickly found four 10mg ampoules of diamorphine stored inside a box that also contained methotrimeprazine (Nozinan). Primrose and their two youngest sons David and Sam stood by as detectives systematically took apart the house. One investigator was astonished at how calm Primrose and the two boys were. 'They were very helpful and quite pleasant, considering,' one investigator later recalled. 'One of the lads even showed us where to find things. He was a nice lad, very polite.'

Investigators were appalled at how filthy the Shipman house was, with clothes strewn everywhere and food left lying around the kitchen. 'It wasn't how you'd expect a doctor's house to be.'

Detectives then discovered Shipman's collection of gold rings, necklaces, brooches and earrings in a cardboard box in the couple's bedroom. When asked who owned this jewellery box, Primrose replied, 'Me.' The detectives were surprised. As one later explained, 'Her fingers were like Cumberland sausages; we couldn't believe she had ever worn such tiny rings.'

One investigator also added, 'It was clear that Primrose knew about the existence of the box or else she would not have claimed it was hers.'

The jewellery was all photographed and put into a catalogue for relatives of Shipman's victims to examine later. Few families had even noticed that trinkets had gone missing when their loved ones were found dead. The police search team also found boxes and carrier bags in the garage, each stuffed with old medical records and labelled with the word 'dead' in red letters. Shipman had chosen to keep some of his old records, instead of handing them over to the West Pennine Health Authority for storage. However, as per his work contract, he was expected to keep them safe, obviously for reasons of confidentiality. The 150 records stuffed haphazardly into boxes and bags were testament to his lax attitude – and some were testament to his murderous habits.

Investigators even employed a nurse from Merseyside, who spread all Shipman's records on her kitchen table and deciphered the doctor's typical scrawl and tried to put them into chronological order. Another expert, Dr John Grenville, was also called on to the team to examine the notes. He noticed how Shipman had recorded that he'd left patient Ivy Lomas – apparently dying of a heart-attack in his treatment room – while he attended the colds and sniffles of three other patients, and he did not even bother sending another victim, Joan Melia, to hospital as 'she would probably have died on the way there'.

Back at Ashton-under-Lyne Police Station, Fred Shipman admitted to investigators that he didn't maintain a controlled drugs register. He said he was aware of the regulations, but since his arrest in 1976 he had made it his policy not to keep controlled drugs and therefore did not need a register. Shipman also claimed that on the few occasions that controlled drugs were urgently required, he would write out a prescription using the patient's name and collect it immediately from a pharmacy. That, Shipman conceded, was why there was no controlled drugs register available.

In fact, Shipman had collected unused controlled drugs following the deaths of patients at home. He insisted that he had destroyed these drugs, but detectives suspected he was lying from the onset. The discovery of ampoules of diamorphine in the Shipman family home was the proof they needed. Many of Shipman's prescriptions for diamorphine were for potentially lethal doses of 30mg.

Shipman said he'd only administered part of the doses and discarded the remainder. Shipman admitted he knew it was an offence under the Misuse of Drugs Act to fail to make a record of the administration of a controlled drug to a patient.

Fred Shipman couldn't wait to show detectives his entries in Kathleen Grundy's medical records because he believed that they would immediately clear him of any involvement in her death. But what Shipman did not realise was that Mrs Grundy couldn't have had an appointment with him on 12 October – as he'd stated in his records – because she'd been with her daughter on that day.

And Shipman's reference in his computerised records to dealing with Mrs Grundy's alleged drug addiction problem occurred on a day when – according to his credit card transactions – Shipman was 200 miles away in the city of York buying one of his beloved tortoiseshell pens.

At that interview, Fred Shipman continued using his medical jargon and even objected to the investigators' interviewing technique. In an adjoining room, DS Postles and DCI Williams felt sorry for their officers who were coping well considering Shipman's condescending attitude. 'Shipman was extremely difficult to deal with in that first interview,' DCI Williams recalled. 'It was a minefield for the officers, who had to establish why Kathleen Grundy had morphine in her body and understand medical issues. He set out to belittle the officers – "I'm the intelligent one here." He saw it as a competition, a challenge between him and us.'

Fred Shipman continued to insist to detectives that Kathleen Grundy was a drug addict. 'I have my suspicions that she was abusing narcotics over a period of a year or so. She may have given herself accidentally an overdose.'

Shipman also told detectives he was 'astonished' to find he was the sole beneficiary of Mrs Grundy's will. The GP insisted he did not inject her with any drug prior to her death and even pointed to comments on her medical records backing his claims about her drug addiction. Asked to explain why the will was typed on his surgery typewriter, Shipman claimed Mrs Grundy had borrowed it several times.

But Fred Shipman's arrogance was about to lead to his downfall. Investigators had also taken Shipman's hard disk from his computer, which held all the patients' records. This was to prove the most damning evidence of all. Shipman was proud of his computerised system and even referred to his practice appeal fund, which had raised £19,000 in six years thanks to the efforts and generosity of his devoted patients. Ironically, some of his patients had donated both in life and in death with money being given instead of flowers to help the surgery's development. Unknown to Shipman, investigators had already established that he'd tampered with the computers to make the women look more ill than they really were.

One of the most telling examples of Shipman's fraudulent use of his computer was victim Maureen Ward, whose medical records showed all the signs of a woman with a brain tumour. Shipman noted on 17 December 1997 that she was suffering from a 'headache, it comes and goes, dull, nauseous, legs not steady, retina of eye is OK, eyesight is normal'. But investigators soon established that the file on Mrs Ward was not created until 18 February 1998 at 2.49pm – 45 minutes before he found her dead.

DCI Williams later spelt it out. 'Maureen Ward was found by Dr Shipman at 3.30pm. He was in the surgery at 2.45pm making that entry. Two minutes later, there's an entry for the day before, suggesting secondary cancer of the brain. Two minutes after that one, for 17 December. He was creating a history, so that having a look at it would show a tendency to the cause of death. He had done the dirty deed. He had called on her, went back to his computer, then went back to "find" the body.'

During that first interview, officers also concluded that Fred Shipman was a pathetic figure in many ways. 'He was like a child who'd done something naughty and couldn't wait for someone to find out. He had to go back and make sure she was found.'

Investigators would soon establish it was the same with three other victims – Pamela Hillier, Winnie Mellor and Bianka Pomfret. Out of a list of more than 3,000 patients, there was no way Shipman could remember blood pressure counts months after the supposed consultation.

In addition to the murder of Mrs Grundy, Shipman was also charged with attempted theft by deception, and with three counts of forgery. He was held in custody that night in the police station cells and appeared in front of Tameside Magistrates' Court the next morning.

At last, investigators appeared to have got their man.

CHAPTER EIGHTEEN

The Victims Speak Again

The town of Hyde found itself even further under siege from journalists within hours of Fred Shipman's arrest. And at Shipman's Market Street practice, Primrose manned the reception desk and patiently explained to callers that her husband would be returning to work as soon as possible. There was absolutely no question of him permanently going to prison.

Vast banner headlines in numerous national newspapers proclaimed Shipman's role as, allegedly, one of the country's most prolific serial killers. But none of this did anything to dampen the support of thousands of his Hyde 'parishioners', many of whom claimed that the newspapers were lying.

Friends, family and associates still refused to accept his guilt and referred enquiries to Primrose, who'd rapidly become extremely adept at refusing to comment and glaring angrily at any journalist who dared to call at the family home in Roe Cross Green. Shipman's son Sam insisted to friends that his father would never be found guilty.

But a few days after Fred Shipman's arrest, Sam slipped into a deeply withdrawn state although he still refused even to consider his father's guilt. For many months afterwards, he barely acknowledged anyone in the street. 'He just seemed to be in a dream world. His face was blank. He was clearly in a state of shock,' one neighbour later recalled. On one occasion, the teenager was even harassed in the street by a group of reporters.

And the rest of the family's confidence in Fred Shipman's innocence also never wavered. The Shipman offspring insisted to friends that their father was the victim of a ghastly mistake and he'd soon be released. They even claimed the family still expected to take possession of Mrs Grundy's house in Joel Lane. All this clearly suggested that Shipman had discussed the old lady's estate in some detail with his family.

In Nottingham, Fred Shipman's estranged family also faced the full onslaught of the fourth estate on their doorstep. All enquiries were greeted with a polite refusal to talk. In Wetherby, friends closed ranks around Primrose's elderly mother Enid Oxtoby and her disabled daughter Mary. And despite everything, Primrose remained out of contact with her family.

* * *

When one of the main whistle-blowers, Dr Linda Reynolds, returned to work after her long vacation in the USA, she was greeted by a chorus at her surgery. 'Have you heard? They've arrested Fred!'

Dr Reynolds was shocked. 'I thought to myself so there was something wrong. I was right,' she later recalled. 'I finally felt exonerated.'

Coroner Dr John Pollard later praised Dr Reynolds. 'She was extremely brave in coming forward. We had to treat her report in a careful and subtle way because she really was laying her reputation on the line by saying something was wrong. If it hadn't been, she would have looked extremely foolish. She had put her career in jeopardy by speaking out, but she was only doing what she thought was right.'

Undertaker Debbie Bambroffe was also on vacation in Spain

when the news of Shipman's arrest broke. She later recalled, 'We saw it on television and instantly there was a sickening feeling in the pit of my stomach.'

She still believes to this day that she should have gone to the authorities sooner and then the lives of some of Shipman's victims might have been saved. 'If only I had believed in my intuition; if only I had been strong enough to speak out earlier; if only I hadn't allowed myself to be persuaded that there was nothing to worry about, then some of the women he killed might be alive today.'

But amongst Shipman's friends and associates there was still a great deal of loyalty. Dr David Walker and Shipman's other drinking friends even agreed to offer to stand bail for the GP because they were so convinced of his innocence. 'I just didn't believe he could do such a thing,' recalled Dr Walker.

Fred Shipman's own GP, Dr Wally Ashworth, was so sure of his innocence that he immediately offered £20,000 towards Shipman's bail. 'What can I say? That is how sure I am of his innocence,' he told one journalist at the time.

Brian Holden, of the Rochdale Canal Society, was just as shocked to hear about Shipman's arrest. 'I thought it was somebody else at first. The photos of him looked so different from the man I knew. He had aged so much and had a beard and I had a job to remember because he was known as Fred or Dr Shipman. I only worked it out because of the frequency with which his name was mentioned. Then journalists started calling me up. I told one person I knew him and soon everyone was asking me about him.' Mr Holden, a teacher for 40 years, then added, 'People who thought of me as nothing more than a respectable teacher of Latin and Greek suddenly all wanted to know what I thought of Dr Shipman.'

On 21 September, Joan Melia's coffin was raised from the earth of St Mary's graveyard in nearby Newton. The following day, the body of Winifred Mellor was exhumed from Highfield Cemetery in Bredbury. A week later, police supervised the removal of Bianka Pomfret's coffin from Hyde

Cemetery. Traces of morphine and diamorphine were found in all their bodies.

In the late afternoon of 5 October 1998, DC Marie Snityhski, 34, and DS Mark Wareing confronted Fred Shipman – supported by his solicitor Anne Ball – across a table in Ashton-under-Lyne Police Station for his second interview. DS Wareing first challenged Shipman over how he'd altered his computerised medical records for 73-year-old Winifred Mellor to create a false history of heart disease. Wareing asked the doctor if he had anything to say and he replied, 'Nothing.'

Wareing then told Shipman he believed he had gone to Mrs Mellor's house in Hyde on 11 May 1998 with the express intention of killing her. Wareing said, 'You attended at 3.00pm and that's when you murdered this lady. So much was your rush that you went back to the surgery and started altering this lady's computerised medical records. We can prove that only minutes after 3.00pm you were fabricating this false medical history.'

Shipman responded, 'There's no answer.'

Then the officer replied, 'There's a very clear answer. You attended that house, you rolled up her sleeve and injected her with morphine, killing her, and that's what you were trying to cover up.'

Shipman replied, 'No.'

The mood of that interview suddenly changed. Fred Shipman had been completely wrong-footed. Questions had been put to him that he couldn't anticipate, questions that he could not answer or fend off with his customary arrogance.

Detective Sergeant Mark Wareing decided to move in for the kill, so to speak. 'I am showing you … I'll put it in the middle of the room because your solicitor can examine it as well then … It's an exhibit, JFA42, and it's an insertion behind your computer. There's a ghost image and it records what's placed in when and what's removed …'

Fred Shipman did not respond. His solicitor Anne Ball, a medical expert, picked up the document, examined it and passed it to the doctor. He examined it.

That document showed Mrs Mellor's record from 1 August 1997, a woman complaining of chest pains, accompanied by a doctor's note. '*?? angina*' was actually typed into the computer three minutes and 39 seconds after the doctor had left Mrs Mellor's house following her death on 11 May 1998.

Detective Wareing then told Shipman, 'I'll ask you again, doctor. Where's that information come from?'

Listening in on an audio link from a nearby room were the two senior police officers DCS Bernard Postles and DCI Mark Williams. They had worked for many weeks for this moment.

'I've no recollection of me putting that on the machine,' is all Shipman could say as he was pressed again and again. He struggled to maintain his composure.

'I still have no recollection of entering that on to the computer ... again, in the same manner as I've explained the other one, I cannot remember putting that on the computer. I'm well aware that that's how an audit trail works ... there's no argument about that ... you say, you're stating the obvious, that doesn't need an answer.'

When interviewed by the two investigators about victim Irene Berry, Shipman was confronted with evidence that he'd faked medical records.

Police: Let me just remind you the date of this lady's death – 11 May '98. After three o'clock that afternoon you endorsed the computer with the date of the 1 October '97, referring to prior chest pains.

Shipman: I have no recollection of me putting that on the machine.

Police: It's your pass code. It's your name.

(*Shipman then paused and took a long, deep breath.*)

Shipman: That doesn't alter the fact that I can't remember doing it.

Police: You attended the house and you murdered this lady and you went back to the surgery and started altering this lady's records. You tell me why you needed to do that?

Shipman: There is no answer.

Fred Shipman had run out of answers, except to point out that the clock on his computer was not set for summer time and it would be out by one hour.

Then Anne Ball asked for a consultation with her client. Left alone with her, Shipman fell to his knees and broke out in uncontrollable sobs, tears streaming down his face. He was unable to go back to continue the interview that day.

As DCI Williams later explained, 'They led him nicely up a particular path. Suddenly he's less arrogant; it takes more time for him to answer. He was floundering; he didn't know a counter-argument. We'd put the pin in the balloon.'

Williams and DCS Postles later listened to the tapes of that interview over and over again. DCI Williams recalled, 'There's a crucial moment where he knows the game is up. I thought he was going to cough it.'

The DCI added, 'It is difficult enough in any interview but that's what we are trained to do. In these circumstances, they had a more difficult job because of the way he reacted to them and treated them. They were extremely skilful. They were under extraordinary pressure but they coped extremely well and did a damn good job.'

DCS Postles never forgot that satisfying moment as he sat in the adjoining room. 'He considered he had won. "I'm up to it, let's get the boxing gloves on." The officers led him along. You get to the point where he can see it coming, when you listen to the tapes.'

Britain's national tabloid newspapers soon reflected the shock felt across the nation about the alleged activities of Fred Shipman. IS GP BRITAIN'S BIGGEST EVER SERIAL KILLER? asked the *Daily Express*.

Fred Shipman was formally suspended from his job several weeks after his arrest, but the health authority was obliged to pay Shipman his salary because he was suspended and not disqualified. That would continue until the day of his conviction, unless, of course, he was acquitted.

Shipman could even still call himself 'Doctor' for the time being, said a spokesman for the General Medical Council whose motto is 'Protecting Patients, Guiding Doctors'. It also emerged that almost £20,000 worth of medical equipment bought by the surgery appeal fund, whose donors included some of Shipman's own victims, had gone straight into the GP's own bank account. This even included more than £200 sent in lieu of flowers at victim Kathleen Wagstaff's funeral.

When detectives tried to turn their attention towards Primrose Shipman and her possible role in her husband's crimes, her solicitor insisted she could only be questioned *after* being arrested and cautioned, and that there was absolutely no evidence to justify doing that. Primrose had become an even more ungainly, plump figure with lank grey hair and eyes that had long since lost their sparkle. Having worked part-time at the surgery and shared the home where Fred Shipman stashed many of the drugs with which he had killed patients, she might well have enlightened investigators in regard to many aspects of her husband's behaviour. As one officer later explained, 'She wouldn't even come to the police station. Her lawyer said she would only be questioned if she were arrested, but we simply had no reason to do that.'

In Hyde, a small, loyal core of friends and family tried to protect Primrose, and they all remained convinced of the GP's innocence. Neighbours even offered help with household chores and one couple continually collected shopping for her and her children. Others called at the family's semi in Mottram to comfort the family and offer support. Primrose told friends she was determined to continue her life as normally as possible.

Through the large window at the front of the house, Primrose could be seen tidying up the living room. Some in the community even began to believe that perhaps Primrose had been secretly instrumental in her husband's arrest and that some kind of a deal had been struck with prosecutors and police, but this has always been steadfastly denied.

For many women, the spectacular downfall of their beloved

husband would have been too much to bear. But Primrose was made of stronger stuff; she'd been with him long enough for his superior attitude to rub off on her, giving her the strength to confront the staring eyes of the people of Hyde. Local taxi driver Michael Kitchen, whose 70-year-old mother was one of Fred Shipman's victims, noted, 'After Shipman was charged, it was disturbing to see Primrose wandering around Hyde.'

In her local ASDA supermarket, one staff member refused to serve Primrose. She later said she felt physically sick that someone could stay with a man after he had been charged with so many horrible crimes. But Primrose ignored all the stares; she and Fred were still invincible and she still believed that it all would be cleared up and Fred would be released from police custody.

Primrose – who throughout life had been prepared to plough her own lonely furrow – was unyielding. She heard the tongues wagging behind her back. Family friends later said that Primrose was 'aware of and prepared for' the life of scrutiny and stigma that lay ahead.

Over at St George's Church in Hyde, some were even saying prayers for the family along with the relatives of those who'd been murdered by Shipman. Curate Dr John Harries said, 'We pray for the family of Dr Shipman – Primrose, Christopher, David, Sarah and Sam – who are also victims of this betrayal and who have suffered so greatly in the last few months.'

* * *

In mid-October, Fred Shipman returned to Ashton-under-Lyne Police Station still in a distressed and highly emotional state. He refused to comment when asked about ten other suspected victims. A doctor then declared him unfit to be interviewed any further by waiting detectives. The police were never allowed to interview Shipman again.

He was then taken across the road to Tameside Magistrates' Court where he was accused of murdering Mrs Melia, Mrs Mellor and Mrs Pomfret. As the charges were put to him, Fred

Shipman visibly shook his head from side to side and said nothing. He sobbed quietly as he was remanded in custody and two security guards had to help him from the court.

The police had no doubt of Fred Shipman's guilt, but remained baffled about his motives. The only time he'd tried to gain from the murders turned out to be his undoing. Revenge and/or a sexual motive did not seem part of the equation. Senior investigator Bernard Postles concluded, 'It appears he just got the compulsion to kill. We looked at greed, we looked at revenge. We examined the possibility that the victims were all women draining his drug fund. But although some of them made visits to him, this was not the case. Rage? Anger? He wasn't annoyed with these people. The clue to the motive is his attitude that he is superior, and wanted to control situations.'

And there lies the key to unlock Fred Shipman's sick and twisted mind. He was fixated at a level of self-esteem that meant his major preoccupation was the idea of intellectual and creative eminence. He frequently treated Primrose and his family in a despotic manner, and expected total, unquestioned obedience, becoming furious at the least sign of resistance. Fred Shipman had an absolute obsession with being right. He completely lacked self-criticism and his killings were a form of self-indulgence.

It gave him the power. But if he was ever proved wrong, he would evade the issue by flying into an even deeper rage at some invented affront or reflection upon his dignity. Shipman's attitude was that if Primrose truly respected him, then she would not tell him if he was in the wrong. If she dared to, then he would consider that the ultimate insult.

Shipman was obsessed with being right. If Primrose had ever left him, he would probably have gone to pieces, maybe even become an alcoholic, or perhaps even killed himself. Her submission to his demands formed the basis of his self-respect; her desertion would have pulled away his psychological foundations.

Shipman's immediate circle – his wife and children – provided him with a much needed psychological vitamin. They had to put up with a certain level of resentment from Shipman. It often took the form of outrageous bullying, even though in many ways Shipman needed his family more than they needed him.

Following Fred Shipman's minor collapse after his interview and court appearance, the GP was prescribed numerous tranquillisers. He quickly regained his iron will to survive and even tried to take control of his circumstances. Initially, Shipman had been remanded to Walton Prison, Liverpool, 50 miles to the west of Hyde, because there was some concern over his safety if he was incarcerated in Manchester's notorious Strangeways Prison where there was a high chance he would find himself facing the relatives of some of his victims among the inmates and staff.

During his brief spell in Walton Prison, Fred Shipman shared a cell with Brian Ratford, then on remand for a drink-driving charge. The GP even informed his cellmate about different ways of killing someone.

But within weeks, Shipman was moved to Strangeways Prison after continual requests from his solicitors because they felt that Walton Prison was too far for Primrose and the children to travel to visit the jailed GP. Shipman was more concerned with seeing his family than any threat from inmates or staff.

Her Majesty's Prison Strangeways is a grim, red-brick, fortress-like building constructed more than 100 years ago. It is a depressing institution where inmates have, over the years, mounted regular roof-top protests at the appalling conditions. Cells line long landings, under a steepled roof which echoes with the noise of men trudging up and down the steel stairway.

Once he'd settled into Strangeways, Fred Shipman took to prison life 'like a natural'. Father Denis Maher, the priest from St Paul's Church, Hyde, who'd lost three of his parishioners to the alleged mass killer, was appalled when he heard how Shipman was 'strolling around the place as if he owned it'.

One of the first people outside his family to visit Fred Shipman was Michael Taylor who'd earlier met Shipman through the Small Practices Association. The two men had even greeted the then Health Secretary Frank Dobson when he attended the organisation's annual meeting at Manchester's Palace Hotel in June 1998, the month that Shipman killed Kathleen Grundy.

'Fred tended to be somewhat grumpy at times,' recalled Michael Taylor. 'He could offend people but he was also very prepared to help. I think it's fair to say that we respected him and those of us who have been to his practice recognised that it was of high quality. He was very energetic, very meticulous.'

Michael Taylor regarded Fred Shipman as a genuine friend but later acknowledged that it was 'a friendship based on acquaintanceship and mutual respect, the need for information and the need to learn together. He was not the sort of man I would seek out for a couple of jars.'

Within seconds of meeting Shipman in Strangeways, Taylor later recalled that the GP told him in no uncertain terms that the allegations against him were false. 'He said it was very upsetting and disconcerting. He mentioned how he'd been on his way back from the post office when a patient crossed the road to see him and support him. He had just burst into tears.'

Fred Shipman showed no regret for his alleged crimes because, in his mind, he had done no wrong. But in letters to other friends soon after his arrest, Shipman did admit that 'even Primrose has started asking me about the deaths'.

Fred Shipman's ability to adapt to prison life didn't surprise those who knew him well. He'd crawled back up from numerous knock-backs during his life. In the corridors, cells and recreation wings at Strangeways, he was going about his manipulative business in the only way he knew. Fred Shipman told fellow inmate Derrick Ismiel, 'My work was faultless. I prided myself on my experience in caring for people who were terminally ill. How dare they question my professionalism? People knew me by my work. How can they actually accuse me of this?'

Fred Shipman still felt himself unquestionable and unassailable. The compassionate, kindly veneer which he'd so carefully perfected for elderly and needy patients was, to a certain extent, discarded. In its place, Fred Shipman seemed a bleak, callous, calculating man convinced of his own infallibility, determined to continue controlling all around him and confident that he possessed the intellect to fool all.

Inside Strangeways, Shipman could barely hide his contempt for most other inmates, with the exception of Derrick Ismiel. In a chilling, monotone voice, he told Ismiel one day soon after his transfer to Strangeways, 'They're never going to find me guilty. I'll show them all. This whole system is full of lies. They should have all died – and died like flies.'

Shipman made a point of counselling inmates whom no one else would speak to. Prisoner Aron Nicholls, who set fire to his 12-year-old girlfriend Lauren Carhart, was one of his favourite 'patients'. Shipman defended his own actions by saying, 'We're all in here for something.'

Shipman believed that by helping people such as Nicholls he was creating a position for himself within the prison hierarchy. Shipman's penchant for looking after certain fellow cons helped him gain a reputation as a combination of Florence Nightingale and Hannibal Lecter. Just as he did with his patients in the outside world, Shipman was successfully keeping people at a safe, admiring distance.

Inmate Tony Fleming shared a cell with Shipman at Strangeways and later claimed that the GP saved his life when he tried to commit suicide. His gasps woke the serial-killing doctor who shouted to the warders for help. Shipman then held Fleming up while the wardens cut him down. Afterwards, Shipman joked with the deeply depressed Fleming, 'Next time, use someone else's shoelaces. Mine are ruined.'

'If he'd really enjoyed killing like they say, then he would have just left me hanging there. He's a good bloke,' Fleming said after his release.

Shipman regularly played Monopoly and Scrabble in prison with inmates and staff members. But he clearly hated losing. 'He was a cheating sod,' recalled Tony Fleming. 'If we bought property [for Monopoly] we put the money in the middle of the board, then he would slip it in his bank. We used to have a laugh about it. He was determined to beat me and I didn't want to spoil his moment of glory.'

* * *

Across Britain and the world, news of the serial killer doctor was hitting the front pages on almost a daily basis. On 12 October 1998, the tabloid London *Daily Mail* ran a headline screaming: MURDER CASE GP: MORE BODIES EXHUMED.

ACCUSED DOCTOR: POLICE PROBING 77 DEATHS hit the news-stands two days later. The article, also in the *Mail*, breathlessly exclaimed, 'The deaths of 77 patients of a GP accused of four murders are now being investigated by detectives, it can be revealed.'

Some of Britain's more serious broadsheet newspapers were rather more conservative with their accounts of Shipman's alleged activities: DOCTOR FACES INQUIRY OVER 20 DEATHS said the *Daily Telegraph*. But they all featured Shipman on their front pages.

Shipman then appeared at Liverpool Crown Court for what was described as a brief 'plea and direction hearing' which would set an initial date for the start of the GP's trial. So far he'd been charged with the murders of Kathleen Grundy, Bianka Pomfret, Joan Melia, Winifred Mellor, Ivy Lomas and charity worker Marie Quinn. Only once during the court appearance did Fred and Primrose Shipman exchange eye contact. That was when Primrose smiled impulsively at her husband and Shipman winked back at her as he was escorted out of the court at the end of the hearing.

In the first week of November 1998, three more victims were exhumed from their final resting places at Hyde Cemetery – Irene Turner, 67, who'd died in 1996, was the first one, followed 24 hours later by Alice Kitchen, who'd died in 1994 aged 70. Then in the early hours of the following day, the remains of Jean Lilley were removed. She'd died only the previous year at the age of 58.

By mid-November 1998, the community of Hyde was stunned to hear the police publicly admit for the first time that they might have to dig up as many as 20 bodies as part of their ongoing investigation. Investigators had initially been hoping that nine exhumations might be sufficient for their case, although they still faced the problem of appeasing anxious relatives who'd reported suspicions about the deaths of their loved ones. In addition to the nine bodies so far exhumed, detectives wanted to recover the remains of another alleged victim from her final resting place in Malta, but the family were completely opposed to the plan.

Little did the investigators know that, so far, they'd only uncovered the tip of the iceberg.

CHAPTER NINETEEN

The Prison Doctor

There were genuine fears that Fred Shipman might try to commit suicide. Any first-timer in jail has the potential to harm himself; there's the noise, the smell, the attitude of other prisoners and the endless indigities that come with the loss of liberty. Every 15 minutes, 24 hours a day, a warder would flip open the spyhole to his cell door. Random searches were also carried out to be sure Shipman had no potential weapons.

In the back of all the guards' minds was the suicide of Britain's last most notorious serial killer, Fred West, who killed himself while in prison in Birmingham awaiting trial. Down the hall from Shipman in Strangeways, a man accused of killing five elderly women hanged himself in his cell. Stephen Akinmurele, a 21-year-old with a hatred of old people, had a history of violence and mental illness.

Another of Fred Shipman's Strangeways cellmates while awaiting trial was 34-year-old heating engineer Peter Hall, who'd murdered his girlfriend and her two children, leaving a callous note for her ex-husband which read, 'You are welcome to your family back.'

Hall's crime was brutal in the extreme; after bludgeoning Brazilian-born Celeste Bates, he used her car to collect her 17-month-old son from nursery, battering him to death with a pick-axe handle. Then he collected her eight-year-old son from school and killed him the same way. Hall, though, was racked with remorse and self-pity while Fred Shipman was behaving as if he was the victim of a gross miscarriage of justice. Shipman even described Hall in a letter to one associate as 'a decent cellmate'. Hall eventually went to trial in March 1999 and was given three life sentences.

Fred Shipman tried to reply to every 'reasonable' letter he received while awaiting trial for mass murder. Even when old classmate Dr Michael Heath sent him a note pointing out that they had gone to school together, he sent back a brief, polite note:

> *Dear Mr Heath,*
> *I'm sorry I cannot remember you being at High Pavement. I feel I have enough on without dredging my memories up. I've learnt never to look back as you always end up disappointed.*
> *Sincerely,*
> *Fred*

But the note gave away a few clues to Fred Shipman's state of mind as he awaited trial. Handwriting expert Patricia Leeson concluded that the writer – whose identity she did not know – was emotionally 'locked in' and could be driven to amoral behaviour by his 'loss of integrity'. Fred Shipman was, in fact, bored out of his brains in prison. His mind needed continual stimulation because he found it deeply stressful being the centre of so much attention. He would give anything to keep a low profile, but his alleged crimes had guaranteed that would never happen again.

Graphologist Patricia Leeson explained, 'This attitude could lead to him being overtaken professionally by people of lower intelligence but with more confidence, causing an irritating sense of under-achievement. His writing shows that he tends to put off decisions and fails to follow through unless the task is important to him personally.

'His low-self image, which brings feelings of insecurity and anticipation of rejection, makes coping with problems difficult, and it is likely he would try to avoid taking final responsibility for his actions. He has been brought up to consider it incorrect to display emotions and to maintain the stiff upper lip at all costs.'

Fred Shipman's emotions were under lock and key and his excellent powers of communication simply masked his inner withdrawal. Shipman became quick to see slights and take offence. But in another sense, life in prison allowed Shipman to reveal a little more of his true self. Everyone knew what he was accused of so he didn't have to put on the façade of being a friendly, harmless GP. The charges he faced brought him a bizarre combination of respect and hatred from both inmates and staff.

There was a strangely childish side to Fred Shipman inside jail. He even wrote in jokey terms about the armed police from the Tactical Support Group who transported him between prison and court.

In the early hours of Monday, 7 December 1998, police exhumed the grave of widow Sarah Ashworth, 75, who was known as 'Sally', and had died at her home in Bowlacre Road, Hyde, on 17 April 1993. Detectives were privately predicting that the number of unexplained deaths linked to Shipman might soon top the 100 mark.

A few hours after the exhumation of Sally Ashworth, Fred Shipman was back in court. The GP seemed to have aged five years in a matter of months as he was flanked by four security guards while standing, shoulders hunched, in the dock of the magistrates court at Ashton-under-Lyne in Greater Manchester. Dressed in a red jumper and blue open-necked shirt, he spoke only once to confirm his name before three more murder charges were put before him. Loyal wife Primrose looked across at her troubled husband from the public gallery and smiled in his direction. But as Shipman was led away, he looked down at the ground, a broken figure.

On Wednesday, 9 December 1998, police investigators exhumed another body – widow Elizabeth Mellor – from Hyde Cemetery. Mrs Mellor had been 75 when she died on 30 November 1994. A post mortem examination was immediately carried out by a Home Office pathologist. Mrs Mellor was the ninth corpse to be removed from Hyde Cemetery.

Tissue samples were sent to the Forensic Science Laboratory at Chorley, Lancashire. The result of the standard screening tests showed positive for morphine but, just to be absolutely certain, hair samples were sent to Hans Sachs, at the University of Munich. Professor Sachs also found that morphine had been administered close to the time of death.

Fred Shipman's first Christmas without his family pushed him close to a deep depression, despite the vast number of tranquillisers he was now taking on a daily basis. Sometimes he was so doped up he slurred his words and prison staff regularly rushed into his cell after seeing him slumped in a corner unable to move because of the powerful tablets he'd been prescribed. 'It was a nightmare situation because we were very concerned that he might have tried to commit suicide on each occasion we had to go in,' one prison staff member later recalled.

Fears that Shipman would kill himself came to a head over that Christmas period when Shipman's cell was raided by prison officers who found a shank – a home-made knife – hidden under the GP's mattress. 'We never found out if it belonged to him or whether he'd been framed by a vindictive inmate, but we stepped up a 24-hour guard after finding the shank. Shipman had to stay alive at all costs,' added the ex-staff member.

On Thursday, 7 January 1999, Fred Shipman was sent for trial on two further counts of murder involving the deaths of Ivy Lomas and Marie Quinn. Once again, Primrose was faithfully in attendance. This time, Shipman appeared calm and collected at the two-minute hearing. Flanked by three guards, he spoke clearly to confirm his details.

During prison visits, Fred Shipman continued to insist to Primrose and his children that he was completely innocent. But he'd spent so much time lying that it's entirely possible he believed his own fabrications. However, Shipman's self-image had faded rapidly since his incarceration and that was why he had physically deteriorated. He was like someone who was partly deaf; he'd become used to never hearing sounds below a certain level, never dealing with certain issues.

Shipman longed for an earthquake of feeling to shake him out of his indifference. The truth was that he could only be shaken out of it by the prospect of another kill. Obeying the same rules as everyone else had long since ceased to satisfy him. He'd crossed the borderline between thought and action long ago. But now he was incarcerated there was little chance of him ever satisfying those urges again.

There seems little doubt that Primrose Shipman sensed her husband's inner feelings. In one letter she wrote to him in the early part of 1999, she commented:

> I am sat at the dining table the rain is coming down like stair rods. I hope it is better with you. You will not notes [sic] you are with yet another women [sic] this is getting silly I must get on with the paper work. Love you and the pain you feel is just how I feel I am coping. But that is all – do not get upset we have an hour a day. All my love, Primrose.

While awaiting trial, Fred Shipman even wrote a series of letters to his local Member of Parliament, Tom Pendry, and a number of fellow GPs. He said he was worried about the standard of treatment being offered to his patients during his enforced absence. The letters also reinforced the GP's complete self-denial of his alleged crimes.

In one letter from Strangeways Prison, Shipman told MP Tom Pendry that his surgery was likely to be closed down. He complained that the locum seeing his patients had been given a restricted list of drugs to use and added, 'I know I was an expensive GP, but few of my patients had side-effects, few failed to be made better.'

In a number of letters to one former medical colleague, Charles Douglas, Shipman further confirmed his complete and utter state of self-denial. As Dr Douglas later explained, 'Time and time he has said it and it has made it difficult for me to write back. There's nothing I can point to as showing who he really was. This wasn't someone who had just had a bad day. This is somebody who apparently committed some horrendous crimes to a level that is quite staggering. Totally out of the norm. There is nothing that I have seen which would explain it.'

And the question of motive continued to baffle investigators. One detective explained, 'It seems that he just enjoyed killing people and being present when they died. He'd developed a taste for it, if you like, and enjoyed seeing the process of people dying and enjoyed holding that power over people.'

So Fred Shipman had been exercising the power of life and death. He was a man who enjoyed playing God. And many were beginning to conclude that he was an evil man – bad through and through.

On Monday, 22 February 1999, Fred Shipman was charged with murdering seven more female patients, bringing the total to 15. He even managed to flash a smile to Primrose as he was led from Tameside Magistrates' Court following a four-minute appearance. Smartly dressed in a jumper and white shirt, and with neatly trimmed hair and beard, Shipman replied clearly 'I do' when he was asked by the magistrate if he understood the new charges. He seemed in a better, brighter mood than during previous court appearances.

Primrose smiled reassuringly at her husband from the back of the court. Six of the seven new charges referred to cremations, not burials, as in the previous eight.

The victims were college lecturer Maureen Ward, 57, who died on 18 February 1998, of Ogden Court, Hyde; Marie West,

81, who died on 6 March 1995, well known in Hyde where she owned and ran a dress shop. She lived in Knott Fold, Gee Cross. Then there was Muriel Grimshaw, 76, from Hyde, who died on 14 July 1997, and lived in Berkerly Crescent, Hyde; Nora Nuttall, 65, from Gee Cross, who died on 26 January 1998; Lizzie Adams, 77, from Hyde, who died on 28 February 1997; Laura Wagstaff, 81, from Gee Cross, who died on 9 December 1997; and Pamela Hillier, 68, from Hyde, who died on 9 February 1998. All apart from Muriel Grimshaw had been cremated.

Hyde Catholic priest Father Denis Maher had been present during five of the exhumations, including those whose families he'd comforted when they had originally died. 'At four in the morning when I was standing at the graveside of those who were being exhumed he [Shipman] should have been made to stand beside me while their bodies were literally dragged out of their graves. Perhaps then he would begin to realise the enormity of the hurt that he had caused the people of Hyde.'

Yet despite condemning Fred Shipman for his crimes, Father Maher stressed he would forgive the GP and added that he 'would love to visit him in prison'. But he made a point of saying that, before that could happen, Shipman would have to face up to the crimes he had committed and admit them openly. Few expected him to do so.

Inside Strangeways, Fred Shipman insisted that staff and inmates called him 'Doctor' and he was considered such a well-behaved prisoner that he was even picked out to welcome visiting VIPs while awaiting trial. Queen Elizabeth II's daughter, Princess Anne, shook hands with the suspected serial killer and chatted with him while touring the tough prison as royal patron of the Butler Trust, a prison welfare organisation. The Princess later commented that she had found Fred Shipman polite and well-spoken and many who were present believed that Anne was intrigued to meet the alleged mass killer. After the Princess left the jail Shipman bragged about his royal connection and then openly insulted Anne's looks. He told one inmate, 'It was nice to meet a normal woman again. Pity she looks like a horse.'

In fact, Shipman was irritated because he hadn't been allowed to tell the Princess about conditions inside Strangeways.

Fred Shipman was becoming a one-man freak show at a circus. Everyone from inmates to officers wanted to take a look at the killer GP. He was the only prisoner on his block without photos of topless women on his cell walls. He preferred his beloved family and steam trains. Shipman saw himself as intellectually superior to the day-to-day riff-raff inhabiting the prison. Shipman's arrogance got him banned from the prison quiz nights because he knew all the answers and always won.

But it was Fred Shipman's penchant for holding unofficial surgery sessions that raised the most eyebrows. One ex-inmate explained, 'He held surgery in his cell on Saturday and even some of the prison officers went to him for a diagnosis.

'He'd give them precise instructions as to which medication to ask for when they saw the prison doctors. He also gave them his expert opinion on medical evidence being used in other inmates' cases, and even helped some of them write letters.'

Shipman continued writing letters to old colleagues and friends out of the blue. The central theme of most letters was, naturally, his innocence and that he was the victim of an appalling mistake. But there were other very down-to-earth references in his letters. In one, he talked about bookmakers William Hill offering odds of 9/5 on for a guilty verdict, 15/1 for not guilty.

Shipman spent much of his time in jail preparing for the court case. He claimed that the only evidence the police had was that he practised as he always had done; he believed he was only guilty of being a good doctor. He also claimed the police were withholding evidence from his solicitors. Eventually, Shipman was given a single cell in Strangeways because of the mountain of paperwork he had to deal with in connection with his trial. He eventually amassed a stack of folders 10ft high, covered in stickers with notes for his lawyers.

And Primrose continued to write regularly to her husband. In one letter, she even referred to his alleged victims and conceded:

> *Well, I am very sorry for them as you happen to be my husband and I love you very much and am not thinking of leaving you. Funny what sets me off. I need all my friends and supporters but that has given me thought. I wonder if other women have looked at it that way.*

In another letter, on 2 March 1999, Primrose, not exactly a scholar of the English language, wrote:

> *My dearest Fred. Only 216 days to go* [until the trial], *good idea, keep my maths going. I have done everything this morning when I should have done the paper work, sorted the clean sock* [sic]*, made bed …*

And so Primrose droned on. It was almost as if she was trying to avoid the most important issue. She even described how she'd listened to a radio programme about secrets of a long marriage on the popular British show *Woman's Hour*.

In the middle of 1999, Shipman wrote to one friend claiming he was supporting Primrose. 'She is being affected by the length of time it is all taking. I'm now comforting her on visits,' he revealed in a letter to a friend.

The children – Sarah, Christpher, David and Sam – seemed to the outside world to be standing by their mother. But behind the scenes, conflict was arising as they began to come to terms with the fact that their father might be a mass murderer. Primrose faced divided loyalties – should she continue in her unswerving support for her husband or begin to concede to the children. At that time, psychiatrist Ian Stephen predicted, 'She will go along with what her husband tells her. If it's "I did not do it, I was set up," she will feel obliged to go along with that.'

Some of the children started questioning why she did not recognise her husband's criminal behaviour sooner. However, it is perfectly plausible she had no idea of her husband's murderous activities. 'Serial killers can act much like the children's cartoon character Mr Benn,' explained Ian Stephen. 'They have that ability to go through a door and become someone else. Shipman was probably able to make a clean split between his activities at work and his home life.'

Inside Strangeways, Shipman was proclaimed 'too clever' to take daily classes with the rest of the inmates. Instead, he became an assistant to the teachers who taught English and art to the prisoners from 9.30 to 11.30 each morning. He also continued regularly to challenge the warders to a game of Scrabble. But most of the time he was bored and obliged to carry out menial prison tasks such as mopping out his cell first thing in the morning, followed by breakfast duty.

Shipman was locked up in a cell between lunch and dinner, but this was usually broken by Primrose's daily visit at 2.00pm sharp. After dinner, at around 6.30pm, he'd find himself locked up for the night. That was when he'd write letters, surrounded by those photos of his family – Primrose and Sarah on a trip to Buckingham Palace; young Sam in his school uniform. They reminded Fred Shipman of the life he'd left behind. It was the normal fragment of his twisted world which had kept him sane through his 'killing years'.

While awaiting trial, Fred Shipman continued to claim to other inmates that he wouldn't get a long sentence even if he was convicted. 'He made it all sound like he'd been doing his patients a favour,' one inmate later recalled.

Shipman's legal team even tried to get his murder trial abandoned during the pre-trial hearings. They requested three separate trials split between the murder of the last victim Kathleen Grundy, the women who were buried, and those who were cremated. But the Judge, Mr Justice Forbes, threw out the request and also turned down their application that the trial should be heard in London because, they argued, he could not have a fair trial anywhere in the north of England due to the intense media coverage.

Meanwhile, the ever loyal Primrose bought a modest second-hand red Mini Metro car after her Ford Sierra had been crashed by joyriders. The Shipmans' daughter Sarah then moved to a new home within a mile of the prison, and his sons Christopher, David and Sam continued to be regular visitors to Strangeways.

One of Primrose's few friends in the months following her husband's arrest was John Gilmore, who'd been sacked from the Donnybrook practice in Hyde some years earlier for gross malpractice. He spent many evenings at Primrose's home comforting her and listening to her confusion over the charges facing Fred Shipman, one of his oldest friends.

Fred Shipman's more distant relatives were naturally shocked by his arrest. His uncle Reg Shipman back in Nottingham said, 'I'm glad his dad isn't alive to see this. He was a good man, a good father. They were a well-brought-up family. I just don't know why this has happened.'

Old schoolfriend Alan Goddard was watching the TV news with his wife when he saw some slow-motion footage of Fred Shipman being led away in handcuffs. 'I didn't recognise his picture, but he looked a lot like his dad,' he recalled with a shudder. 'I can't believe it's true.'

Another childhood friend, John Soar, was convinced Fred was mentally ill. 'I feel sorry for him and his family, as well as the victims. Such a waste of talent. If I was asked why Fred Shipman would be in the newspapers at 53, I would say because he was an exemplary GP doing something for his community, not this.'

Former classmate Terry Swinn agreed. 'You need strength of character to become a doctor, put in the graft. I liked him. I'm perplexed, as everyone else is.' Another classmate Bob Studholme put it, bizarrely, in sporting terms. 'He has rather let the side down,' he said, referring to the infamy Shipman had brought to High Pavement Grammar School. Studholme believes to this day that Shipman's problems began when he struggled to get the grades he needed for medicine, especially after his mother died. Then there was that shotgun wedding to Primrose when he was still a student. Studholme also said it was significant that his old classmate stopped doing any sports the moment he met Primrose. 'I was very shocked to hear that. He'd been so keen on rugby.'

Studholme added, 'Fred needed to work hard to get qualifications and he would take everything seriously. He would have been equally serious about that marriage and about his children. His focus was taken away from sport, concentrating on family and being qualified. If I saw him now I would say, "Hi, Fred, how are you?" Then I would ask him about it man to man – "What the bloody hell have you done?"

'Doctors have to have a degree of detachment. Life is full of people who die; you can't win them all. We have to respect that aspect. We all have a bill to pay in life. It's not malice that led to Fred's actions, there's a kink that allowed that, perhaps overwork. People setting him up, going to him when things go wrong. All of us are only one inch from this. Women with small children under threat are capable of killing. The Germans have a saying – let the pig out. It means letting off steam, getting rid of frustration. Like he did on the rugby pitch. Maybe that was it. He didn't permit himself to let go; now he has in the worst possible way.'

Over at Lord Derby Road, where the family first settled when they arrived in Hyde, neighbours refused to speak ill of the Shipmans. There were still many who simply could not believe that Shipman was a mass murderer.

There was intense speculation about Shipman's eventual trial since mass killers often changed their plea to guilty at the last minute once they were confronted with the enormity of the crimes they'd committed. Then the main argument in court would concern their sanity at the time they committed the crimes. But Fred Shipman made it clear he was going to plead not guilty. He planned to make the most of his court appearance and drag the case out for as long as possible. He insisted to his lawyers that he would give evidence himself, and that he'd be proclaiming his innocence to his last breath.

Shipman even wrote from prison to his old friend and GP Dr

Wally Ashworth, protesting that he had had nothing to do with the deaths. Dr Ashworth later recalled, 'He never doubted he would be acquitted. I do feel rather guilty that I haven't visited him in prison and probably never will. Despite everything, he was remarkably attentive to me when I was ill and I owe him a debt for that.'

The reaction to Shipman's incarceration continued to confuse the entire community.

Tried and Tested

CHAPTER TWENTY

Tried and Tested

In the early summer of 1999, psychiatrist Dr Richard Badcock interviewed Fred Shipman in Strangeways on behalf of prosecutors. He gave the GP a series of tests involving putting shapes in different relationships to each other, and then consulted some papers about the case.

Badcock's job was to report on the state of Shipman's mind following a general check-up which established that the GP was in reasonable physical condition. Shipman knew perfectly well that this meant establishing whether or not he was insane.

It was all a question of whether he had been responsible for his actions, and that involved a variety of factors, including how easy Shipman found it to adjust to other people, and so on. Shipman had long since ceased co-operating with investigators, but Badcock was interested in the death of Fred Shipman's mother all those years earlier.

The psychiatrist, who had an account of Vera Shipman's death in front of him, asked Shipman if he had been very upset at the time.

'Yes,' replied Shipman dryly.

'It must have been a terrible experience for you,' the psychiatrist said in his warmest voice. Then he pointed out to Shipman that, soon afterwards, he'd left home. That's when he asked Shipman about his early career as a medical student.

But Shipman insisted on answering in single words – 'Yes' then 'No' then 'Maybe'. He saw himself in a psychological duel with Badcock. Shipman eventually emerged far from bewildered by this session. He knew why he had killed so many people but he objected to Badcock digging into his childhood and the death of his mother. He tried to block out everything the psychiatrist had said but he knew that Badcock had touched on some sensitive subjects which he would rather not have considered.

Thinking about his mother made him realise for the umpteenth time how much he missed her. Everything about her had long since gone, except a series of pictures which ran through his mind like projected slides, showing images from his childhood – walking through Nottingham holding his mother's hand; her tying his bow-tie as she prepared him for school; her pride at opening the letter saying Fred had been accepted to High Pavement.

When people die, those closely linked to them reconstitute their personalities in terms of what they wish to remember and, following her death, Shipman's mother had become – in his mind – the only woman who had truly loved him and whom he truly respected. The dream of one day joining her in heaven was ominpresent, a dream all the sweeter because he knew that one day it would be fulfilled. Nothing could take the perfection of that dream away from him.

Throughout his meeting with Dr Badcock, Shipman continued to deny the murders, so there were few clues as to his motive. Dr Badcock later claimed that Shipman was a 'classic' necrophiliac, a man obsessed not with having sex with the dead, but with the act of inducing death, and controlling and observing the moment when life leaves the body.

Shipman had been meticulous at positioning his victims

before he injected them. He enjoyed waiting with them while they died and was excited at being present when his handiwork was discovered by others. He also relished having evaded capture for so long, and he gained an extra buzz of excitement from those he murdered inside his own surgery. He even enjoyed breaking the news to his victims' relatives.

Psychiatrist Dr Badcock later surmised that Shipman's necrophiliac tendencies were triggered by the death of his mother. Killing others made perfect sense to Shipman's twisted logic. Shipman's perceived arrogance and his fascination with state-of-the-art computers were manifestations of his need for control, whether that be of people or machines.

Deep inside, Fred Shipman was nothing more than a shell of a person having to re-invent himself continually for the outside world. Sooner or later, his obsession with control would mean he'd have to make others do things they didn't want to do. A form of sadism had taken over Shipman's mind. At work, he frequently humiliated people in such a way that they knew they were being demeaned. Inflicting pain or torture on his victims and seeing them take it was part of his addiction. It was the only way Fred Shipman could see himself remaining in control.

Fred Shipman had become like a country that only had an atomic bomb as a defence policy; a person with the ultimate control but little else. Shipman's own special brand of necrophilia was a psychological disorder rather than an illness. But it was undoubtedly a disorder which transcended the conventional disciplines of medicine.

There was also one apparent link to Shipman's sexuality; he regarded the act of sex itself as messy and difficult and to be avoided because he couldn't control it and be successful. Sex was one of the few times when he lost control of his surroundings. That's why he grew to prefer the huge intellectual buzz of committing murder. It became the power base replacement for real sex.

Fred Shipman's relationship with Primrose remained an enigma. He still retained total control over her both mentally and physically, yet he held her accountable for everything that either went wrong for him or displeased him. He was not an easy master by any means.

Despite languishing in Strangeways, Fred Shipman was awarded a 7.3 per cent pay rise. The increase consisted of 3.5 per cent for all GPs in the UK and a further 3.8 per cent in back-dated pay. As well as his wages, Shipman also had a contributory National Health Service pension scheme to which his employers paid £3,000 a year and he contributed £4,500. Shipman even instructed Primrose to cash in two financial policies believed to be held at a Manchester-based investment company. The policies were thought to be worth at least £30,000.

Behind the scenes, Fred Shipman's vast legal costs were to be paid jointly by the Medical Defence Union and legal aid. They were expected to reach several hundred thousand pounds once the trial was completed.

During the summer of 1999, Dr Linda Reynolds, one of the GPs responsible for bringing Shipman to justice, was diagnosed with terminal cancer. Her husband Nigel and children Caroline, 21, and William, 18, were naturally devastated. She wasn't even certain she would live long enough to see Shipman brought to trial. 'I just hope I live to see the conclusion of all this,' she said stoically. 'And I hope he stays in prison for the rest of his life.'

But even in her eleventh hour of life, she was able to joke about the Shipman case. 'I had a 90-year-old patient who joked, "You are a terrible doctor; if I had Dr Shipman I would not have all this pain now."'

Dr Reynolds could not have been more different from Fred Shipman. 'I loved my job, being part of the community, looking after generations of the same family; the intellectual stimulation of making a diagnosis, just being able to help people, be kind to them,' she said sadly. 'I would have liked ten more years to look after the people of Hyde – I was just getting started with them.'

The morphine, diamorphine and various other drugs seized from Fred Shipman's home in a grey C&A store bag in September 1998 lay untouched in an exhibits bag without a contents label for nearly a year at the headquarters of the Greater Manchester Police. It was only re-discovered when Detective Constable Dave O'Brien was sorting out exhibits to be returned or destroyed in August 1999. He later explained, 'I entered it on the computer and I assumed what was written on the label was in the bag.'

O'Brien admitted he did not look inside the bag and the exhibits were not examined between 7 September 1998 until 26 August 1999. During police interrogation, Shipman had insisted he did not keep any drugs or even have a register to do so. The police had been incredibly inefficient and had almost overlooked a vital piece of evidence which they had failed to log correctly when it had originally been found in the house. The drugs in question had been reported by Fred Shipman as being destroyed in 1995 in his surgery. Shipman told detectives he'd not kept any drugs and said he had not had a register to do so since 1976.

Numerous grief counsellors stood by to help the friends and relatives of Fred Shipman's victims cope with the publicity expected when the GP's trial started at Preston Crown Court later in 1999. Local health authorities set up a confidential helpline for any concerned relatives of possible Shipman victims. 200 people had already been referred by police for support and more than 70 had contacted the helpline.

* * *

The town of Preston, 40 miles from Hyde, was chosen to host the Shipman trial because it would be virtually impossible to find an impartial jury any nearer to the scene of the alleged crimes. Preston was very similar in size and character to Hyde with its prosperity built on the thriving cotton industry of the Industrial Revolution.

The Crown Court at Preston was known as 'the Old Bailey of the North', a reference to the most famous court in Britain, the Old Bailey in London, where many of the most famous criminals of all time had been tried. It was set amongst grandiose Victorian

buildings with a statue of Justice, blind and carrying scales, just
like the one that tops the London original.

Fred Shipman's trial was to be heard in Court One, decorated
in bright green tiles, and rich oak panelling with ornate cornicing.
A stained-glass centre to the curved ceiling allowed daylight to
pour into the courtroom. Hanging from the walls were portraits
of past chairmen of the Lancashire Quarter Sessions. Next door;
Number Two Court was transformed into a media centre to cope
with the vast number of journalists expected from across the
globe. There was even an audiolink allowing reporters who could
not get seats in the actual court to follow the proceedings.

Thirty-eight press seats were allocated on a first come, first
served basis for Britain's national newspapers, TV and radio
news organisations. Extra power points for laptops were
installed in Court Two and another room was set aside for court
artists as no cameras would be allowed to record the
proceedings.

Chief prosecutor in the Shipman trial was Richard Henriques,
who'd also prosecuted in the James Bulger case. Henriques, 55,
was leader of the Northern Circuit of barristers which made him
the most senior and respected barrister in the north-west of
England. He came from a long line of barristers; his Madeira-
born father had been a celebrated divorce lawyer. Henriques
earned in excess of £500,000 a year. Both he and his junior, Peter
Wright QC, were based in nearby Manchester.

Fred Shipman's lawyer, Nicola Davies QC, 46, was born in
South Wales. She read Law at Birmingham University and had
been involved in several well-known cases, including a child
abuse inquiry in Cleveland, the Bristol heart surgery scandal and
a British Government inquiry into BSE. Slim, fair-haired and
always immaculately dressed, Nicola Davies was particularly
adept at dissecting expert evidence.

Judge, 61-year-old Thayne Forbes, had been presiding judge
of the Northern Circuit for two-and-a-half years. He'd gained his
law degree from London University. Forbes had a reputation for
being scrupulously fair and meticulous: none of his trials had

ever been successfully appealed against. His owlish, patient and occasionally amused expression often defused some awkward courtroom battles.

So the scene was set for the trial of one of the most prolific cold-blooded killers in British criminal history.

* * *

At 8.50am on 4 October 1999, Fred Shipman was driven into the back yard of Preston Crown Court in a prison van. His wife Primrose and sons David and Sam had arrived in a nearby parking lot and were walking up the steps into the court shielded by a burly 6ft 'family friend', when the boys found themselves having to protect Primrose from paparazzi surging towards them.

In court, Fred Shipman was dressed like the doctor he was, in a grey suit, white shirt and dark tie as he entered the dock for the first time. But his clothes hung off his shoulders and his thinning hair was combed forward. He'd lost at least two stones in weight, shrinking from a 36-in waist to 32in. He was 53 years old but looked as if he was about to hit his seventies. As Fred Shipman walked in that morning, a sense of expectation gripped the courtroom but then the GP shuffled into view; a small man, with a neatly-trimmed beard and a large bald patch, wearing a dark suit and white shirt. Shipman immediately peered at the jury through his shiny, gold-rimmed, round glasses.

The trial was opened and immediately adjourned after just 15 minutes for legal arguments. Just across the court in the public gallery, Primrose, Sam and David plus several friends sat and watched the proceedings. Primrose, in a maroon-and-green checked jacket, looked as matronly as usual.

Dozens of camera crews, photographers and journalists from across the world were also present. Three documentary teams were covering the case along with at least a dozen TV news crews. Special arrangements had also been made to seat the relatives of some of Shipman's victims.

The following day – 5 October 1999 – was a day when world events, such as a horrific earthquake in Turkey, ensured that the uneventful first day of the Fred Shipman trial did not make the front page of many newspapers.

As part of their legal argument, the GP's defence team were making numerous submissions to the judge. Court officials predicted that the trial would not properly get started until the following Monday once a jury had been sworn in. Prosecutor Richard Henriques had already warned the judge that his opening evidence would take at least three days to deliver.

Shipman faced 16 charges – 15 of murder and one of forging Mrs Grundy's will. The 15 female victims were Kathleen Grundy, Joan Melia, Winifred Mellor, Bianka Pomfret, Marie Quinn, Ivy Lomas, Irene Turner, Jean Lilley, Muriel Grimshaw, Marie West, Kathleen Wagstaff, Pamela Hillier, Norah Nuttall, Elizabeth Adams and Maureen Ward.

Outside the court, a small crowd appeared each morning to watch the 'stars' of the case. Many were local women shoppers anxious to examine Primrose, the wife of the so-called 'monster' Shipman. Heavyweight Primrose was usually loyally flanked by at least one of her children when taking her place in her pre-designated spot in the public gallery. Often, she was greeted by a chorus of 'Morning, Primrose' from the WI-lookalike group, as the regulars gathered outside the court before opening time at 10.30am. Primrose returned the greeting with a friendly enough expression, before being ushered away to her specially reserved seat inside the court.

Primrose sat every day at her place in the front of the public gallery with her hands clasped in her lap. Occasionally, she exchanged pleasantries with people around her, but mostly she kept to herself. She even handed round chocolates to those sitting beside her in court. Primrose referred all press enquiries about the case to the Medical Defence Union, but happily chatted to people at the court kiosk where she bought regular coffees.

Bianka Pomfret's ex-husband Adrian found Primrose's attitude very disturbing. 'I used to see Primrose on the TV but, on the day I was in court, Primrose was walking down the corridor. She was laughing and joking. It was like she was enjoying a day out.' During breaks in the hearing Primrose even retired to a private room in the court.

At the end of each day, Primrose and her brood were often pursued to a nearby multi-storey car park by photographers and TV cameras, but they never once reacted angrily to the onslaught of flashguns. Not even when two youths shouted obscenities from the crowd gathered on the courtroom steps. However, the beginning of the trial was so low-key that even the dozen or so police crash barriers seemed a gross over-reaction. Inside the courtroom, officials didn't need to use the 'Public Gallery Full' sign during those first few days of the trial.

Over the following five days, a panel of 60 potential jurors were warned by lawyers that the trial could last five months, and then asked if there was any reason why they could not serve for that long. More than 20 immediately put their hands up. The judge excused a single mother, a woman who regularly suffered from bronchitis in the winter, a man who'd planned a fortieth wedding anniversary holiday. Others, like a man who was planning a trip to Disneyland, were denied permission to leave. On Monday, 11 October 1998, seven men and five women, ranging in age from their mid-twenties to late fifties, were sworn in.

Prosecutor Henriques initially referred to how Shipman had 'exercised the ultimate power of controlling life and death, and repeated it so often that he must have found the drama of taking life to his taste'.

In the dock, Fred Shipman cut a modest, slightly disorganised figure balancing a vast pile of papers on his lap, then passing notes to his lawyers. A table was eventually brought in the dock to allow him to spread out the paperwork. The prosecution case was scheduled to last 25 days and was to be punctuated by two breaks of a few days. There were even a few laughs; prosecutor Henriques brought smiles to the jurors' faces when he asked pathologist Dr John Rutherford to explain his medical evidence more simply by saying, 'Can you put that in layman's terms, bearing in mind that we are in Preston, not a city?' There was consternation in the local press. Was the prosecutor suggesting that the people of Preston were not as clever as those who lived in cities?

On 12 October 1999, Fred Shipman's so-called joke as his victim Ivy Lomas lay dead in front of him earned front-page banner headlines in the *Manchester Evening News* – much to the horror of many of the respectable middle-class inhabitants of Hyde. The newspaper began its coverage with the headline: GP'S JOKE AS VICTIM LAY DEAD and then published the following:

> Family GP Dr Harold Shipman made no attempt to resuscitate one of his alleged victims and carried on treating others as she lay dead on a treatment table at his Hyde practice, a court was told today.

The paper devoted three entire pages to what was only the second full day of Shipman's trial. Not surprisingly, every copy in Hyde was sold out within minutes of hitting the streets.

Preston Crown Court then heard how lawyers received the will from one of Shipman's last victims, Mrs Kathleen Grundy. Conveyancing manager Brian Burgess told the court he became suspicious after taking a phone call from a distressed man informing him that Mrs Grundy had only just died. Burgess said that his firm, Hamilton Ward, usually insisted on first meeting people who asked them to be executors of their will.

The court was told how Kathleen Grundy's will was a crude forgery and that the portable typewriter seized from Fred Shipman's home was almost certainly the one used to write the documents. Michael Allen, a forensic document examiner for 16 years, told the court, 'My opinion is that these two questioned signatures on the items were not written by K Grundy. Rather, they are poor, crude forgeries of her signature written by some other person.'

Asked if it was possible to determine the real author of the signatures, he replied, 'No.' Allen also explained to the court how forgers covered up their natural style which made them impossible to identify. Asked by prosecutor Richard Henriques whether a signature may be genuine, but different from usual because of old age, Mr Allen replied, 'No.' He conceded that old age could have an effect on handwriting, but would not fundamentally alter its style. He also said the signature featuring on a covering letter about the will was a crude forgery.

On the letter, Mr Allen found an indentation of Mrs Grundy's home telephone number, while on the will there were indentations which appeared to be forged versions of K Grundy's signature. 'At some time or another, a sheet of paper had been resting upon the will and upon that sheet of paper another forged K Grundy signature had been written,' said Mr Allen.

Another expert called Andrew Watson told the court that Dr Shipman had left a fingerprint from the little finger of his left hand in the bottom left-hand corner of the will. Asked if he thought anybody else could have left it, he said, 'No, not at all. It's a unique identification system.'

Then the court heard how Fred Shipman had made an entry in Kathleen Grundy's medical records on the day after she died. But the computer had dated his remarks one year earlier. DS John Ashley of the Greater Manchester Police Computer Examination Unit told the court how he came across an entry dated 23 June 1997, stating, *Term: malaise symptom. Comments: nothing definite, just feels tired, nothing specific. Blood fresh from morning … old? Anything at all? Depressed although always happy. Lives on own, socially active.*

DS Ashley said that the record had actually been created on 25 June 1998. The court then heard how six computers were networked together at the three-storey surgery on Market Street. The password for the system used by all the staff were Fred Shipman's initials – HFS. DS Ashley took a copy from the hard disk on which patients' records were kept and examined those of Mrs Grundy. A 365-day, 24-hour clock recorded when all notes were actually made.

Mrs Grundy's records included an entry concerning wax in

her ear, stating: *'Comments: So little leave alone.'* It was dated 23 June 1998, the day before she died and was created that day.

Throughout all this, Primrose watched her husband from the public gallery with the couple's only daughter and eldest child, Sarah. When she tried to catch Fred Shipman's eye, he turned away.

The court also heard from patient Claire Hutchinson, whom Shipman persuaded to 'witness' Mrs Grundy's signature on a piece of paper in Shipman's surgery on 9 June 1998. The court was told how Shipman even admitted to nurse Marion Gilchrist he should have had Mrs Grundy cremated to 'save all this trouble'.

Then the court heard how the son and daughter of one of Shipman's victims had been left hurt and confused by Shipman's explanations about their 'very fit' mother's sudden and unexpected death. Pamela Hillier's two adult children said they finally accepted the GP's diagnosis of natural causes, even though he had 'been going round in circles'. Shipman had even warned the family that a post mortem could prove a very unpleasant thing for their mother to go through.

On Monday, 8 November, the former mental patient known as 'Czech Andy' – who'd encountered Shipman when he visited Bianka Pomfret's house just before her death – turned up in the public gallery. Twice during evidence he drifted off to sleep, snoring off the contents of a beer can he'd left on the court steps. The first time he was awoken, he muttered the word 'Murderer' loud enough for those in the gallery to hear, including Primrose.

Eventually, Czech Andy screamed 'Murderer!' even louder and everyone in the court turned towards him, except Fred Shipman. The Judge and jury left the court while security guards tried to convince Czech Andy to leave. He refused to budge, gripping the side of his seat. Then he was dramatically manhandled out of the courtroom shouting 'Fuckin' murderer!' as he went. He had no doubt that Shipman was guilty after their encounter in Bianka Pomfret's house.

One of the most moving pieces of testimony came from Ann Brown, daughter of victim Muriel Grimshaw, after she'd given evidence about the last days of her mother's life. She talked about the death of her first husband, Raymond Jones, in November 1993. She described to the court how he had died in the early morning and how Fred Shipman attended soon afterwards, and took away two or three boxes of diamorphine. The court went quiet as the notion that Ann Brown's mother might have been killed with diamorphine stockpiled after the death of her own husband crossed everyone's minds.

Hyde Catholic priest Father Denis Maher also gave evidence in court about his encounters with Shipman. He later claimed that the GP had tried to 'eyeball' him during the hearing. 'He avoided all eye contact when he pushed past me inside the court earlier in the day. But once I was in the witness box he stared at me. I was quite afraid. It was as if he was daring me to talk about him, deliberately looking straight at me. I could see him looking straight through me. It was chilling. I'll never forget the look on his face.'

The court even heard how Fred Shipman prescribed heroin for patients who were already dead. The GP also wrote heroin prescriptions for a further 18 people, who either did not receive it, or only received part of it.

That, according to prosecutors, was how Shipman stockpiled the drug in order to murder his female patients. Thousands of milligrams of heroin remained unaccounted for. One patient, 72-year-old James Arrandale, was prescribed 1,000mg of heroin over two days in July 1995. Shipman took away ampoules of the drug which were not used before Mr Arrandale's death, saying he would dispose of them. But when police later raided Shipman's home, four ampoules from that batch were found.

In court, Primrose was having a profound and disturbing effect on many of the relatives of Shipman's victims assembled near her in the public gallery.

'She'd blotted it out, but many of the family members in the public gallery were quite wound up about the fact that she appeared to be smiling all the time,' Bianka Pomfret's ex-husband Adrian recalled. 'When I looked across, I could see she was in a heck of a state, but mentally gone overboard. She was shaking her head and everything.'

Primrose Shipman remained a long way from accepting that her husband was a mass murderer.

CHAPTER TWENTY ONE

Under Oath

Just after noon on Thursday, 25 November 1999, Fred Shipman rose hesitatingly to his feet, turned to his right, and shuffled past the jury sitting 6ft away and climbed into the witness box. The whole courtroom held its breath as the GP accused of mass murder prepared to make his début.

He took the short walk from the dock to the witness box escorted by a prison officer and affirmed that he would tell the truth, rather than swearing an oath on the Bible.

'My full name is Harold Frederick Shipman,' he said. The voice was strong and confident to begin with, but soon fell away. He even apologised as his voice faltered, saying it was because of tablets he was taking. Primrose watched intently from the public gallery.

Shipman's grey suit hung loosely on his shoulders and he wore a white shirt with a grey striped tie. He spoke in low, virtual whispers and was frequently asked by the Judge to speak more clearly.

The court then heard how in 1992 he left the Hyde practice he'd shared with six other doctors and set up his own one-man operation. Asked why, he responded, 'It was at the time of fund-holding. The other doctors were not as committed.'

The light through the stained-glass ceiling caught the gold rim of his glasses as he looked up at the jurors. They all looked straight back. Fred Shipman's earthy Nottingham accent was betrayed by his pronunciation of words such as 'blood' or 'past' and 'once a month'. Yet at the start of that first day in the witness box he tried to sound reasonably positive. He clearly wanted the jury to know what sort of doctor he was. His pride was unmistakable when he disclosed he didn't have much time for word processors, adding, 'I'm one of the few doctors in the area who still hand-writes letters.'

Note the present tense. Fred Shipman used it through much of his evidence. He talked of 'my practice' as though he had left it only the previous day and would soon be back behind his desk.

Shipman took a transfixed court audience through his weekly work routine. His hands on the rail of the witness box tapped out the rhythm of his words when he needed help to get them out. He said Monday was the day he did most of his administration before afternoon surgery. Friday was reserved for minor operations, 'removing warts, or in-growing toenails', he said, 'nothing glamorous'.

Then a smile began breaking across his face more often. He talked about making home visits, and how, if he had time on his way back, 'I might pop in and have a word with the wife.'

'The wife' remained seated at the back of the court listening avidly to every word. Occasionally, she fingered her wedding ring. Across the oak-panelled court, the couple's eyes seldom met. Next to Primrose that day was 20-year-old son David.

It wasn't until more than two hours after Shipman had entered the witness box that the name of any of his alleged victims was mentioned in court. Kathleen Grundy was the first. Fred Shipman maintained that she had been a drug addict. Her daughter Angela Woodruff stopped taking notes and fixed the doctor with a stare as he gave his evidence.

Speaking in a hoarse voice, Shipman said he believed 81-year-old Mrs Grundy had simply died of old age, although he repeated that she'd shown symptoms of drug use. Shipman said, 'Abuse of drugs in the elderly is becoming more recognised. I began to suspect that she was actually abusing a drug. It had to be something like codeine, pethidine or perhaps morphine.'

Shipman then referred to the day in June 1998 when Mrs Grundy asked him to witness her signature on what he claimed were 'some papers'. He went on, 'I jokingly said to her that if it was a will and she was going to give me some money, then I couldn't do it. There was a moment of pause when I realised it was something like that.'

Shipman admitted then asking two other patients in his waiting room to sign the papers. Asked if he thought he would be beneficiary of her will, he said, 'I thought the patients' fund would benefit by one or two hundred pounds, I didn't want to get entangled.' Shipman said it was that same day that he noticed Mrs Grundy appeared to be suffering a decline in her health. He added, 'She used to be very bright, very talkative, with enormous enthusiasm. But on that evening I thought she looked old, not well, going downhill.'

Shipman then told the court that a fortnight later he went to her home to do some blood tests. He added, 'Her face was more wrinkled than normal and she appeared slow in her movements.' The court then heard how later that same day a friend found Mrs Grundy dead in her living room. Shipman wrote on her death certificate that the cause had been old age.

Then the jury finally heard the question they had been asked to consider: 'Did you murder Kathleen Grundy?'

'No,' Dr Shipman replied firmly. 'I did not.'

Sometimes, Fred Shipman muttered silently into his close-cropped beard and shook his bird-like head in irritation. But as his evidence progressed, he became curiously more detached, as though he felt the worst was over. Every few moments, he'd take off his gold-rimmed glasses, wipe them methodically with a handkerchief, hold them aloft then peer closely through narrowed eyes as though searching out the slightest smears.

Away from the actual courtroom, Primrose smiled and nodded amicably to reporters and officials. But once back in her designated spot in the public gallery, her face returned to an emotionless mask with her eyes fixed on her husband. He rarely glanced up at her. Was she keeping an eye on him, making sure he didn't say anything which might implicate her?

That afternoon, Fred Shipman's starring role in the witness box giving evidence brought queues around the block for the 40 available public gallery seats. A gaggle of women also sat on the steps outside Court One, eating biscuits and sharing cans of soda, waiting to replace anyone who might decide to leave the proceedings early.

Then Fred Shipman revived his flagging confidence, frowning when his QC shared a joke with the Judge. As Fred Shipman left the court building at the end of his first day of giving evidence, a film crew from Britain's Murdoch affiliate Sky TV network grabbed footage of him being led to the prison van which took him back to Strangeways. He looked shattered, like a man with the weight of the world on his shoulders.

The next day, Shipman's only admission was that he did back-date his computer records. He claimed that was because he had to bring his files in line with when the patient said they had first noticed the symptoms. Then Shipman gave the jury a glimpse of his finest bedside manner when he talked about one alleged victim's medication. 'I'm sure you all know people who, when they have an angina attack, put a tablet under their tongue – this is a souped-up version. Aspirin, as you are all aware, has had lots of publicity, and I expect everyone knows that it is what we give to make the blood less sticky.'

But many remained far from convinced. Some of the reporters covering the Shipman trial looked at his evidence with a certain degree of cynicism. Antonella Lazzeri wrote in the *Sun*:

He painted a picture of a surgery that was cosy, friendly and welcoming. There was even a pink piggy-bank in the waiting room for patients to contribute to new equipment.

According to his own testimony, Harold Shipman was a

good-hearted, old-fashioned GP who could never do enough for his patients. Yesterday, he looked more like *Alice in Wonderland*'s White Rabbit as he peered through wire-rim glasses at a bundle of papers in front of him.

Wearing a brown suit with striped tie, he occasionally glanced at his wife Primrose in the public gallery. But mostly he stared straight at defence QC Nicola Davies. He even laughed several times.

But as the day wore on, he seemed more thoughtful, continually champing on his lower jaw ...

Those who attended court during Shipman's testimony were struck by the utter normality of his appearance and verbal delivery to the court. Many spectators who'd attended religiously since the start of the trial claimed to have 'medical backgrounds' and were fascinated by the Shipman case. Some, such as David McGrady, admitted being fascinated by the ghoulish aspects of the case. 'It's disturbing, but fascinating,' he admitted to one reporter. He even conceded that it made him nervous about visiting his own GP. Other members of the public who attended even included a handful of loyal patients from Fred Shipman's practice.

Fred Shipman, referring back to Bianka Pomfret, told the court, 'She told me she was having chest pains and had some pain to other parts of the body, including the left arm. I told her I thought the diagnosis was angina, lack of oxygen getting into the heart, and I said we needed further investigation.' He said he advised Mrs Pomfret to see a cardiologist and left her to think it over.

When asked by his defence QC Nicola Davies if he had given her a dose of morphine or diamorphine he said, 'No, I did not.' And when asked if he murdered her, he replied, 'No, I did not.'

Shipman regularly looked down to refer to two large files in front of him. Primrose and 20-year-old son David sat in the public gallery just a few feet away. Shipman told the court how Mrs Pomfret had just returned from seeing her family in

Germany and her state of health was quite good but she had relapsed after a couple of weeks back in Hyde. Shipman said, 'She felt tired, listless, had no energy and even after a sleep she felt she should sleep longer.'

Shipman insisted that he had changed her medication to a weaker drug so as to reduce the side-effects which were causing her tiredness. Shipman then told how, less than four hours later, he received a call to say Mrs Pomfret had collapsed at home and was requested to attend. 'I believed she had had a heart-attack because of the history she had given me earlier in the day regarding chest pains.' He repeated that he did not give Mrs Pomfret either morphine or diamorphine.

Asked why he'd recorded coronary thrombosis as a contributory cause of death, Dr Shipman replied, 'I was told Mrs Pomfret was found sat on a settee with a cold mug of tea or coffee by her side and a burned-out cigarette either in her hand or in an ashtray. It seemed obvious she had made no attempt to get to the phone or kitchen, or anything. Whatever happened was fairly rapid.'

On Monday, 29 November 1999, Shipman admitted in court that he should have called an ambulance for alleged victim Ivy Lomas when she collapsed at his surgery. Shipman told the jury, 'In hindsight, it may have been better to have called for an ambulance immediately.' Shipman described how Mrs Lomas was a regular visitor to his surgery complaining of chest pains and depression. He said she 'looked grey and sweaty' at her appointment. He took her to the treatment room to be tested on the ECG machine, but as she climbed on to the bed she collapsed. Shipman admitted he did not call his receptionist Carol Chapman for help because there were three other patients in the waiting room. He tried to resuscitate Mrs Lomas on his own because he believed he knew what to do because he was fully trained in first aid. Shipman said he could carry it out 'better than the average person'. But after 15 minutes, he claimed, he found that his efforts had completely failed.

Shipman then told the court he decided that Mrs Lomas had died of a heart-attack because she smoked and had a family history of heart disease. He even admitted he dealt with three more patients while Mrs Lomas lay dead in the treatment room. Shipman said he treated them in order to get them out of the surgery swiftly. The prosecution alleged that Shipman had administered a fatal dose of morphine or diamorphine to Mrs Lomas while she was in the treatment room.

Fred Shipman then admitted to Preston Crown Court he let one patient die in front of his eyes because he thought it better 'to let nature take its course'. The GP told the jury how he was called to the home of widow Marie Quinn, 67, and found her lying on the kitchen floor. Although he could feel a pulse, she was not breathing and felt 'floppy'.

Earlier, Mrs Quinn had called the surgery and said she was paralysed down one side and would leave the door open for him to visit her. Shipman said he diagnosed a stroke but decided to do nothing rather than reviving the widow and condemning her to life in a nursing home.

Asked to explain this decision by his barrister Nicola Davies QC, he said, 'I'm sure GPs all over the country get the same problem. They have to decide whether to attempt resuscitation or let nature take its course. Whatever happened to Marie Quinn was on a major scale. She was deeply unconscious. I made the decision that I would not attempt resuscitation. I would review the situation in a couple of minutes' time. If she was starting to improve, I would get her to hospital, but two minutes later there were no signs of life. She was dead.'

Shipman then added, 'Patients who survive often have loss of personality, loss of use of the body, and often end up in a nursing home. Mrs Quinn was an independent, likeable person, and to go from that to being dependent on someone she did not know was something I couldn't envisage her doing.'

That day the jury also heard about Irene Turner, 67, who was found dead on 11 July 1996, within minutes of Shipman leaving the house. Then there was victim Jean Lilley who, he claimed, he left alive but needing hospital treatment on the day she died. Shipman described Mrs Lilley – who suffered from angina, high cholesterol and a serious lung condition – as a 'courageous patient'.

On 1 December, Shipman collapsed weeping in the witness box as he answered questions about the death of Kathleen Wagstaff. He said she had collapsed and died in front of him in her home. She had earlier called him after complaining of chest pains. When he examined her, he informed her she should go to hospital.

Shipman explained, 'I looked around for the phone and looked at Mrs Wagstaff, who was sat in the chair with her mouth open. I asked her if she was OK but there was no response. I shook her but she was floppy. She had a coronary.'

He said he tried to resuscitate Mrs Wagstaff but failed. Shipman then told the court he drove to a nearby school where he knew her daughter-in-law Angela worked.

He said, 'I explained that her mother had died. I should have made it clear it was her mother-in-law. I thought I had done so, but she became extremely distressed and drove to her mother's house.'

He said he was 'more upset than her relatives', and sank into his seat weeping, his head in his hands. His breakdown came just before the lunch adjournment. After regaining his composure, he said his distress over the 81-year-old's death was to blame for the error he made on her cremation certificate which had said a neighbour was present when she died.

Asked by his defence lawyer Nicola Davies why he had made the mistake, Shipman replied, 'I was quite upset. I don't think I was quite clear in my own mind when I completed this document. This was one of the few times I was possibly more upset than the relatives.'

Then, as his legal team looked up at him, Shipman sank back into his chair, put his head in hands and began sobbing again. He continued crying for at least two minutes, his head barely visible above the sides of the oak-panelled witness box. He even wiped his eyes with tissues handed to him by an usher.

Then Nicola Davies, asked the Judge, Mr Justice Forbes, for an early lunchtime adjournment so that her client could regain his composure. As the jurors left the courtroom three minutes earlier than scheduled, Shipman walked the ten paces back into the dock and then down the stairway leading to the cells. The entire scene was witnessed by Primrose who fidgeted nervously but showed no other signs of emotion or concern for her husband.

That afternoon, Fred Shipman gave the court his account of what happened to patient Winifred Mellor, 73, when she visited his surgery in May 1998 without an appointment and complaining of chest pains. Shipman explained, 'I said it sounded like angina and talked to her about what we should do.' He said he asked her to return to the surgery later in the day to arrange an appointment with a cardiologist. When she failed to get in touch, he decided to visit her house which was on his way home.

After knocking on the door and getting no reply, he said he looked in the window and saw her sitting motionless in a chair. A next-door neighbour who had a spare key to the house let Shipman in and he certified that Mrs Mellor was dead. He recalled to the court, 'With the history she had given me earlier in the afternoon, I considered that the likely cause of death was that she had had a heart-attack.'

Once again, Fred Shipman was asked if he had administered any morphine or diamorphine to Mrs Mellor and he replied firmly, 'No.'

Then Shipman was again asked if he had murdered any of his patients.

'Did you murder Bianka Pomfret on 10 December 1997?' asked Nicola Davies.

'No, I did not.'

'Did you murder Winifred Mellor on 11 May 1998?'

'No, I did not,' responded Shipman, looking straight ahead.

'Did you murder Joan Melia on 12 June 1998?'

'No, I did not.'

CHAPTER TWENTY TWO

Defending Himself

Fred Shipman looked irritated when his lawyer Nicola Davies QC sat down at the end of his testimony to her. He'd wanted her questioning to go on beyond the actual deaths. When prosecutor Henriques stood up to start his cross-examination, Shipman broke down, telling the Judge he was unwell. He was given a 15-minute break but he still looked uncomfortable when he returned to the witness box.

Prosecutor Henriques continued to pick over Shipman's evidence, highlighting inconsistencies in the GP's records of the deaths, and the uncanny similarities between many many of the circumstances. Shipman admitted 'a bad habit' of prescribing very large amounts of morphine for patients in need of it, claiming he had no idea what had subsequently happened to it. He said that the morphine found at his house was 'an oversight'.

While speaking to the court about the death of Ivy Lomas, prosecutor Henriques came back at Shipman like a shot when discussing the doctor's claims.

'If this lady died at 4.10pm, she must have been administered, or administered to herself, diamorphine between 4.00pm and 4.10pm, mustn't she?'

With a sigh in his voice, Shipman replied wearily, 'You could put the evidence that way and, yes, I would agree.'

But Shipman said he had no knowledge of where the drug had come from.

Then Henriques's tone became much sterner. 'Dr Shipman,' he said, 'there is no sensible explanation, is there?'

A long pause followed, before Shipman replied pedantically, 'Was that a statement or a question?'

Clearly irritated, Henriques snapped back, 'You know very well it was a question.' Then, for good measure, he repeated it.

Shipman admitted, 'I don't know of any explanation.'

'Save except for your guilt,' replied Henriques quick as flash.

Just as fast, Shipman volleyed back, 'That's what you're saying and I disagree with it strongly. I didn't administer anything to this lady and I had no idea how she got it in her body.'

Once again, Henriques suggested there was no explanation – other than Fred Shipman's guilt. Again the GP denied it. 'I can think of no explanation at all. I'm not guilty of administering anything to this lady.'

Henriques then changed tack and condemned Shipman for leaving a dead patient while he attended to three others at his surgery.

'To leave a deceased person without any attempt to contact next of kin is a disgrace,' he said tersely.

'In your opinion,' the GP responded sharply.

But the prosecutor would not let go. 'It's unprofessional to leave someone for dead in the back room.'

Shipman insisted to the court there was no 'terrible rush' considering the patient was dead.

And so the duel continued, with Henriques in his black robes with large, black-framed glasses. A tall formidable figure who tended to lean over the podium when standing during his delivery to the courtroom. Henriques even put it to Shipman that he'd treated other patients because he was waiting for Ivy to die. If she was dead, then there'd be no need for an ambulance to be called and she wouldn't be seen by another doctor who might have discovered the morphine in the system.

But perhaps the most dramatic moment of the day came when Henriques asked Shipman, 'Have you any sadness?'

The GP's face was completely expressionless. Silence enveloped the courtroom. You could have heard a pin drop. Eventually he answered, 'I'm not quite sure what you are asking me.'

'Did you have any sadness?' boomed Henriques at the top of his voice.

In a flat voice, devoid of emotion, Shipman replied calmly, 'You're always sad when a patient dies.'

As the court rose that day, Fred Shipman was led from the witness box, staring resolutely at the ground, wringing his hands as he went.

The following morning, Primrose appeared in her usual seat in court but this time she had younger son, Sam, alongside her. He wore a smart dark suit and, during breaks in proceedings, could be found talking and joking on his mobile phone in the corridor. On one occasion he was heard commenting to the ladies at the snack bar that he was always having trouble staying awake in the courtroom.

That day, Henriques laid into Shipman as the court heard about the details behind the death of 81-year-old Maria West. Initially, Shipman said, 'There was no doubt in my mind that the lady had a sudden and lethal stroke.'

'Or a sudden and lethal dose of morphine,' retorted prosecutor Henriques.

When questioned about resuscitation, Shipman told the court that he did not attempt it and neither did he call 999, because she was already dead. He told Henriques that 'the effort put into resuscitating her would not have given good results'.

The prosecutor then asked, 'Have you not heard of people's lives being saved by resuscitation?'

The GP answered, 'Yes, I have done it myself.'

Henriques hit back, 'The lady was beyond defribillation and resuscitation because she had a massive dose of morphine.'

'No, she had not,' insisted Shipman.

The following day – Thursday – Shipman and Henriques continued their duel while discussing the death of Kathleen Wagstaff.

'It is an unhappy coincidence,' the prosecutor told the court, referring to the fact it was two years to the day when 81-year-old Mrs Wagstaff had died.

'Have you any disturbance that we should deal with this on the second anniversary of this event?' asked the QC.

'No,' Shipman replied.

Mrs Wagstaff's relatives watched from the gallery. Her sons Peter and John, both smartly dressed, sat with Peter's blonde wife Angela listening intently as Henriques said to Shipman, 'You had no reason whatsoever in the world to visit Mrs Wagstaff, did you?'

Shipman replied, 'Mrs Wagstaff rang the surgery, I answered the phone, and she complained of chest pains.'

But then the prosecutor produced phone bills that proved there was no call from Mrs Wagstaff's house to Shipman's surgery. There was also no written surgery record.

'I'm going to suggest you made up a phone call from Mrs Wagstaff to your surgery,' Henriques said.

But according to Shipman, he and his patient went inside and sat down and she told him she had been having chest pains. Shortly afterwards, she collapsed.

Shipman explained, 'The situation was she clinically had a coronary.'

Yet, Henriques pointed out to the court, the doctor failed to call for an ambulance, just as he failed to make any record of his examination of her.

Henriques added, 'It is a fact, isn't it, that not once in any of the 15 cases did you yourself – as opposed to the surgery or a relation – summon an ambulance?'

'That's correct,' replied Shipman coldly.

Then Henriques asked, 'Do you accept any blame or responsibility for the death of Laura Kathleen Wagstaff?'

'No, I don't,' replied Shipman without any hesitation.

And that is how the hearing proceeded as prosecutor Henriques took the court through case histories of the dead women. Shipman in turn explained why he was not guilty.

But in some cases, particularly that of Ivy Lomas, the GP offered no real explanation of her death. He even admitted that, despite writing 'heart disease' on her death certificate, she must have died from morphine poisoning. He agreed the morphine level was so high that death would have occurred within five minutes.

Shipman told Preston Crown Court he should have had a post mortem for his alleged victim Muriel Grimshaw, because it would have prevented him from being accused of murder. He said he had discussed Mrs Grimshaw's death with her daughter Anne Brown, and they'd decided a post mortem was not required. 'In hindsight, I would have had it done but at the time I didn't think it was necessary,' he said.

On 3 December 1999, Shipman repeated to the court that he thought victim Kathleen Grundy had had a drug habit – and she knew of his suspicions. He denied smearing her good name by placing his claims on her medical records after he realised that police had carried out toxicology tests on her body which would uncover evidence of morphine.

Shipman claimed Mrs Grundy must have taken the morphine between his visit on the morning of her death and when her body was found. Prosecutor Henriques then asked, 'So she might have got into her motor car and driven to some drug-dealers and obtained diamorphine and then gone home and administered herself?'

The GP replied, 'I don't think it is my role to ascertain where she was getting diamorphine from, if she was taking it.'

Shipman even admitted to the court there were no signs on her body that Mrs Grundy had taken drugs at her home on the day she died. Then prosecutor Henriques questioned Shipman about his conversation with district nurse Marion Gilchrist, in which he said he would have found himself guilty on the evidence, before his arrest and before the toxicology results were known.

Shipman insisted to the court that this was his own special brand of black humour and explained, 'I was under suspicion. I could see my name as a GP would vanish and you could see from the police side there was reasonable evidence that I had killed Mrs Grundy.'

He later added, 'The police told me they were looking into her death and possibly forging the will. I didn't raise any objection of the fact it was typed on my typewriter. I knew the police would go very hard and very enthusiastically to get me. And that explains the comment; it was black humour so I could survive the next two weeks until they arrested me.'

Then Henriques asked Shipman, 'Do you know of anybody who would wish you to have Mrs Grundy's estate?'

Shipman responded, 'I couldn't think of anybody unless Mrs Grundy took it into her head that's what she wanted to do.'

The prosecutor hit back, 'Are you suggesting Mrs Grundy forged her own will?'

Shipman said, 'That's not true. It was a rhetorical question and a rhetorical answer.'

On 7 December 1999, Shipman even claimed in court that he was not surprised four of his victims had 'suddenly' revealed secret medical problems which he subsequently blamed for their death. Prosecutor Henriques asked Shipman, 'They gave you medical histories of which you were previously unaware? In three cases on the day they died and, in the case of Miss Ward, the day before?'

Shipman replied, 'I was given those histories, yes.'

Then Henriques steamed in, 'Does it happen with any regularity that patients see you and say, "I have a medical history I have not previously disclosed to you?"'

Shipman simply replied, 'No.'

The following day, Fred Shipman was accused in court of

telling his receptionist a lie as victim Ivy Lomas lay dead in his surgery. The jury heard that he claimed he'd been delayed because of a 'technical problem' when, in fact, she had just died in the treatment room. He was asked by prosecutor Richard Henriques, 'You told her a bare-faced lie?'

Shipman admitted it 'wasn't the truth', but said he was worried about other patients hearing.

Shipman also agreed that if Mrs Lomas had died at 4.10pm, she must have had morphine between 4.00pm and 4.10pm. The GP also accepted that he did not leave her side, nor did she administer the drug herself, but he had no explanation to offer.

The next case brought to light was that of 81-year-old Marie West, whom Shipman stood by as she died unaware that a neighbour was in the kitchen all the time. Prosecutor Henriques projected those minutes as the so-called 'silent period' when Shipman waited for the drug to take effect on Mrs West.

Shipman hit back from the witness box, 'No, it was not.' He claimed he was surprised to find neighbour Marion Hadfield in the kitchen. He told her he was looking for a telephone to call relatives.

Prosecutor Henriques insisted to the court, 'What had happened was you had been caught out by Mrs Hadfield's presence, and there you were trapped, Mrs West barely dead, you were taken by surprise, coming up with the best explanation you could. That is the real truth.'

Shipman replied, 'No.' But he did agree that he made no attempt to resuscitate Mrs West.

'The simple reason was this lady was beyond resuscitation because she had had a massive amount of diamorphine,' Henriques told the court.

But Shipman insisted, 'There is no doubt in my mind that the lady had a sudden lethal stroke.'

'Or a sudden lethal stroke of diamorphine,' Henriques hit back.

Later, prosecutor Henriques told the jury, 'Not once in all these cases did you call an ambulance ... Not once did you admit any patient to hospital ... Not once did you permit a post mortem ... The simple explanation for all the evidence in this case is your guilt.'

On Monday, 12 December, the Judge adjourned the case for Christmas. The proceedings would reconvene on 5 January 2000.

* * *

In the middle of his trial, Shipman's former Strangeways cellmate Tony Fleming was surprised to receive some letters from the GP. In them, he discussed his trial and how impressed he was by his solicitor Anne Ball, 'she of the steel-tipped heels and intimidating nature'. Shipman also seemed to be revelling in his notoriety. 'I never thought court would be more interesting. Fascinated to see the QCs set out their wares with booby-traps hidden. No applause which I feel would help the audience.'

Cellmate Fleming – now back in the outside world – added, 'I miss him. He'd sit there and listen to all my problems. He was very caring. He was also a very intelligent, very interesting bloke.'

Fleming's words had a familiar ring about them; they could so easily have been uttered by so many of Fred Shipman's patients.

CHAPTER TWENTY THREE

Justice Prevails

Prosecutor Henriques addressed the jury calmly and precisely, reminding them they had heard the evidence of more than 120 prosecution witnesses. He told how Shipman had abused the trust of his victims and their families. 'They trusted him to care for them, their relatives trusted him to tell the truth about the circumstances in which the patients died, and the community trusted him to complete records with honesty and integrity.

'As they grieved, this determined man deployed any and every device to ensure that no post mortem took place. He would overbear, belittle, bamboozle and disadvantage relatives until they accepted the doctor's words that they should not "put their mother through it".'

Fred Shipman, wore his usual charcoal grey suit and white shirt with a striped green-and-red tie and continually wrote notes on a legal pad. His solicitor, Anne Ball, frequently glanced at him, as if she was genuinely unsure he would survive the day.

Prosecutor Richard Henriques told the court that Fred Shipman had betrayed the trust of his patients with a 'trail of murder', then lied to save himself. Henriques said the only alternative to believing Shipman was guilty was to imagine there had been a serial killer following the doctor.

Henriques even pointed out that if the families of some of Fred Shipman's relatives had met earlier, then his 'trail of murder would have been halted sooner'. He told the court, 'He took advantage of their grief and their lesser knowledge of medicine and procedures. As they grieved, this determined man employed every device to make sure no post mortem examination took place.'

Prosecutor Henriques ended his summing up to the jury by repeating Fred Shipman's own description of his situation, as given to the practice nurse before his arrest, 'I read thrillers and I would have me guilty on the evidence.'

Defence counsel Nicola Davies opened her summing up by saying, 'A doctor's primary objective is to care for his patients. A doctor's training is directed at that one aim. Doctors are expected to care for their patients, not kill them.'

She said that by the time of his arrest, Shipman's patient list was 3,100, which was much bigger than the national average. 'No patient had to register with Dr Shipman, but the fact that so many did must be something upon which inferences can be drawn. It is not an unreasonable inference that patients who followed him were satisfied with the care he provided.'

Davies insisted that in all professions, including the medical profession, individuals carried out their duties with their own 'idiosyncrasies'. She said that Shipman's Market Street practice had a spirit and ethos where every member of staff, including Shipman, would carry out tasks to help one another.

Nicola Davies said Shipman would also call on patients when not required to do so, but when he wanted to see how they were. 'In the context of this case, the way the prosecution put it, that has taken on a sinister inference. But the fact is doctors do cold-call and have every right to cold-call. It's part of their duty of care.'

Nicola Davies painted a portrait of a dedicated doctor who

frequently went beyond the call of duty. Keeping records was not his specialty, she said, because he was 'more interested in the patients than the paperwork'. Nicola Davies told the court, 'It is alleged this doctor failed to care for his patients and killed them. Such an allegation requires a high degree of proof and detailed analysis of the evidence. There is no clear and cogent truth of what substance was administered in what quantity or in what form. The prosecution have also manifestly failed even to raise the question of motive. They claim there was a power complex behind the doctor's actions. It is said he enjoyed all this killing. But where is the evidence?'

She then accused prosecutors of failing to find a true motive for the killings, dismissing the 'power complex' argument as amateur psychological theory. And she described the stockpiling of morphine by the GP as 'a red herring'. With regard to the forged Grundy will, Nicola Davies said the crude attempt could not have originated with Fred Shipman. 'Are these the letters the sort a devious, clever and cunning man would write?' she asked, before also claiming the scientific evidence from the bodies was 'inherently unreliable' and that the prosecution case 'stands and falls' on that evidence.

Nicola Davies said that Shipman had sought to spare families the unpleasantness of a post mortem, but this, too, had been turned against him. 'Dr Shipman can't be the only doctor practising in this country who could wish, and properly wish, to spare the relatives this grief. On the scale of things, what is more important – that his patients were cared for or that immaculate records were being kept?'

On 7 January 2000, three months of evidence ended with defender Nicola Davies claiming that the scientific evidence against the family doctor was also 'unreliable'. Miss Davies also suggested that the youngest victim Bianka Pomfret, 49, had suicidal thoughts just two days before her death. In a final plea to the jury, she said, 'We come back to this. Before the court is a doctor faced with 15 counts of murder and one of forgery. In respect of these 15 counts, they are wholly reliant on the base findings of toxicology and that toxicology is based on scientific evidence. It is our submission that scientific evidence is unsafe and unreliable. It is our submission to you that because of the inherently unreliable nature of that scientific evidence, the very basis of the Crown's case has to go. And in the absence of such scientific evidence, the inference to be drawn from it relating to the behaviour of the doctor, relied upon by the Crown, also fails. With it fails the entirety of the prosecution case.'

Judge Mr Justice Forbes's summing up began on Monday, 10 January. He described it as a deeply disturbing case. 'The allegations could not be more serious – a doctor accused of murdering 15 of his patients. Inevitably in the course of this case, you will have heard evidence that will have caused anger, disgust, profound dismay and deep sympathy. They must not be allowed to cloud your judgement. You must consider the facts dispassionately.'

The Judge urged the jurors to 'be fair' as they considered their verdict. He asked them to put aside any strong feelings and emotions aroused by this 'tragic and deeply disturbing case', and told the jury that they had to make allowances for the strain of giving evidence in court. 'You must, of course, apply the same fair standards to the evidence given by Dr Shipman. Do not hold it against him that he came to give evidence to you from the dock. Make every possible allowance for the strain Dr Shipman must have been under giving his evidence. It cannot be easy giving evidence in circumstances in which you face charges as serious as those faced by Dr Shipman.'

The Judge added, 'It is Dr Shipman's case that he did not forge Mrs Grundy's will and did not administer morphine or diamorphine, whether by injection of otherwise to any of the alleged victims.'

Thursday, 14 January passed without anyone mentioning the fact that it was Fred Shipman's fifty-fourth birthday.

On Monday, 24 January 2000, the jury at Preston Crown Court finally retired to decide whether Fred Shipman was guilty of being one the world's most prolific serial killers. The jurors were sent out after an eight-minute address by Mr Justice Forbes on the fifty-second day of the trial. The Judge told the jury that they had to consider each of the cases separately. 'These counts do not stand or fall together,' he said. Mr Justice Forbes also told the jurors to consider their verdicts only on what they had heard and seen in the court. He reminded them that the burden of proof lay with the prosecution and added, 'Dr Shipman does not have to prove anything.'

He also reminded the jurors that the prosecution had to be sure of the doctor's guilt in order to convict on each and every count. 'It is clear to me that you have paid very careful attention throughout the whole of this case and throughout my summing up. You have also made your own detailed notes. You must not feel that your deliberations involve you in some exacting memory test.'

Meanwhile, Fred Shipman stood silently in the dock wearing a pale brown suit, white shirt and tie. In the public gallery, Primrose and their eldest son Christopher, as well as relatives of some of the alleged victims, sat silently. After five hours of deliberation, the jury were sent home for the night. Primrose constantly looked reassuringly at Shipman while the jury was out. 'Wifely support' was how she later described it.

While the jury was out, the British Medical Association took the extraordinary step of circulating Shipman's previous convictions to members so that they were prepared for media questions in the event of a guilty verdict. The e-mails included a question-and-answer document to make sure the doctors were briefed. But by sending it out while the jury were still considering their verdicts it constituted a serious risk to the judicial process.

Judge Mr Justice Forbes demanded that lawyers acting for the organisation, which represents the medical profession, appear in court to explain why details of Shipman's previous conviction had been passed over to its members before the trial was completed. By making the information public, the BMA had risked the details being leaked to the trial jury, which would have made it impossible for them to reach unbiased verdicts. A re-trial would have been out of the question because the case had attracted so much publicity it would have been impossible to find a fresh, untainted jury.

Mr Justice Forbes told BMA lawyers, 'The outrage and horror that the public would necessarily have felt cannot possibly be exaggerated. This is such a serious matter it would not be appropriate for me to accept the apology to bring the matter to an end.'

But he decided not to abandon the trial.

On Friday, 28 January 2000, the jury at Preston Crown Court were sent out to consider their verdicts for a fifth consecutive day. It wasn't until late in the afternoon of Monday, 31 January – a week after they'd originally retired – that the jury returned. Everyone assembled in the courtroom expected them to be sent home for the night once again. Then a whisper went through the ranks that the jury had asked for another ten minutes.

At 4.33pm, the jury trooped back into the courtroom and the foreman strongly announced that all their verdicts were unanimous. The court became deathly quiet.

'Guilty ... guilty ... guilty ...' Sixteen times.

Fred Shipman remained motionless. A stony face gave nothing away. Primrose, wearing a black suit, sat next to son Christopher with David just behind her. Perhaps she'd decided on black because she knew the end was near. An audible sigh from Primrose as the first guilty verdict was returned was the first and only time she publicly registered the enormity of her husband's crimes. But both Fred Shipman's sons lowered their eyes and shrank in their seats. David looked close to tears.

A jubilant cry of 'Yes!' accompanied one of the later verdicts. A clenched-fist salute punched the air for another. The relatives of the victims were finally having their day in court.

Mr Justice Forbes then told Fred Shipman, 'Harold Frederick Shipman, stand up. You have finally been brought to justice by the verdict of this jury. I have no doubt whatsoever that these are true verdicts. The time has now come for me to pass sentence upon you for these wicked, wicked crimes. Each of your victims was your patient. You murdered each and every one of your victims by a calculated and cold-blooded perversion of your medical skills for your own evil and wicked purpose.

'You took advantage of and grossly abused their trust. You were, after all, each victim's doctor. I have little doubt each of your victims smiled and thanked you as she submitted to your deadly ministrations. None realised yours was not a healing touch. None knew in truth you had brought her death, death disguised as the caring attention of a good doctor. As your counsel rightly states, on each of the 15 counts which I pass sentence upon you, the sentence is prescribed by law. However, I take the view that justice demands I pass in respect of each and every one count of murder the sentence of life imprisonment. In the ordinary way, I would not do this in open court, but in your case I am satisfied justice demands I make my views known at the conclusion of this trial.'

After passing 15 life sentences and a four-year sentence for the forgery, the judge then broke with the usual tradition of sending his recommendations about the length of the sentence to the Home Secretary in writing.

'I am satisfied justice demands that I make my views known at the conclusion of the trial. I have formed the conclusion that the crimes you stand convicted of are so heinous that in your case life must mean life. My recommendation will be that you spend the remainder of your days in prison.'

Every word of the Judge's withering criticism of Shipman was savoured by the relatives of the victims. When the court was told of Shipman's previous convictions for forging prescriptions, it provoked gasps from the public gallery, brimming with relatives of the victims.

Judge Mr Justice Forbes then removed his wig to address the relatives directly, paying unusual tribute to their 'courage and quiet dignity'. His own voice quivered as he addressed them. 'I am very aware this trial has been harrowing and painful for all of you. Many of you had to relive in public the shock and grief and sorrow resulting from the death of your loved one. I would like you to know how much I admire the courage and quiet dignity you have shown. Your evidence was, at times, immensely moving and touched the hearts of all who heard it. Each of you has made a significant contribution to the course of justice.'

The Judge also commended the investigating police officers, DCS Bernard Postles and DCI Mike Williams, for their work. 'As far as I am aware, there has never been another case in this country which has required the investigation of so many murders by a single individual as there has been in this case. This has been a deeply disturbing trial and the significance cannot be understated. This has also been a historical trial.'

Fred Shipman remained aloof to the last. The small man with steely grey eyes staring into the distance as the litany of his crimes was put before him. It seemed almost an inconvenience to Shipman that he should be made to listen as Mr Justice Forbes, his voice sometimes faltering under the awful weight of his words, continued addressing the court.

Behind the dock, the relatives of his victims sobbed and held out their hands to each other. But Fred Shipman didn't bat an eyelid. Then, after a few moments, he gazed distractedly at the mahogany carvings above the Judge's chair.

Relatives of the victims left court quietly, as Primrose and her family were escorted away by security guards.

Primrose had been making copious notes earlier in the trial. But now her pen was stilled. The nervous hand-kneading that betrayed her anxiety had gone, too. She had no intention of leaving him, especially as his legal team were expected to mount an immediate appeal. She even shared his optimism about the outcome of the trial, after it emerged that she had ordered flowers to be sent to the family home for his 'welcome home' party.

After sentencing, Primrose had wanted to join her serial-killer husband immediately, but that was out of the question. She later said she was 'devastated' by the verdicts. But for 20 minutes or so she had to endure the agony of all eyes switching to her as the court slowly emptied. Just then, a mobile phone went off in her handbag. The tune it played would have been familiar to most of his victims: 'Jesu, Joy of Man's Desiring'.

Primrose emerged briefly for photographs outside the court, but when she later answered the door to the family home, she appeared tearful as she uttered, 'No comment.' Her son David, 20, also red-eyed, said, 'There will be no comment now. No comment in the future. No comment at any time.'

Throughout the trial, Primrose had made the journey to Preston Crown Court and also paid visits virtually every day to Strangeways Prison to see her husband. Her unbowed loyalty was fascinating and it perhaps held the key to much of Fred Shipman's behaviour. Always modestly and plainly dressed, Primrose was unswerving in her duty to stand by her husband. But why? It must truly have been a remarkable marriage to withstand all the secrecy that Fred Shipman had indulged in. Perhaps he had confided in his wife. Maybe he told her the reasons behind his crimes. On the other hand, perhaps she simply refused to accept the truth. Shipman's bedside manner had worked miracles on his own wife. He was a Godlike figure to Primrose and nothing would ever change that.

The now slightly ungainly, plump and otherwise unremarkable wife with her grey hair cut in a practical bob had taken the same seat in the public gallery each and every day. Barely a flicker of emotion was revealed by her throughout the 50-plus days of the trial. To many, she seemed to have battened down the hatches and done what she had always done best – she kept the family together.

Few doubted that Fred and Primrose were as much in love after his arrest as throughout their 34-year marriage. She seemed to revel in his brilliance, even as he had stood in the witness box blandly denying the heinous crimes he had committed.

What no one in the court that day could fail to appreciate was the unique and deeply moving mixture of grief and relief that swept over the faces of the victims' relatives. One by one in the public gallery, like a living map of Hyde, little clutches of people

broke down in tears as the verdicts had been announced. They
hugged each other for support – different families, but sharing
the same burden. The sound of weeping continued on and off for
more than half-an-hour. It had been punctuated with muted
shouts of delight as it became clear that Fred Shipman was not
going to get away with murder.

But none of this highly-charged emotion seemed to register
with Fred Shipman. His witness box performance had been
unimpressive. With the same lifeless, methodical manner that
had dominated his character as a doctor, he'd tried to convince
the jury that he was right, and that everyone else was wrong.
The jurors were mostly young, ordinary men and women,
charged with the responsibility for testing everything he said.
He'd failed the test miserably. Shipman was then taken
downstairs to the bowels of the court, and ushered into one of
a row of empty cells.

* * *

Within hours of his last court appearance, tributes for some of
Shipman's alleged victims were recorded in the local *Manchester
Evening News*. A friend of Maureen Ward told how the widow
was about to go on a Caribbean holiday days after she died. 'She
was a lovely woman, so kind and thoughtful. She would often
pop into the neighbours and ask them if they needed any
shopping.'

Retired secretary Pamela Hillier, who was a member of the
Friends of Mottram Parish Church, would never be forgotten by
Friends Secretary Katherine Elwood. 'She was a lovely, kind
person. She would help anybody if they needed it.'

Outside Preston Crown Court, victim Jean Lilley's family –
Albert, Odette and Wayne – issued a statement saying, 'Jean
Lilley was a loving, caring wife and mother who dearly cared
about her family and friends. She will always be loved and
missed. Dr Shipman may have taken her life from us, but he can
never take our memories.'

Liz Hunter, who saw Shipman leave the home of her friend, Jean Lilley, just minutes after he killed her, said she was still coming to terms with the verdicts.

She said, 'At the moment, I am still trying to take it all in. The biggest thing I keep asking myself is why I didn't go down to stay with her. Even if I had stayed with her and I had seen him give her something, I wouldn't have known what it was, I'm not a doctor. I do know that if she had thought she was dying, she would have asked me to stay with her. She didn't want to die alone – that was her biggest fear, to die alone. Technically, she didn't, he was there. You want someone with you who cares about you – not someone who wants to kill you.'

The family of victim Kathleen Wagstaff said, 'We feel a sense of relief that this part of the nightmare is at an end and justice has been done. To lose our mother in such circumstances leaves us with a feeling of deep sadness that we were so badly betrayed by someone in whom we had great trust.'

And so the tributes went on. But they clearly hid the true feelings of the entire community who were so shell-shocked by the news that they still refused to believe their favourite GP was capable of mass murder.

Immediately after Shipman's sentencing, it was announced that he was likely to be charged with another 23 murders and may have been responsible for many hundreds of other deaths.

The Shipman case sent ripples of concern and indignation through Britain; the Government's Health Secretary Rt Hon Alan Milburn made a statement in the House of Commons on the Shipman case on the day of sentencing. He said, 'Our sympathies lie with the very many families who have been victims of these dreadful crimes. As an individual, Harold Shipman betrayed the trust of his patients. He also betrayed the professionalism of our country's dedicated family doctors.'

There was a public outcry when it was openly disclosed that Shipman had been drawing his £100,000 salary – taxpayers' money – right up until he was convicted of mass murder. His earnings as a GP had increased since his arrest in September

1988, because his own practice was having to offer more services, such as bereavement counselling, for many of his victims' families and extra nursing hours to support Shipman's stand-in, Dr Haz Lloyd, at the Market Street surgery. In the weeks following his sentencing, Shipman waited for a final cheque from his paymasters at the West Pennine Health Authority.

It was only when the Health Secretary stepped in that the payment was stopped. He also promised to prevent Shipman claiming his sizeable pension. An average GP in Britain earned approximately £54,000 per year, but Shipman was getting at least 20 per cent more because he was running a single-handed practice.

Despite the trial and subsequent conviction, Fred Shipman's practice only lost 200 patients out of a total of more than 2,000. Yet many of the relatives of the GP's victims discovered they would only get derisory compensation payouts estimated at no more than £10,000 under the Criminal Injuries Compensation Act. Alternatively, the victims' families were advised that they could try to sue Fred Shipman if they could prove they suffered post-traumatic stress.

Within days, it was announced that safeguards on family doctors would be tightened to prevent any similar cases in the future. Health Secretary Alan Milburn announced that an inquiry would be launched which would also review the rules on death certificates and the procedures for allowing cremations and burials. Milburn also promised to close the loophole which allowed Shipman to draw his NHS salary for another month. He also was considering removing the doctor's pension rights.

There was astonishment amongst the general public that Shipman was still registered as a GP under the rules of the General Medical Council, despite being Britain's worst serial killer. It would be some weeks before he'd finally be struck off for good.

CHAPTER TWENTY FOUR

Life, after Death

The truth for thousands of Fred Shipman's patients was going to be extremely hard to swallow. They'd trusted him implicitly and now many faced a struggle to rebuild their lives and their confidence in a professional figure who should have been a pillar of the community. At the presbytery of St Paul's, Hyde, Father Denis Maher's phone rang constantly. He'd been there when his parishioners were bereaved. He'd been there when those same loved ones were exhumed for re-examination and he'd been there in court giving testimony against Fred Shipman.

Now, following the trial, Father Maher was once more on hand to provide comfort and support to the families of the GP's victims. Father Maher knew only too well that the community of Hyde was still in shock. The outcome of Fred Shipman's trial hadn't really made it any easier for the families of his victims. So in the midst of the grief and confusion, many turned to their priest. 'The question I was asked many times was: "Is he evil? Can he be forgiven?"'

Father Maher explained, 'What he did can be seen as

intrinsically evil. He murdered people but he also betrayed their trust. His patients would have opened the door with trust to him, let him in with a smile. He violated that very sacred trust. I believe we can forgive; if we refuse forgiveness, we perpetrate evil. If I refuse to forgive, I am making pain for myself. Forgiveness is for people who have done evil. You can condemn what has been done but still forgive the person.'

Father Maher was also chaplain to the local police so he soon heard how the number of Shipman victims was expected to go into the hundreds. He even acknowledged that Fred Shipman himself probably had no idea how many he had killed. Father Maher explained, 'Who knows how many he may have killed? It could have been going on for a long, long time. As chaplain, I have seen the people engaged in forensic work every week. They have been affected by it; they have never been involved in anything like this before.'

Following the end of the Shipman trial, Father Maher gave numerous informal counselling sessions and even held a service at his own church for anyone who felt they might have been touched by Fred Shipman's supposedly evil deeds. Father Maher also appealed to many of his flock not to vent their anger at Fred Shipman's family.

'I am aware what an ordeal it must be for his wife. His family are as much victims as anyone else. They must be going through a terrible time and will be hounded.'

The Shipman trial verdict dominated the British newspapers in the days following his sentencing. Among a host of issues raised, much criticism was pointed in the direction of the medical authorities. The *Sun* wanted to know why Shipman was allowed to carry on practising after spending six months in a drug addiction clinic. And why was his conviction for forging prescriptions glossed over?

Other newspapers agreed. As the London *Daily Mail* pointed out, 'We shall never know exactly how many patients died as a result of that outrageously complacent decision.'

The *Daily Telegraph* cautioned against an over-reaction by

arguing that the worst outcome of the case would be if, whenever a patient died, suspicion fell upon his or her doctor.

But there was no getting away from the fact that Fred Shipman had shaken, albeit temporarily, that vital bond of trust between doctor and patient.

Just after the trial, the ex-husband of Shipman's special friend and victim Bianka Pomfret encountered Primrose Shipman. 'She was at York Station taking photographs,' explained Adrian Pomfret. 'She looked totally undamaged and really happy. How could she look so unbothered about what had happened?'

The day after sentencing, the muffled bells of St George rang for an hour-and-a-half and produced an eerie echo which carried right across Hyde. Many of Hyde's still shocked residents filed into their parish church to remember Fred Shipman's victims. Emotions overflowed during the 40-minute Church of England service which featured hymns and prayers carefully chosen to try and console and reconcile a horrified community.

The 400-strong congregation included many of the detectives who worked on the murder inquiry plus Tameside's mayor, Frank Robinson. As schoolgirl Julia Mann sang 'Pie Jesu', a middle-aged man pulled out a handkerchief and dabbed at his eyes. One woman sobbed openly when five candles were lit in front of the altar by local people representing every generation of Hyde's community. But the most moving moment came when the Reverend John Harries told his congregation, 'We will never be the same as we were yesterday. Our innocence has been lost. Nothing anyone can say or do can take away the pain and hurt that we feel. For so long, many in our midst have been grieving and wounds opened time and time again as we sat through the trial or heard the stories of others.'

And still many in Hyde found it hard to believe that their respected GP was a serial killer. A couple of days after Shipman was sentenced, one of his patients called at his surgery after being treated by Fred Shipman for more than 20 years. Dorothy Heywood, 69, said she was 'in total shock'. She added, 'He was the best doctor I've ever been to. This is very hard to come to terms with.'

Over at the Shipmans' home in Mottram, a policeman stood guard in the driveway. Behind drawn curtains, the flickering of a television could be seen as Primrose and at least two of her children watched the countless news broadcasts about Fred Shipman's murderous activities.

Within 48 hours, Shipman had penned yet another letter to Primrose. He still retained the upper hand in the relationship and clearly continued to view himself as a towering intellect, a man whose judgement should never, ever be questioned. Primrose had stuck by him throughout everything. The couple had even brought up four fine, seemingly well-adjusted children in a wholly responsible manner.

However, in the aftermath of the trial, it seems that the two youngest, Sam and David, suffered. Both had been school captains at West Hill School. But the stress of his father's trial meant that David, now 20, had to re-sit his latest set of exams at Newcastle University where he studied engineering. Sam had left school and was studying to be a nurseryman at an agricultural college near Preston. 'He wanted to get as far away from medicine as he could,' explained one schoolfriend.

By the time of his father's arrest, oldest son Christopher had moved to Dartford, Kent, in the south of England, although he did remain in close contact with his family and even travelled up to attend court on a number of occasions.

And despite his incarceration, Fred remained Primrose's Svengali figure. He had complete power over her. She was prepared to do anything for him. Many later speculated that Fred Shipman's power was equal in strength to the way that the other notorious British serial killer of recent times, Fred West, had control over his wife, although there is no indication that Primrose actually took part in any of her husband's crimes.

Primrose was a classic example of a less confident woman drawn in by a powerful man. In many ways, the relationship was similar to those in which battered women remain in abusive relationships. Basically, Primrose could not manage her life on her own and that's why she continued visiting Fred at every available opportunity. Of course, she knew something wasn't right, but she chose to ignore it. Fred Shipman was a dominant character, full of his own self importance. She didn't dare cross him. In any case, he would never have allowed that.

And when it came to making contact again with her family, she was so consumed by guilt and shame over the pregnancy that she couldn't face up to her mother, even more than 30 years after that hastily arranged marriage. Primrose also hung on to her husband because, in some ways, she felt debased and that she was not worthy of Fred Shipman or his attentions. He made her feel grateful for his existence.

There was a complete imbalance of power in their relationship, but it suited them both. She was completely submissive. But Primrose's self-esteem had been at rock bottom for many years and that was why the house remained in such a mess. She blocked out all the unpleasant thoughts and considerations. Primrose did not want to do or say anything that might jeopardise her relationship with her husband. The purpose of her life was to serve him – she had nothing else.

From Fred Shipman's point of view, he desperately needed Primrose to remain completely dependent on him. His partner had to continue to adore him and bow to his every whim.

* * *

Fred Shipman may have appeared outwardly calm as those life sentences were announced in court, but by the time he got back to Strangeways Prison he was in a state of complete and utter shock. One warder later recalled, 'He totally went to pieces – whimpering, bleating, pining for the world he had forfeited.'

Shipman sat and rocked backwards and forwards saying over and over again, 'How can they do this to me of all people? After all I have done. I am a great doctor, a caring man. This is an affront.'

There was no remorse. No consideration for those whose lives he had taken or the families left behind. The previously charming, relaxed demeanour was replaced by a manic stare and the sight of Shipman shuffling along the corridors looking as if he lived in another world from everyone else. He spent increasing amounts of time curled up like a baby in a body suit on a bare plastic mattress. One ex-inmate who encountered Shipman in Strangeways later said, 'I do not think he will last more than a year inside now. I think he will top himself at the first opportunity he gets.'

Fred Shipman found himself once again on 24-hour, round-the-clock suicide watch in prison. But as the weeks passed, Shipman tried to adjust to his fate. He wanted to retain control even within the prison system. For jail is a world where the rules are clear cut, where he could feel cleverer than many around him and the sheer number of his victims accorded him a great deal of respect.

Primrose saw her husband for the first time after his sentencing accompanied by sons David and Christopher, for a one-hour visit at Strangeways. Handsome David resembled his father at the same age in many ways with his dark, Latin looks. Primrose, wearing a dark skirt and turquoise jacket, walked straight into the prison reception area without having to go through the usual procedure of collecting a security pass from the visitor centre. But she and both sons were thoroughly searched before being escorted through a maze of corridors to meet Shipman. The Shipmans were told they'd initially be allowed to make four visits a month to see Fred Shipman before he was moved to another prison to serve out his sentence.

After the visit, Primrose maintained her traditional grim silence for the waiting reporters as the three family members climbed into her Metro car which had been hurriedly reversed up to the reception area doors by a friend. Shipman's sons David and Chris looked stunned at the barrage of press cameras.

* * *

A few days after sentencing, Father Denis Maher decided that the Shipman family deserved some mercy – despite the doctor's horrendous crimes. He later recalled, 'I felt a lot of sympathy for his family, especially his sons. I heard from many that they were nice kids, so I took it upon myself one night to go to their house and see them. I wasn't sure which house they lived in, but eventually I found the next-door house and the couple in there asked me in and talked to me. They encouraged me and told me where the Shipmans lived.'

Then Father Maher went and knocked at the front door of the GP's home. 'One of the sons answered it. I could see people milling about behind. The house was a complete mess.' The priest heard the Shipmans' son go back inside and ask his mother what he should do. 'She said, "Don't talk to him,"' recalled Father Maher. 'Then he came back and said they didn't want to speak to me. That was it. I never even got in the hallway. They shut the door firmly, but politely.'

Fred Shipman's sentencing on 15 counts of murder did not bring the families of many of his numerous other victims any nearer to an emotional closure on the subject. One Greater Manchester Police source admitted privately to a local newspaper reporter, 'Where will it all end? There could be hundreds.' And a relative of one suspected victim said, 'We feel like we are in a limbo. At one time, we thought our loved ones died a natural death, but now we can never be absolutely sure.'

Gradually, dozens of family members began to speak out about their worst fears. James Ashton, 60, whose widowed mother Dora died in Shipman's surgery in 1995, said, 'Shipman told me it was a stroke. I didn't doubt him and that is what he put on the death certificate, but now we just don't know what to believe.'

Joe Kitchen, 42, endured the torment of seeing the body of his mother Alice exhumed as part of the police investigation. He said, 'Shipman has left a trail of lies and deceit in his wake. He may have been handed 15 life terms, but the sentence is only just beginning for many people in Hyde.'

Spinster Joan Harding, an 82-year-old retired council worker, was another patient who died in Shipman's surgery. Close friend Winnie Richards said, 'We mourned her once and I feel like I'm having to mourn her again.'

Marion Higham, a retired wages clerk, died at her Hyde home in 1996. A neighbour said, 'As soon as we realised what Shipman had been doing, we thought Marion had fallen victim to him.'

Widowed mother-of-two Josephine Hall died aged 69. Daughter Josephine Allen said, 'I wrestled with my thoughts and felt I had to go to the police. I wanted them to say, "No, you're wrong," but they didn't.'

Retired mill worker Elsie Cheetham, 76, died in April 1997. Neighbour Ken Houlsworth said, 'She didn't deserve to have her life cut short.'

Businesswoman Joan Dean – once an extra on the popular British TV soap *Coronation Street* – died at her Hyde home in February 1988. *Coronation Street* actor John Savident, who plays butcher Fred Elliot, was a close family friend and read two Shakespeare poems at her funeral. Afterwards, Joan's son Brian found that an 18-carat Omega watch and a £5,000 engagement ring were missing.

Gladys Saunders, 82, died in June 1996. A friend said, 'Dr Shipman was there. A neighbour went out to get some milk from the shop and when she got back Shipman said Gladys had gone.'

Widow Hilda Hibbert, 81, died in January 1996, just minutes after Shipman left her house. Granddaughter Jane said, 'I'm 95 per cent sure he murdered her.'

Irene Heathcote, 76, died in 1996 after a visit from Shipman. Son-in-law Duncan McAlpine said, 'My wife Susan feels Shipman should be hanged.'

Lively Edith Brady, 72, was found dead in 1996. Daughter Pam Turner said, 'I just want to know why. I owe it to my mum.'

Other alleged victims included Marie Fernley, Edith Brock

and Bertha Moss who died in 1995; Valerie Cuthbert and Marjorie Waller who died in 1996; Marjorie Bennison who died in 1997; and Cissie Davies and Mabel Shawcross who died in 1998.

And police knew only too well there would eventually be even more deaths to investigate.

On 18 February 2000, families of 23 of Fred Shipman's alleged victims reacted angrily when told that the GP would not face any more murder charges. David Calvert-Smith QC, the director of England's Public Prosecution Service, had decided that, after the mass of publicity given to Shipman's trial, it would be impossible to give him a fair trial. Calvert-Smith told the families of his 'reluctant' and highly unusual decision not to proceed in letters delivered to the homes of the relatives by special courier early that morning.

Calvert-Smith said, 'I have reluctantly concluded that there are insurmountable legal difficulties to further trials taking place.' After giving his reasons, he added, 'I hope my explanation is to some degree helpful to you and that you will in time be able to come to terms with your tragic loss.'

Calvert-Smith had overruled detectives convinced of Shipman's guilt in the deaths of those patients. But police promised to continue their enquiries into many more cases involving Shipman. They still believed there was enough evidence for a second or even a third trial.

But Calvert-Smith insisted, 'I have had to consider the effect of the enormous publicity upon any further trial of Harold Shipman on new charges, and he has already been sent to prison for the rest of his natural life. In reaching this decision, I have been acutely aware of the distress of relatives of the deceased and the understandable desire for some of them for a further public trial in a criminal court.'

He claimed that 'a considerable majority' of the relatives of the alleged victims had accepted that a new trial could not take place and added that further proceedings could delay or hamper the progress of a public inquiry into Shipman's activities.

'Normally, a decision to prosecute would automatically follow if there is enough evidence for a realistic prospect of conviction of murder,' he said. 'But this has been an exceptional and, I hope, unique case.'

Calvert-Smith then said any decision about the deaths of Fred Shipman's other alleged victims would now be a matter for John Pollard, coroner in Tameside, Greater Manchester. 'I am going to assess the whole Shipman situation fully,' responded Pollard.

But many of the relatives of Shipman's numerous victims still wanted Shipman prosecuted. 'I'm outraged that the Crown Prosecution Service is not going ahead,' said Suzanne Bennison, whose grandmother Edith Brock died in November 1995. 'If they think they can appease me by shoving a letter through my door and thinking I will go away quietly, they have chosen the wrong person.'

John Hibbert, son of Hilda Hibbert, who died in her armchair at home four years earlier, said, 'Shipman has literally got away with murder.'

The families of many of Fred Shipman's alleged victims also became angry about the British Government's decision to hold an independent inquiry into his murders in secret. Lead investigator Lord Laming promised that 'care and sensitivity' would be used when relatives were asked to give evidence. He also said the inquiry would be swift and thorough, although the decision to hold it in private had been made because, under the terms of the National Health Service Act, it had to be held behind closed doors.

* * *

Some weeks after the end of Fred Shipman's trial, moves were finally made to close down completely his one-man surgery in Market Street, Hyde. Many felt it served as a constant reminder to the relatives of victims and any incoming GP should be given an opportunity to make a clean start. The decision to move to new premises was endorsed by the Tameside and Glossop Community Health Council. 'We think it would be very unsettling for patients to be treated in premises where at least five women have died at the hands of their GP,' said Pauline Davenport, Chairwoman of the Council.

But the local West Pennine Area Health Authority did not expect any move for at least three months. 'In the short term, the only realistic option is to keep the surgery open,' said a spokesman.

Back in his prison cell, Fred Shipman continued to lobby the health authority about the poor standard of care being provided by the temporary doctor who had taken his place. Fred Shipman clearly remained in a complete state of self-denial about his murderous habits.

CHAPTER TWENTY FIVE

Suicide Watch

Inside Manchester's Strangeways Prison, two members of staff whose mothers may have been among Fred Shipman's numerous victims were sent home until the GP could be transferred following his conviction. Shipman was held on the healthcare unit while being carefully monitored by medical staff. A prison spokesman explained, 'It is routine for newly convicted prisoners to be monitored in this way if there has been a long trial of this nature.'

Warders still believed Shipman might yet try to commit suicide and he was categorised as a high-risk inmate. Shipman would normally have spent at least a month being assessed before being transferred to another high-security jail, but the process was speeded up because of the suspension of those two prison officers who needed to return to work as quickly as possible.

Shipman found himself segregated in a similar way to sex-offenders because his victims were all elderly and female. 'There is little doubt that he would be targeted because he was such a prolific murderer and his victims were someone's mum or grandparent,' said one member of the prison staff.

Then Fred Shipman was transferred out of Strangeways to the high-security Frankland Prison in County Durham. He had asked to be transferred to Wakefield Jail in nearby West Yorkshire, because he thought Durham was too far for his family to travel to visit him. But that request was turned down.

Frankland Jail is the sort of place that gives the prison service a respectable name. It's not the usual grim, grey collection of typically British Victorian buildings, even though it contains many of the nation's most deadly criminals. Relations between staff and inmates are reasonable most of the time, although there's little to smile about if you're facing up to the prospect of spending the rest of your life in prison.

Within weeks of Fred Shipman's incarceration in Frankland Prison, his family moved house to be closer to him. They also wanted to escape the memories associated with their home in Mottram. Primrose informed a select group of friends that she was moving to Whitby, North Yorkshire, midway between Frankland and Wakefield Prison, where Shipman still hoped eventually to be transferred.

A family friend explained at the time, 'Primrose is standing by him. She used to see him almost daily when he was on remand at Strangeways, but now it's a lot harder. By moving, it also gets the family away from the house and all its bad memories.'

Around the same time as Primrose was packing her bags, the *Sun* newspaper revealed that Fred Shipman's surgery had been re-listed in a new phone book despite his conviction for killing 15 patients. The Market Street surgery was included in the 2000–01 Manchester South telephone directory. It gave his name, the surgery's address and its phone numbers.

On 10 February 2000, Fred Shipman was finally struck off the medical register by the General Medical Council. He did not appear before the GMC's professional conduct committee in London and was not represented by solicitors. The hearing had been speeded up following Shipman's conviction. Committee Chairman Rodney Yates said, 'The committee are appalled by the evidence. It is abhorrent that Dr Shipman cold-bloodedly murdered 15 patients, using his medical skills. He greatly undermined the trust the public place in the medical profession, in particular their family doctors.'

On the same day, Shipman made it clear though his lawyers that he still intended to appeal against his convictions. Shipman's representativess claimed that pre-trial publicity linking the GP to the murders of more than 100 people may have influenced the jury. Shipman was told he had until the end of the month to lodge papers requesting an appeal against the 16 convictions, which included the forgery of the Grundy will. A death toll running to 146 was mentioned, and many believed that was only a conservative estimate. There was every chance that that figure could more than double.

On Monday, 6 March 2000, one of the doctors who helped bring Fred Shipman to justice died of cancer. Dr Linda Reynolds, aged just 49, put her career and health on the line by speaking out about her fears concerning Shipman. She'd noticed that the death rate amongst Shipman's patients was three times higher than at her surgery nearby. Dr Reynolds – who worked with the Brooke group practice in Hyde – was diagnosed with terminal cancer in August 1999. She died at her home in Stockport with her husband Nigel at her side. The couple had two children – Caroline, 22, and William, 18. Mr Reynolds later explained, 'What she did was against her nature, she was not interventionist. I have utter respect and admiration for my wife and know what this cost her.'

Coroner Mr Pollard said, 'I will never forget how brave she was to come forward and put her profession on the line. Dr Reynolds was a very courageous and stoical person who acted in a very helpful and brave manner.'

In April 2000, it was revealed that three of 26 alleged new victims had been exhumed during the original police inquiry and inquests on those victims – Sarah Ashworth, Alice Kitchen and Elizabeth Mellor – were to be held imminently. South Manchester coroner John Pollard even wrote to the then Home Secretary Jack Straw seeking permission to open the inquests.

Pollard stressed that, unlike in a criminal trial, an inquest would not seek to establish Shipman's guilt or innocence but simply establish the facts which would mean his role coming under the spotlight. Pollard explained, 'It is my intention to inform Dr Shipman of the inquests and to notify him of his right to attend.' That meant Shipman could be called from his prison cell to give evidence. But he was highly unlikely to co-operate.

The following month – May 2000 – police investigators revealed that their long-standing investigation into Shipman's activities now suggested that he'd killed close to 200 people. His case was now Britain's biggest ever murder inquiry. Investigators already knew that Shipman's guilt could never be determined from cases dating before 1985 because itemised phone bills, medical records and cremation certificates on which detectives relied did not exist.

The Shipman case was now dwarfing some of Britain's most historically significant murder investigations; Dennis Nilsen, who admitted killing 16 gay men in London between 1978 and 1983; arsonist Bruce Lee, jailed in 1981 for murdering 15 people by setting their houses ablaze; Yorkshire Ripper Peter Sutcliffe, who killed 13 times; and Fred and Rose West, who murdered at least 12 young women. Even the world's most notorious serial killer, Andrei Chikatilo, stood accused of murdering a mere 52 women and boys in the Soviet Union between 1978 and 1990.

A team of 20 police officers continued investigations out of a moral obligation to families, despite the fact that prosecutions were unlikely. 'There was a need to find them some sort of closure,' explained one investigator. Then the Shipman incident unit at Ashton-under-Lyne, Greater Manchester, was moved to a smaller office in nearby Stalybridge.

The fall-out from the Shipman case continued for many months following the end of his trial. Dr Alan Banks, medical adviser to the authority who paid Shipman's salary, was suspended from his job. He'd examined the files of 14 Shipman patients during the first police investigation but told detectives he could find nothing wrong. After Shipman's trial, 49-year-old Dr Banks was ordered to remain at home until further notice by his bosses at the West Pennine Health Authority.

Dr Banks said, 'I do not feel that I have done anything wrong or behaved in anything but a professional manner. I have already talked things over with my legal people and I have no doubt about being completely vindicated when all the facts are known.'

Even Fred Shipman's small group of drinking pals in Mottram were now convinced he was a mass killer. But despite their feelings about Shipman, his friend Dr David Walker made a special effort to look after the GP's youngest son Sam. 'He's a lovely lad and he needed to be helped to pull through all this,' added Dr Walker.

Dr Walker and his friends were convinced Fred Shipman would probably kill himself. 'I thought he might do it before the end of the trial. I still think he might. He'll need to be carefully watched,' said Dr Walker. Many in Hyde believed that the sooner Fred Shipman died, the better.

Fred Shipman – now the nation's most famous serial killer – was soon making a lasting impression on other inmates and staff at Frankland Prison. Many quickly dubbed him, 'The Good Doctor' rather than the evil, psychopathic genius portrayed in court during his trial. Fred Shipman dispensed death and sympathy to hundreds of innocent old ladies in Hyde, but that didn't stop him setting up his own, very special practice within the red-brick walls of Frankland.

Other lifers in Frankland believed Shipman was more trustworthy than the prison doctor. 'It's only injections he's a bit dodgy with; he can't get the drugs in here, so we're all safe. He told me he wouldn't trust the prison doctors to treat his cat – if he had one,' one old bank robber later recalled. An inmate suffering chest pains went to see Shipman because prison doctors had not prescribed any treatment for him. Shipman diagnosed a cracked rib and the man was immediately treated properly.

Fred Shipman soon overcame the fear and suspicion of an entire prison to gain the respect of his fellow inmates. As one who was recently released explained, 'At first we thought he was a right nutter, but he's a cool guy. He's interested in us and he's proved he's a decent fellow.'

Shipman – described at his trial as a fanatical control freak – clearly had excellent coping skills. 'The only difference is that he can't knock any of us off without the screws noticing,' added the former inmate, with tongue firmly in cheek. Shipman continued to insist to all and sundry inside Frankland that he was innocent of the murders connected to his name. 'Most inmates say they're innocent, but the doc, as we call him, is pretty convincing and, you know, if you look at the evidence against him, it does look, well, flimsy,' added one former inmate. Others might disagree.

But there were some disturbing side-effects to Fred Shipman's incarceration. Warders at Frankland feared that Shipman – by now a frail 54 years old – was being pressurised by certain heavyweight inmates (including three notorious armed robbers) to give them a worse diagnosis so they could get lighter duties or go into the prison hospital. Eventually, prison staff prevented Fred Shipman from treating his 'patients' by putting him in permanent solitary confinement in the jail's hospital.

And Shipman's moods continued to roller-coaster with alarming regularity. He was still being prescribed four different types of tranquillisers on a daily basis. 'One minute he was up, smiling and full of himself then the next he was virtually slumped in a depression in his cell,' explained one fellow inmate.

But by placing Shipman in a cell alongside the prison's hospital wing, they had further isolated the GP from his new 'patients' – the other inmates. Within weeks, Shipman tried to hang himself, with a piece of towelling he'd stolen from the washroom area. There are few details of the never before revealed incident but a relative of another inmate explained, 'Shipman was completely cut off from everyone apart from those inside the hospital wing. No wonder he got desperate. I heard they managed to grab him just after he'd tried to hang himself off the cell door handle.'

Meanwhile, Primrose moved into the house she'd bought in

nearby Whitby so she could be as close as possible to her beloved husband. Primrose strolled casually up to the prison gates each and every week, taking numerous calls on her mobile, which still played the haunting melody of the hymn 'Jesu, Joy of Man's Desiring'. Primrose usually arrived with sons David, 21, and Christopher, 29, for a one-hour visit. The couple's two other children Sarah, 33, and Sam, 18, also made regular appearances at Frankland.

Primrose – increasingly heavyweight – tended to dress in long skirts and baggy jumpers and jackets. Her distinctively tatty ten-year-old Metro car soon became a familiar sight to local journalists camped outside the prison. The family were allowed two weekday and two weekend visits per month. But reporters who tried to quote her found she never uttered anything other than 'No comment'.

Primrose's first impression of Frankland Jail was its starkness. Along with all visitors, she was obliged to book in at the entrance and then sit in reception to wait for her name to be called out. Then she had her photo taken in keeping with prison rules. She was only allowed to take £10 in change into the prison which could be used at the various vending machines inside the visitors' hall.

Then Primrose was escorted to another building where her fingerprints were taken and her shoes, watch and cardigan were carefully examined for contraband. She then walked through an X-ray machine and was escorted to yet another building through more glass doors.

Then a dog sniffed her for drugs before she finally got into the visitors' hall. Shipman and other segregated inmates such as child molesters and killers were made to greet visitors in a separate room just off the main hall. Two members of staff stood by at all times.

It's known as 'the nonces' [child molesters] area' to the rest of the prisoners. Fred Shipman – still refusing to concede his crimes – was categorised with the child offenders 'for his own safety'. Other inmates say to this day that Shipman is deeply offended to be classified with 'the nonces'. Undoubtedly, prison authorities moved Shipman 'to try and water down his influence amongst the other inmates'.

Primrose seemed determined not to miss one visit. In the visitors' room, she could be seen hanging on to Fred's every word. Nothing – not even the prospect of him never being a free man – could deter her from her duty as the faithful wife. Shipman even told one inmate about how supportive his family were being. 'I have talked to all of them. Primrose and my children are being very supportive, particularly Sam. They are standing by me and they will get me through this. They are loyal because they know I am innocent.'

Many of Shipman's family associates were seriously concerned about the health of Primrose. 'She is losing the whole focus of her life,' said one. Even Shipman confided to one Frankland prison officer, 'Primrose is affected. I'm now comforting her on visits.' Not even Fred Shipman's incarceration could prevent him from controlling his wife's life.

Shipman bitterly complained about being held in the hospital wing at Frankland. His cell had a clear plastic door to enable warders to continue to watch over him round the clock. One source said, 'He has ranted and raved about being called a monster. He insists he is innocent and he will fight his conviction. It seems as if he has shut out all the killings from his mind.'

Back in the outside world, one of Fred Shipman's former cellmates from Strangeways – Tony Fleming – decided to speak out about the killer GP who he claimed saved him from committing suicide. 'I miss him, you know. He would sit there and listen to all my problems, take it in. He was very caring. He was also very intelligent, a very interesting bloke. I will never ever believe he killed all those women. He saved me life – that's the man he is.'

Soon after arriving at Frankland Prison, Fred Shipman began suffering serious eyesight problems and made his only trip out of Frankland for treatment at the Sunderland Eye Infirmary. The visit – Shipman arrived handcuffed to two warders at 10.00am one Monday morning – was shrouded in secrecy. It sparked criticism from other patients who claimed that Shipman 'was being treated like a royal'. Patients were ordered to stay inside rooms and banned from corridors while Shipman was in the hospital.

Back inside Frankland, Shipman received visits at least once a month from detectives still trying to urge him to co-operate with their enquiries into the hundreds of other deaths among his patients. When a video link was set up for Shipman to give evidence at one of the new inquests into yet another victim, it remained blank. He even refused three invitations by the coroner examining one victim's death – Sarah Ashworth – to exercise his right to question witnesses.

By the middle of 2000, Shipman was translating *Harry Potter* books into Braille inside Frankland. Some newspapers expressed horror that this so-called 'monster' should have been given such a pleasant job. But then not many prisoners would have the intelligence to translate into Braille. 'Shipman started in the unit not long ago and had to undergo training, but he's learned very quickly,' one prison source explained. 'He's really enjoying having something more interesting to do and he's impressed by the fact it's *Harry Potter*.'

Inside the healthcare centre at Frankland, Shipman didn't even get woken up until 7.45am each morning. But he remained on a supervised suicide watch because staff still feared he might try to kill himself. Officially, prison authorities stated that Shipman was shattered by his incarceration, but that's not the picture painted by other inmates – or the murdering medic himself.

In one outburst to prison officers and other inmates at Frankland, Shipman shouted, 'I am not going to commit suicide because I am going to fight to prove my innocence. I am not a monster. I have given injections to tens of thousands of patients in my 30 years so it is ridiculous to suggest that I would start killing them at the end of my career.'

But physically, Shipman had deteriorated since his

incarceration. At one stage, he wrote his beloved Primrose a poem which seemed to sum up his predicament:

> Despair.
> Those words, 'I'm arresting only you.'
> Despair. Who can help me? Now it's only you.
> Despair. Clang goes the door, I cannot even see you.
> Despair. Wait, waiting, no time passes. Night is as day, waiting, loving you.
> Despair. To let you go at visits. Can you, will you come back?
> Loving you.

Primrose's reply was slightly more business-like: 'I love you very much and I'm not thinking of leaving you …' she wrote. In another letter, she wrote, 'Love you – and the pain you feel is just how I feel. I am coping but that is all. Do not get upset. We have an hour a day.'

Another letter contained the words 'Lust and passion, dull and boring, falling out of love then falling in love again and the happiness, and then true love. I am not sure we have been through all these.'

Primrose was facing up to humiliation in the only way she knew – by ignoring everyone else in the world apart from her beloved Fred. She knew only too well that if her father George had still been alive, he would have been telling her that the day she met Fred Shipman on a bus in Leeds was the start of an inevitable downfall.

Other inmates in Frankland found Shipman devoid of emotion and extremely arrogant. 'He seemed to have no trace of emotion,' explained one prisoner. 'He never even mentioned the women he'd killed by name. The only person he talked about was Kathleen Grundy. The other women were just numbers.'

Shipman told one friend in a letter that a fellow inmate had advised him to treat jail like a foreign country. He wrote, 'You go along with the local customs and it will not impinge on you too much. The problem is getting to know the customs.'

Many recognised that he was heavily reliant on visits from his wife. One said, 'He always made sure he looked his best for her and would change into his own clothes before he went to the visiting hall.'

By the time the police had concluded their secondary investigation in the Shipman case in May 2000, detectives believed he was responsible for an additional 192 deaths, even though many cases were dropped from the statistics because the patients were already suffering from terminal illnesses.

* * *

Over in Shipman's original killing ground of Todmorden, West Yorkshire, local newspaper reporter Pete Devine was undertaking his own investigation into suspicious deaths that had occurred when the GP practised in the town. He identified most of the apparent victims through the deaths column of his own newspaper, the Todmorden *News and Advertiser*.

Those figures seemed to indicate an increase in the number of deaths in the area during Fred Shipman's 'reign', with 401 deaths between 1 March 1974 and 30 September 1975. Fred Shipman had undoubtedly 'honed his skills' as a mass murderer in Todmorden. Despite being a young, relatively inexperienced doctor, he'd signed 22 death certificates, considerably more than any of his colleagues during the 16 months he worked in the town. And when Shipman departed, the death rate dropped again. Local MP Chris McCafferty immediately called for a public inquiry into Shipman's activities in Todmorden.

Meanwhile, Fred Shipman still had not lodged a valid appeal against his conviction. He'd submitted a request for an appeal to Preston Crown Court, but the document – believed to be a handwritten note by Shipman – was not in order. The killer GP had also parted company with his trial solicitor Anne Ball. Shipman struggled to find a new lawyer to represent him. He told friends and family that other members of the legal

profession he approached were coming up with excuses and he
was considering conducting his own defence. The old, defiant
Fred Shipman was never far from the surface.

CHAPTER TWENTY SIX

The Death Toll Rises

In Frankland Prison, Fred Shipman came across another notorious British multiple killer called Roy Archibald Hall. Hall – known in prison circles as 'The Perfect Gentleman' – was allowed to stay in the healthcare wing while visiting a friend who was dying of cancer at the time. 'Fred was kept away from the main prisoners because of the crimes he'd committed,' Hall later told this author.

'I found him very polite and lent him copies of *Country Life* magazine and the staff seemed to like him.' Shipman even told Roy Hall he was desperate to help his wife earn some money so she could survive in the outside world without him. Hall, who had committed a series of brutal murders before being hunted down by the police in the 1960s, found the killer doctor fascinating 'but very guarded'.

But after many hours of conversation, Roy Hall is convinced the GP killed his patients to feel in control of them 'as they passed under his control to death'. Hall explained, 'Fred seemed very cold within. He had few friends. In fact, I'd go as far as to say he was either a freak or insane.'

Before Roy Hall left the hospital wing at Frankland, Fred Shipman struck up a conversation with him about writing his own book. Hall's own memoirs entitled *A Perfect Gentleman* had just been published. Shipman even said he swore his fellow inmates to secrecy whenever they were released because he wanted to 'save up' his life story so that one day he could put pen to paper.

To date, Fred Shipman has not yet come to terms with the crimes he has been jailed for committing, let alone writing a full, honest account of his murderous habits.

It was then announced that the story of Shipman's murderous reign in Hyde was to be made into a £1.5 million TV movie starring 62-year-old British TV actor James Bolam as the good doctor. The film's makers insisted that they would be concentrating on the police investigation into the killings. Filming was due to start in March 2001.

Meanwhile, Greater Manchester Police mounted an investigation to find out who was responsible for tipping Shipman off about their initial enquiries. They believed Shipman initially avoided arrest thanks to his mystery informant keeping him one step ahead of investigators. If they discovered the identity of the mole, that person would face a charge of conspiracy to pervert the course of justice.

And the crimes of Fred Shipman were forcing people across Britain to re-examine the behaviour of their own GPs. One inquiry into the activities of a doctor was triggered after his wife rang ITV's *This Morning* programme to contribute to a discussion about Shipman's crimes. The caller claimed that her husband had deliberately given lethal doses of diamorphine to two female patients. One of the women was understood to have been given 15mg of the drug and the other 20mg. Both died within hours of the injections. The show – hosted by well-known British TV personalities Judy Finnigan and Richard Madeley – did not broadcast her call, which was made without her husband's knowledge. But her comments led the programme makers to inform police.

It eventually emerged that the case had already been

investigated by the General Medical Council, the British medical profession's regulatory body. The doctor was understood to live in South Yorkshire, near Shipman's old killing ground of Todmorden. He had at one time more than 2,500 patients on his list and had been allowed to continue to practise after 350 patients signed a petition supporting him. There was no doubting the shades of Shipman in the case. Police immediately contacted the local medical authorities seeking details of his past. The officer in charge of the case, Detective Chief Superintendent Mick Burdis of South Yorkshire Police, said, 'It is early days regarding any inquiry. We have not received any formal allegations.' But there was a feeling throughout Britain that there might be quite a few other potential 'Doctor Shipmans' across the nation.

And the fall-out from Fred Shipman's murderous activities continued. A row broke out between the two most senior bodies of Britain's medical profession – the British Medical Association and the General Medical Council. The dispute was sparked by attempts to restore public confidence in doctors in the wake of Shipman's conviction.

A MORI opinion poll, commissioned by the BMA, reported that 89 per cent of the public still regarded doctors as the most trustworthy of professions. But the GMC was completely contradicting this by working on a set of proposals for improving self-regulation of the profession.

In Todmorden, Yorkshire, local reporter Pete Devine continued to dig up more and more suspicious deaths connected to Fred Shipman's stay in the area. On 16 June 2000, the situation came to a head when he hosted a meeting at a Todmorden hall to talk to worried relatives. Devine told them how his three-month investigation had uncovered some 'worrying statistics'.

Local politicians demanded that more than 100 mystery deaths which had occurred during Fred Shipman's stay in the town should be re-examined. West Yorkshire Police had already confirmed that they were looking at 22 death certificates signed by Shipman.

Many wanted Shipman to end the uncertainty of countless relatives by making a full confession. But Fred Shipman still had no intention of admitting his crimes. 'Under these circumstances, we may never know the full extent of his actions, but it is important that every lead is investigated,' one local politician told the packed Todmorden hall.

One Todmorden patient who nearly died at the hands of Fred Shipman in 1974 came forward and revealed her close escape for the first time. Elaine Oswald was by now a professor at Tennessee University in the USA. She revealed that Shipman had told her she had an allergic reaction to a painkiller after injecting her with what is now thought to have been diamorphine. She even admitted she would like to face Shipman once more to ask him why he had tried to kill her. 'I would love to meet him in person, face to face. I am consumed with wanting to know why he tried to kill me. Did I remind him of his dead mother? Was I wearing something which triggered this?'

And Elaine Oswald pointed out that her young age at the time contradicted the assumption that he only killed older patients. 'It makes me wonder how many others there have been. How did he manage to get away with killing so many? He obviously didn't start with older people, judging by what he did to me.'

In June 2000, many of the families of Fred Shipman's victims went to the High Court to try and force Health Secretary Alan Milburn to hold a long-awaited Government inquiry in public. The families of victims also demanded to know why the GP had been allowed to go on killing for so long.

The British press even mounted a legal challenge to a ruling denying them access to the inquiry. Journalists and relatives of the victims wanted the answer to three questions: why were local GPs allowed to stockpile a staggering 13,000mg of diamorphine? How was it possible for Shipman to hoodwink his colleagues, having become a junkie, and then go on a killing spree that would stun the world? And who was responsible for a series of devastating errors that allowed Shipman to go on wiping out innocent victims long after he should have been caught?

The Government capitulated and announced that the inquiry would be held in public, although it would still be some time before it was opened.

It wasn't until six months after Fred Shipman's conviction that the first full-time doctor was appointed to step into Shipman's shoes. Dr Amy Cumming, a GP for 30 years, bravely agreed to take on Fred Shipman's former patients at her premises in nearby Denton. Many were still dazed by Shipman's propensity for murder. Dr Cumming explained, 'It will be an uphill struggle, but I feel I have a responsibility to the people of Hyde. I find it amazing that no other practice has applied to do the same.'

Incredibly, almost a third of Shipman's patients still expressed a reluctance to move. Dr Cumming had known Fred Shipman well, but was surprised by the patients' loyalty to the jailed medic. She later recalled, 'Like many, I believed he was innocent. I couldn't believe he would be capable of killing. But gradually, as the evidence in his trial came out, it became obvious. The number of people dying in his surgery was extraordinary, as were his methods of disposal [of the bodies].'

Dr Cumming added, 'If a doctor works in an isolated environment, nobody questions his or her work. People come in to do audits, but they tend to trust what you, the doctor, say – partly because its so hard to cross-check the facts.'

But Dr Cumming did encounter some patients who were not so keen on Fred Shipman. 'I had a young woman in my surgery the other day who did one day's work experience with Shipman when she was a teenager. Someone died in the surgery that very day. She was traumatised. It put her off being a doctor for life … Several of Shipman's former patients have told me they feel glad to be alive. They say, "I'm lucky to have got away."'

Coming bruisingly close to death has made many of his patients anxious at the thought of seeing a new doctor. One or two have said, 'I think my aunt/mother/sister was helped on her way by Shipman, but I won't take it up with the police as I don't want to re-open old wounds.'

In the middle of August 2000, coroner Dr John Pollard ruled that Mrs Sarah Ashworth had been unlawfully killed, although he was prevented by law from specifically naming Fred Shipman as her murderer. Pollard told the court that there were striking similarities between Mrs Ashworth's sudden death and those of the 15 other women he was earlier convicted of killing. He also said it would be 'an affront to common sense' to seek to explain them as mere coincidence.

Weeks later, coroner Pollard was re-assessing his verdict on yet another of Shipman's alleged victims. He labelled the death of 77-year-old Nellie Mullen as an unlawful killing after hearing how she'd died during a visit by Shipman to her bungalow in Lanegate, Hyde, on 2 May 1993. The GP had recorded on her cremation certificate that she died two hours *after* a witness said he had found Mrs Mullen dead. Shipman had also told Mrs Mullen's niece, Patricia Rooke, that her aunt had died even later in the day, while he waited for an ambulance.

The inquest also heard that Shipman's notes gave the cause of death as coronary thrombosis, yet this was incompatible with the state in which her body was found. Specialist GP Dr John Grenville said he would have expected such a patient to have suffered pain and distress and be lying down when she died. But yet again one of Shipman's patients had been found sitting upright in her chair, dressed to go out and with a peaceful expression on her face. It backed the suggestion that all Shipman really wanted to do was ensure that his patients died a 'happy death'.

As Dr Grenville later stated, 'None of it rings true. It's like throwing six lots of sixes on a dice. It may happen once, but if it happens twice you suspect the dice is loaded. If it happens 192 times you can bet your life it's loaded.'

Experts trying to analyse Fred Shipman's murderous ways were now privately admitting there could be close to 400 victims. They concluded that Britain's worst ever serial killer mainly went about his business in the afternoon. For reasons still only known to himself, Fred Shipman appeared to prefer administering lethal injections after a light lunch prepared by the ever-loyal Primrose.

This macabre twist was one of the most baffling but inescapable conclusions from an official report published into the true scale of Shipman's career of murder in January 2001. The report – commissioned by the Department of Health – struggled to put a definitive figure on the total number of Shipman victims, and it did not have the detail that would be expected of the public inquiry. Report Chairman Professor Richard Baker of Leicester University said there were 236 deaths among patients that were directly suspicious, but added that the true death toll could be as high as 345. His analysis showed that more than half the patients who died under Shipman's supervision were recorded by the GP as dying of heart failure or old age. They may all have been murdered.

Liam Donaldson, Britain's Chief Medical Officer, said it was 'inexplicable' that Shipman could have murdered for so long without being caught. He said part of the Baker report portrayed a cycle of 'death in the afternoon' with 55 per cent of Shipman's patients dying between 1.00pm and 7.00pm – most of them between 2.00pm and 4.30pm – compared with 25 per cent of other GPs.

Families of some of Shipman's numerous victims met with Professor Baker when he briefed them at Dukinfield Town Hall, near Hyde. There was criticism that Shipman himself did not give evidence to the Baker inquiry. Some believed that the doctor would have agreed to help the inquiry but he was never asked. MPs were particularly interested in how Shipman had managed to obtain such large quantities of controlled drugs.

The Baker Report itself concluded the following:

- Shipman issued in excess of 297 death certificates.
- There were 236 more deaths in the homes of Shipman patients than would be expected.
- Highest death rates were among female patients aged between 64 and 75, but also among older men.

- There were excess deaths from the beginning of Shipman's career, but they did not occur every year.
- Shipman was more likely, and relatives and carers were less likely, to be present when patients died.

The report concluded, 'There is convincing evidence that the observed numbers of deaths among Shipman's patients was in excess of what would have been expected.'

A total of 166 deaths were described as 'highly suspicious' and 43 were described as 'moderately suspicious'.

Professor Baker explained, 'I am conscious that these findings are going to be distressing to the families of the victims of Shipman, but I hope that understanding the facts will be useful in coming to terms with what has happened.' Baker said he felt rage about the way Shipman had 'abused the trust of the people who depended on him completely'.

A newspaper headline on the same day summed it all up: DOCTOR SHIPMAN 'MURDERED 265' OF HIS PATIENTS. Now the only certainty about the figures being released was that they would continue to rise.

Health Minister John Hutton promised that a public tribunal following on from the *Baker Report* would look carefully at the issue of controlled drugs. Hutton even promised a closed circuit TV link to Hyde Town Hall so that residents could keep in touch with the hearings.

However, no actual date was given for the inquiry, although it was announced that the Chairman, High Court Judge Dame Janet Smith, would be based in offices next to Manchester's Piccadilly Station, and Manchester Town Hall would be used for the witness hearings.

But many still believed it was all a matter of too much, too late.

CHAPTER TWENTY SEVEN

Establishing Fact
from Fiction

Fred Shipman spent his fifty-fifth birthday – 14 January 2001 – behind bars in Frankland Prison. With police enquiries continuing, he found himself still regularly receiving visits from investigators armed with an obligatory tape recorder hoping he'd decide to capitulate and face up to the enormity of his crimes. But Shipman said nothing each time and referred them to his lawyer.

Much of Shipman's time by now was occupied with writing letters to his family and a select band of friends who'd remained in contact with him since his trial. On the surface, his mood never seemed to alter. He was often seen holding Primrose's hand in the visiting room, whispering instructions to her. One prison visitor later explained, 'She seemed to listen avidly to his every word. She just kept nodding her head in agreement. She didn't seem to say much back to him.'

Shipman continued claiming that he was planning to write a book, but since that would involve confessing or, at the very least, explaining why he'd committed his crimes, it seemed unlikely he would ever really put pen to paper. [Repeated written requests to

Fred Shipman to co-operate with this author have gone unanswered.]

Greater Manchester Police then announced they'd opened investigations into the deaths of a further 62 of Shipman's patients. This was in addition to the 192 cases they had already examined.

And, not surprisingly, many of Britain's sensation-seeking tabloids soon got word of the ever-rising toll. The London *Evening Standard* claimed: SHIPMAN'S DEATH TOLL COULD BE AS HIGH AS 345.

In Manchester, police drew up a list of 13 'characteristics' describing Fred Shipman's so-called technique which might help worried relatives conclude if their loved ones could be among his numerous victims. They were:

- She was of a certain age.
- She was a widow or living alone.
- She died in the afternoon.
- She died at home.
- She complained of minor ailments before her death.
- She saw Shipman on the day of her death.
- Shipman asserted he had telephoned for an ambulance.
- Her door was open or 'on the latch'.
- Her body was found upright in a chair or on a settee.
- The victim looked peaceful or appeared to be asleep.
- She died wearing normal day clothes.
- Shipman made no attempt at physical examination of the dead woman.
- Shipman informed relatives that no post mortem was necessary.

Back in prison, Fred Shipman has even become addicted to many of the anti-depressants prescribed to him before and during his trial. 'It's as if he's replaced his addiction to killing and pethidine with something else,' says one ex-inmate.

And one visitor to Frankland Jail in the summer of 2001 said, 'It's easy to see when Shipman is doped up because he shuffles around the place mumbling to himself. Some of the other inmates are furious that he's been given so many drugs as they consider it a form of escape which none of them are allowed.'

Back in Manchester, police have sworn to continue trying to establish the identity of Shipman's 'deep throat' who enabled the GP to stay one step ahead of investigators for months before he was finally arrested. 'This person must be held responsible, as at least three of Shipman's victims would not have died if he had been arrested earlier,' said a Greater Manchester Police spokesman.

* * *

Inevitably, Fred Shipman's notoriety led to him joining Jack the Ripper and Adolf Hitler in a TV advert aimed at turning teenagers off smoking. The 30-second ad was screened on Britain's National No Smoking Day, 14 March 2001, for the Cancer Research Campaign and was written by 12-year-olds. It's tag line included a pile of cigarette ends and the slogan 'The Biggest Serial Killer of All'. Six boys from the independent City of London School came up with the idea which beat 2,500 other entries in a national competition.

And police finally conceded they were investigating every single death certificate signed by Fred Shipman in Todmorden. A West Yorkshire Police spokesman said, 'Following publication of Professor Baker's report, and continued media speculation, West Yorkshire Police is widening its investigation to include all 22 patients' deaths certified by Shipman during his time in Todmorden. West Yorkshire officers will continue to work closely with officers from Greater Manchester Police. This process is likely to take some time.'

Then an inquest into yet another Fred Shipman victim heard how he had certified the death of a patient he had not seen for two months. Shipman was called to the home of Mabel Shawcross in Stockport Road, Hyde, on 22 January 1998, by police who had found her dead after being alerted by neighbours. Police Constable Stephen Broadbent found the 79-year-old spinster sitting bolt upright in a chair, but when Shipman arrived on the scene he insisted he had not seen her for 'a couple of months'. Then Shipman said he could certify the death and recorded that Miss Shawcross had died of a stroke.

A few days later, another new inquest into an alleged Fred Shipman victim heard how he'd once more been callous when dealing with the relatives of a patient who had died in his surgery. Widow Bertha Moss, of Newton Hall Court, Hyde, died in the doctor's treatment room during a check-up in June 1995. Her daughter Ann Whelan told the coroner's court that Shipman said her mother had suffered a heart-attack while his back was turned.

When she asked him why the relatively fit 68-year-old had died so suddenly, he replied, 'If her heart hadn't killed her, she would have had to have her legs chopped off because of her diabetes. She would not have wanted to spend the rest of her life in a wheelchair and be a burden.'

Mrs Whelan was upset by the GP's comments but did not have the courage to question Shipman. 'It was like he was shouting at me,' she later recalled. 'Like he thought I was stupid. I was very intimidated by him.'

Shipman later noted on Mrs Moss's cremation certificate that practice staff were present when she died. But former surgery receptionist Jane Kenyon – who was alone on duty that day – told the court she was not aware of what had happened and Shipman never spoke to her about Mrs Moss's death. Coroner John Pollard recorded his twelfth unlawful killing verdict following inquests into the deaths of suspected Shipman victims since his trial.

Then the daughter of one of Shipman's victims announced that she was planning to sue the police after their initial, bungled investigation had enabled the GP to continue killing patients. Kathleen Adamski was the daughter of Winifred Mellor, one of at least three people killed by Shipman after the police abandoned their initial investigation into the doctor's activities.

She planned to seek substantial compensation if she could

prove that she suffered post-traumatic stress as a result of discovering that her mother's death could have been avoided if the police had arrested Shipman earlier. Mrs Adamski explained, 'I am sick of the whole notion that doctors are untouchable. There have been many cases where the doctor has had previous problems, and Shipman had a previous drugs conviction. Who else has this tremendous protection of reputation? Police officers can't have criminal records and teachers are rigorously checked, too. There are bad apples in every profession, including medicine. Now I am very, very angry. From what I have been told, it seems the police did not want to upset anybody because it was such a sensitive issue. But we are talking about people dying unnecessarily. I think the police should have rigorously investigated it.'

Greater Manchester Police responded, 'We are entirely sympathetic to all the families involved in this case, particularly at this time.' There really was little else they could say.

A few days later, Kathleen Adamski announced she'd changed her mind about suing the police. She decided that she wished to grieve in private and stopped her plan for action against Greater Manchester Police. But the fact remained that she had highlighted a situation that still needed to be properly answered.

Then it also emerged for the first time that a man who survived Shipman's attempts to kill him could also receive a six-figure compensation award. Derek Webb, 58, suffered brain damage when the GP suddenly doubled the medication he was receiving to control epilepsy. Now, after ten years of legal wrangling and the rejection of an out-of-court settlement worth tens of thousands of pounds, Mr Webb's family were at last on the verge of a full settlement.

Meanwhile, yet another inquest into one of Shipman's new victims heard how pensioner Mary Wall, 78, had been playing energetically with her grandchildren the day before she died during a visit by Shipman, who'd recorded her death as coronary thrombosis. Coroner John Pollard concluded that Shipman's version of events was 'extremely unlikely' after hearing how the

GP had called the victim's niece Elizabeth Lomas to say that her aunt had died. Lomas then went straight to the widow's house in Werneth Avenue, Gee Cross, near Hyde, where she was greeted by Shipman.

Inside the house, Mary Wall was still sitting in her favourite armchair, fully clothed and 'looking very peaceful – as if she had fallen asleep'.

Shipman told Lomas that Mrs Wall had been unconscious when he arrived. But later, Mrs Wall's daughter Eileen Morris said that Shipman told her a different account. Shipman had informed her that Mrs Wall had told Shipman where to find her phone book in order to contact relatives after he had arrived at her house to find her 'in shock'. Both women said it was unlikely that, as Shipman had claimed, Mrs Wall had left her front door unlocked so he could walk in.

Coroner Pollard concluded that, beyond reasonable doubt, Mrs Wall had been unlawfully killed by Shipman.

By this time – early spring 2001 – some of the relatives of Shipman's victims were pressing harder for compensation. Criminal Injuries Compensation Board Chief Executive Howard Webber and members of his team even held a special meeting in Dukinfield Town Hall to talk to family members and answer questions. The meeting had been organised by the Victim Support Group and solicitors Alexander Harris, who represented many relatives of victims and suspected victims. Solicitor Ann Alexander said at the time, 'We are delighted the Board's Chief Executive has agreed to attend. Compensation has never been an important issue for many of the relatives but it is important for those who believe Shipman may have murdered their loved ones to understand the compensation system.'

Ironically, the CICB soon received dozens of fraudulent claims made on behalf of supposed Shipman victims. One Victim Support source later explained, 'We couldn't believe it at first, but people were reading about the Board's compensation offer and sending in claims that they were related to Shipman victims when they didn't have any connection with them.'

In the second week of March 2001, there was a predictable outcry from the respectable citizens of Hyde when it was revealed that shooting of the TV movie about Shipman was taking place on their Hyde streets. Many of his victims' families were said to be appalled that the film-makers had hired Shipman's actual Renault Espace van which had became so famous thanks to the one piece of TV news footage of the GP leaving his house shortly after the police investigation was finally made public.

Soon, the people of Hyde were lining up to take a swipe at the TV film. Jane Ashton-Hibbert, whose grandmother was one of Shipman's victims, told her local newspaper, 'It's just too soon. He was only convicted last year and the wounds are still raw. There are many relatives of victims here who would have a heart-attack if they saw James Bolam [the actor playing Shipman in the movie] walking down the street looking the spitting image of Shipman. Also, it would be very macabre to see him driving past in the car as he did on his way to kill.'

Veteran British actor James Bolam, 62, was slated to play the good doctor, but Tameside Metropolitan Borough Council sought advice from the Broadcasting Standards Commission to see if they could do anything to stop the project. But there seemed little chance that the film would be delayed, let alone cancelled. 'This is a matter of record and it's a case that has fascinated the world. People want to know more about Shipman,' was the justification.

Leaders of the local Tameside Council flatly refused to help the programme's makers. They explained, 'It was felt filming of this nature would be very distressing for local people.' It then emerged that the producers of the Shipman movie were under so much pressure from local people that they'd switched many of the locations to a similar-looking town called Ossett, in Yorkshire, to avoid any embarrassing scenes with angry Hyde residents.

Meanwhile, chilling 20-year-old footage of Fred Shipman talking about caring for patients in the community instead of hospitalising them was broadcast. The archive film was shot in 1982 at a time when the GP had already amassed up to 35 victims. Interviewed at the desk of his surgery in Hyde, Shipman seemed enthusiastic about a new type of treatment for the mentally ill. The film had been shot for the *World in Action* current affairs programme and had been first screened almost 20 years earlier when Fred Shipman was regarded as a deeply caring and widely respected doctor. This time, the footage was shown on *Tonight with Trevor McDonald*. Shipman even talked about the need to 'break down the barriers' between doctor and patient.

Police investigator DCS Bernard Postles said of Shipman's TV performance, 'Anybody who has met him will see that he is a very confident individual, very able to put together a story quite coherently.'

Dr John Grenville, who was called as an expert witness during the Shipman trial, told the *Tonight* show, 'He certainly comes across as being very arrogant and I'm sure that the only way that he could get through the trial was to think himself invincible.'

* * *

By the beginning of spring of 2001, more than £700,000 had been paid out to relatives of Fred Shipman's victims, even though each payment did not exceed a £10,000 ceiling. A total of 160 people had made the claims in relation to 70 deaths. At least 120 awards had already been made, while about 30 were still under consideration. Only 12 applications had been rejected, relating to cases which both the police and Crown Prosecution Service had been unable to offer any evidence in support.

And the £10,000 sum handed out to relatives was reduced to £5,000 if more than one family member made a claim. Relatives were also offered an additional award of up to £20,000 for mental injury if they could show they were psychologically scarred by a death, but only a dozen applications of this type were ever made in connection with the Shipman case.

Meanwhile, the Chairman of the newly formed Shipman

Public Inquiry promised to establish just how many victims the former Hyde GP had claimed. Dame Janet Smith wrote to families of suspected victims and told them she would also consider the methods he employed and the period over which the killings took place. She added, 'I will do everything possible to give an indication of whether a patient died from natural or unnatural causes.'

The families of Shipman's numerous victims were promised a video link from the hearing so people in the area could 'keep in touch' with the evidence. Health Minister John Hutton told MPs, 'We owe it to families and friends of victims to implement whatever steps are necessary to prevent a repetition of these terrible crimes.'

In June 2001, Dame Janet Smith's public inquiry finally began hearing evidence at Manchester Town Hall. The day before proceedings got under way, coroner Dr John Pollard called for reforms that would stop any future serial-killing doctor in his tracks. Dr Pollard admitted that the current system was unco-ordinated and provided insufficient safeguards to the public. He conceded that one of the main reasons Shipman got away with murder for so long was because not all deaths had to be reported to the local coroner. Even when they were, there was no centralised system that might identify emerging criminal patterns. Pollard said that a single organisation should be set up for all aspects of the investigation and registration of deaths throughout England and Wales.

The new service would be headed by a legally-qualified coroner and two deputies. In each area, these officials would receive reports from registrars plus a number of full- and part-time medical referees. Pollard explained, 'For the future, not only would it be much more likely that all deaths requiring further investigation would receive the attention they require, but also the system could be interrogated to spot unusual patterns.'

If the proposals went ahead, then the deceased's doctor would be required to provide a medical history and it would no longer be legally possible for him or her to issue a death certificate without having examined the deceased in a post mortem. As one coroner said, 'A very admirable list of recommendations. But in the case of more than 400 Shipman victims, it is all a little late ...'

* * *

But Fred Shipman's residence at Frankland Prison, in County Durham, was far from comfortable. At one stage, during the early summer of 2001, he was attacked by another prisoner inside the jail's hospital wing.

One visitor to the hospital wing later explained, 'Shipman upset a couple of the tougher inmates by refusing to talk to them when they tried to strike up a conversation with him. These two fellows got well narked and one of them pulled a shank on him one evening as he was coming out of the toilets.'

Luckily for Shipman, the attack was spotted on closed circuit TV and three prison guards overpowered the assailant within seconds. A shaken Shipman was kept locked up in his cell alongside the hospital wing for the following 48 hours until things had cooled down.

Being the Good Doctor who once thrived on playing at being God didn't help when it came to life inside prison.

* * *

In the early summer of 2001, investigators from the Shipman public inquiry headed by Dame Janet Smith secretly interviewed Susan and Mark Orlinski about the death of their one-day-old baby son Christian in Todmorden in 1974.

'Shipman killed my baby and my husband and I have waited a long time to hear the truth about what really happened,' explained Mrs Orlinski. The Orlinskis are now considering suing the local health authority for negligence because Shipman was injecting himself with pethidine at the time her baby died. 'It's scandalous that he was allowed to work in such a shocking condition.'

Back on 5 August 1974, Shipman filled in a death certificate for the baby stating Christian had died of 'sudden death infancy syndrome' without even bothering to return to examine the body.

'He just lied,' says Mrs Orlinski. 'My baby died because Shipman didn't bother to get him checked over when he was born prematurely. He simply left him to die. Everyone goes on about how Shipman only killed old people, but that is nonsense. He's responsible for what happened to Christian. You can call it murder or neglect, but it boils down to the same thing – he would not have died if Shipman had done his job properly.'

Mrs Orlinksi and her husband Mark were astonished when officials from the Manchester-based public inquiry into the Shipman killings contacted the family to say they were investigating the circumstances surrounding little Christian's death. 'We were really surprised because we thought they'd never bother to go back that far, but it seems that Shipman was killing other patients even back then,' explained Mrs Orlinksi.

Mrs Orlinski remains furious that Shipman was not made to step down as a doctor after his drug addiction was uncovered by colleagues at the Todmorden practice a year after baby Christian's death. 'How could they have let him carry on as a doctor? It's disgraceful and someone has to take responsibility. He should never have been allowed to practise.'

The inquiry team even brought a midwife with them to talk Mr and Mrs Orlinski through the precise details of the day their baby died. 'It was very painful, but I was glad that at last someone was taking some notice. And the midwife agreed that Shipman was at least guilty of neglect.'

'This whole Shipman business stinks. Why was he allowed to get away with it for so long? If someone had bothered to come and see us at the time perhaps we would have been able to stop him in his tracks and all these hundreds of other people would not have been murdered.'

Mrs Orlinski's words once again highlighted the errors that allowed Fred Shipman to turn into a killing machine.

CHAPTER TWENTY EIGHT

Struggling On – The Living Victims

These days, Primrose Shipman does her shopping on a Sunday when the supermarket tends to be quieter. That means there's less chance of her or her children being recognised. And for that same reason, Primrose hasn't been on a bus for two years. It's all part of her legacy as the wife of mass murderer Fred Shipman.

Primrose's life since her husband was exposed to the world as one of Britain's most prolific serial killers of all time has been changed for ever. But what she and her four children do not yet truly know is how long it will take for the finger-pointing and sly remarks to stop.

The victims of Fred Shipman extend well beyond those he actually killed. They include, of course, the families of his victims, but often forgotten are the families who have to live with the shocking fact that one of their number has joined a select criminal roll-call of infamy. Fred Shipman was responsible for more than 400 murders. The home where he escaped the pressures and guilt of his life as a doctor is now owned by another family. But in the community where the Shipmans lived,

Primrose has lost many of her friends. They've stopped calling her at her new home close to the prison where her husband resides. She is no doubt feeling lonely and she must surely sometimes feel like shouting, 'This has nothing to do with me.' But, for the moment, her loyalty to Fred Shipman remains intact. As one friend explains, 'All they've got is each other and there's no way Primrose is going to let go after all they've been through together.'

Following Fred Shipman's trial and its worldwide coverage, Primrose called up many of her friends and associates to tell them that she still believed her husband was innocent. In the small community of Whitby, Yorkshire, where she now lives, Primrose has long since learned to harden herself against outright abuse from some quarters, including passers-by. Although it has to be said that, on a few occasions, she has beaten a hasty retreat from a local shop when confronted by an angry crowd.

Primrose also receives at least ten anonymous letters a week, including the classic threatening paste-and-scissors notes using the print from newspaper headlines. 'It's not so much what they say that disturbs Primrose,' says one old Shipman family friend. 'It's the fact that someone bothered; someone disliked her husband so much that they would cut up these newspapers.'

Ever since Primrose bought the house in Whitby she's kept a very discreet distance between herself and her new neighbours. She has virtually no contact with anyone in the community. She thinks that many have already made up their minds as to what sort of person she is.

On a personal level, Primrose has recommenced one of Fred Shipman's closest relationships with former Market Street surgery manager John Gilmore. He has become very close to Primrose and has spent many evenings at the Shipman house in Whitby talking to her. Staff at Frankland Prison have even spotted Gilmore dropping Primrose at the gates before she visits her husband. Many even speculated that the couple might be having a relationship, but one of Primrose's friends pointed out, 'That's highly unlikely. Primrose is still devoted to Fred and would never do anything to hurt him.'

Shipman's Hyde GP Dr Wally Ashworth explained, 'John Gilmore and Fred Shipman were very close when they worked together and Gilmore refused to believe that Shipman had committed any murders, even after his conviction. I'm not surprised that he is still closely involved with the Shipman family.'

John Gilmore also agreed an out-of-court settlement with the local health authority after claiming unfair dismissal from Shipman's surgery and four other single-handed practices in the Hyde area between 1994–98 while managing their funds. Gilmore had been responsible for the GP's drug budgets while becoming one of the Shipmans' closest personal friends, staying at the family home even after the GP's arrest.

Today, two years after the trial's worldwide banner headlines and global TV coverage, Primrose remains incredibly cautious about meeting new people. One of her few long-standing friends says that Primrose is determined to fight on and one day hopes to clear her husband's name. She refuses even to concede that he might be guilty of anything more than simply being a good doctor.

The Shipman children – Sarah, now 32, who works in a ticket agency; Christopher, 28, who is an engineer; 20-year-old university student David; and Sam, 18, at agricultural college – will no doubt also be haunted by their father's evil deeds for the rest of their lives. But as Stephen West, son of serial-killing couple Fred and Rosemary West, recently explained, 'The first thing you have to remember is that there's nothing you could have done to prevent it. You have a life that's as precious as anyone else's; you have to think you're number one, because no one else will think it of you.

'You can't forget about what happened, and if you try you will end up damaging yourself. I have spent a time each week when I have five minutes to myself just thinking about what happened. It makes you understand a little bit more each time.'

Stephen West is, for the most part, remarkably well focused

when he talks about his situation. He becomes less so, and is clearly emotional, when he addresses his feelings for his parents, the parents who killed so many innocent people. 'I believe you can still love a person – your mum or dad – as detached from what they have done, but they are your parents, and it's so difficult to let go.'

'People say to me, "How can you still love them?" There's a fine line between love and hate anyway, and people shouldn't judge 'til they have had to live with something like this. You can't make yourself hate someone. If I have anything to thank my parents for, it's that I'm healthy and I'm alive. The Shipman family should know that things will get better.'

Primrose and her children have seen their figurehead in the dock for mass murder. They've seen Fred Shipman taken off to prison, and yet they've continued wholeheartedly to back his plea of innocence. Even when the jury found him guilty, they refused to condemn him. They all saw him within 24 hours of that guilty verdict and told him they would support him until their dying day.

There will not be a day in their lives when they won't be hit by the magnitude of what has happened. The Shipman family's image to the outside world is one of solidarity in the face of irrefutable facts. They have all become tougher and more cynical as a result of Fred Shipman's conviction but then that is how they survive. No doubt, some of the Shipman children must have wondered if they have inherited from their father any of his genetic predisposition to murder. But experts say there is no point in lingering on such thoughts.

Stephen West believes the Shipman children simply have to try to live as normally as they can, however hard that might be. He says, 'I enjoy my job, and take a lot of pride in my work. Everyone needs something, whether or not they're the son or daughter of a mass murderer. And people won't appreciate you for stopping working. And they won't forgive you, either. This kind of thing will never go away – but it can make you a stronger person.'

Meanwhile, Primrose Shipman had even, admirably,

volunteered to help care for the vulnerable elderly and disabled residents of a care home 15 miles from her own house in Whitby, Yorkshire. She happily cooked, cleaned, shopped and even washed patients as part of her regular duties. But behind her decision to help those less fortunate than herself was an attempt to mend her broken relationship with her elderly mother and sister.

Primrose's sister Mary, who suffered from severe multiple sclerosis, was amongst the 50 residents of the home. Few people at the establishment and none of her neighbours in Whitby had any idea that Primrose was working there. Most mornings she'd leave the family home at 7.30am and spend the entire day at the centre.

Psychologists warn that Fred Shipman's crimes will have an everlasting effect on his wife and children. Some believe the children will be unlikely ever to fully recover from their father's betrayal and could even turn on Primrose as they try to make sense of his horrific double life. Consultant forensic psychologist Ian Stephen believes that Primrose, having married Shipman as a pregnant teenager and having relied on him totally for the previous 32 years, will be feeling utterly alone for the first time in her life and might see suicide as the only way out.

'She has lost the whole focus of her life,' he explained. Stephen believes that Primrose's weight problems could well be a sign of long-standing depression. Her composed exterior, as she posed for photographers on the day after her husband's sentencing, was a typical sign of emotional shut-down. Now she must try to build a life for herself in the outside world while still clinging to her all-powerful husband – a doctor who took the lives of more than 400 patients.

CHAPTER TWENTY NINE

Too Little
Too Late

In May 2002, police apologised to the families of Shipman's victims after it was disclosed that their 'flawed' investigation had initially cleared the GP of any wrongdoing. This was revealed during the second phase of Dame Janet Smith's public inquiry into the Shipman case, although it did little to quell the anger of those still furious about the earlier police inquiry.

In the middle of May, cameras began filming for the first time at the public inquiry although Dame Janet was prepared to allow recorded excerpts only. Her goal remained to try and find out how many people actually died and how Shipman had escaped undetected for so long. Meanwhile Shipman continued to refuse to leave his cell at Frankland Prison, near Durham, to give evidence to the inquiry.

The screening of 'Shipman' – the TV film about the case – in July 2002 no doubt extended the grief for the relatives of his victims. The programme, starring Likely Lads actor James Bolam as Shipman, reminded millions of viewers about the course of events which had culminated two years earlier with the sentencing of the doctor to 15 life sentences.

Many remained highly critical of the film because it didn't really highlight the failure of the medical profession to halt Shipman's obvious inclination to flout the rules.

However TV critic Peter Paterson insisted in the Daily Mail, 'This was an honest and interesting piece of work, but in all likelihood only marks the starting point for a minor industry that will keep dramatists and documentary makers busy for years to come.'

Tony Blair expressed sympathy for the relatives when he was challenged about the screening of the Shipman film at Prime Minister's Questions. New stringent checks had already been introduced with regard to the signing of death certificates and Health Secretary Alan Milburn promised to introduce changes to the law, which would require all GPs to submit their criminal records to primary care authorities. They'd also be required to report all deaths in surgery.

A few days later, Dame Janet Smith presented stage two of her report on the Shipman killings to the world by saying, 'He betrayed patients' trust in a way and to an extent that is unparelled in history. He has caused unimaginable grief and distress.' Dame Janet also asked in her report, 'What kind of man works hard to become a doctor, takes the Hippocratic oath and, within only a few years, embarks on a career of killing his patients?'

The 2,000-page, two-volume report made grim reading as it outlined every single death, but Dame Janet found space to pay tribute to the 'heart-warming' conduct of the ordinary people of Hyde and Todmorden whose relatives became Shipman's victims.

According to the inquiry psychiatrists, Shipman may have wanted to be caught when he forged the will. It explained, 'Shipman might have had mixed subconscious motivations in forging the will. He might have felt an overwhelming need to stop killing. He might have been, as it were, "throwing himself to the gods". Either his plan would succeed and he would leave Hyde and run away with the money or he would be caught. Either way the killing would be stopped.'

In her report, Dame Janet also painted a picture of a typical killing by the GP. 'Shipman would visit an elderly patient, usually one who lives alone. He would make a routine visit, for example, to take a blood sample or to provide repeat prescriptions, sometimes he would make an unsolicited call. During the visit he would kill the patient – afterwards he would have a variety of explanations for what had happened.'

Dame Janet also commented in her report that 'psychiatrists think it is possible that the fact and circumstances of his mother's death might have had a profound effect on his psyche.' But because Shipman never confessed, the report admitted that his personality remained beyond the bounds of understanding.

The end of the latest stage of the public inquiry sparked yet another torrent of front page stories about the case. It seemed an excuse for the media to rake over the stories of the victims once again. The Times even ran a front page map of Hyde covered in black dots where Shipman's victims died. It made chilling viewing and seemed to hammer home the sheer scale of the crimes he'd committed. The Times also re-visited the so-called 'Street of Death' – Garden Street, in Hyde – where Shipman murdered at least six patients.

By this time – the summer of 2002 – there were few if any clues to identify this leafy street as the place where the mass murderer went about his business. Only the occasional appearance of a TV crew sizing up properties for the best creative shot could be linked to the past. A new generation of young families now occupied most of the 34 miners cottages and none of the adults would agree to discuss what had happened in their homes. But one older resident Mrs Ellen Middleton did tell one reporter, 'They call it Death Street but they should call it Sad Street.'

In late September, 2002, it was revealed that Shipman bragged to one fellow prison inmate that he used his 'power' to kill for all those undetected years. Prisoner Jon Harkin was assigned to be a 'listener' to Shipman when he was in custody in Preston Prison soon after his 1998 arrest. Harkin claimed in one newspaper that Shipman put the number of his victims at 508 rather that the 215 confirmed kills quoted in Dame Janet Smith's second report.

Harkin said, 'When I first met Shipman he was just a guy in glasses, sat facing the wall crying. There was a suicide watch on him. I was put in the cell with him for extra protection – so he wasn't going to swing. But his moods were always changing – highs and lows. It all depended on who he had seen that day.'

Harkin continued, 'He looked proud of himself as he said he'd been doing it for the last 25 years – since his days in Todmorden. I said, "Doing what?" And he replied, "Acts of God." He told me he had got away with it. I said, 'But you haven't.' Yet it was as if I wasn't there. He was laughing at the police and medical profession.'

In May 2003, Shipman once again hit the headlines when it was revealed that he'd been carrying out hospital 'work' with the elderly at Frankland top security jail. One source was quoted as saying, 'It's like putting a paedophile in a children's ward.'

Shipman's disturbing new prison duties came to light after he was permanently transferred to the healthcare centre at Frankland. There he was allowed to wheel patients from room to room, help them back to bed and even serve them food.

After being exposed in the Daily Mirror, worried prison staff described Shipman's duties as 'highly irregular' and 'totally wrong'. MP Phil Woolas, whose constituency Oldham East was part of Shipman's health authority area, said, 'We need to get to the bottom of this – fast. It beggars belief that the world's most notorious mass murderer should be allowed anywhere near sick people, let alone be allowed to work in a hosptial.'

Inside prison, Shipman had grown increasingly arrogant, aloof and sarcastic. He kept mainly to himself and spoke to few of his fellow inmates. On the whole, he steadfastly refused to talk about his crimes and continued to take no responsibility for them.

As a result of the newspaper expose, Shipman was then transferred to Wakefield Prison, in West Yorkshire. With him he took his reputation for being a troublesome prisoner. Staff at Wakefield found him just as aloof and cut off from the other inmates – and he continued complaining every aspect of his life in prison.

In July 2003, a nurse who was asked by Shipman to resuscitate a patient he'd just murdered announced she was suing the former GP and the Health Service for damages. Gillian Morgan, a nurse at Shipman's Hyde surgery, was claiming £100,000 for the stress she'd suffered since the incident.

Back in January 1994, Shipman had asked surgery nurse Morgan to help revive 82-year-old Joan Harding after he had given the patient a lethal injection in his consulting room. He even directed Mrs Morgan to perform cardiac massage whilst he gave her the kiss of life. It wasn't until Dame Janet Smith's second report was published that it could be confirmed that Mrs Harding was one of Shipman's victims. Mrs Morgan recalled, 'Inevitably the "resuscitation" failed and, after an appropriate interval, he called it off and called the ambulance.'

In September 2003, it was revealed that fifteen family doctors were being investigated to find out whether they made proper checks before counter-signing cremation forms for many of Shipman's victims. A spokesman for investigators at the General Medical Council explained, 'The body is determined to root out any GPs who could have acted differently to stop these killings.'

Just before Christmas 2003, Shipman's television was removed from his cell at Wakefield prison as punishment for 'obnoxious behaviour'. He was also barred from wearing his own clothes, received £3 instead of £12.50 a week for pocket money and was locked up 90 minutes earlier than other inmates. The lost priviledges were only restored in early

January, 2004, under the incentives and earned privileges scheme when Shipman appeared before a board and agreed to sign up to a number of educational courses.

Shipman was returned to 'standard' prisoner classification but because of his generally poor behaviour he was never considered for 'enhanced' status, which would have allowed him more access to the gym and playstation. But he was still able to make regular phone calls to Primrose.

The following Monday, 12 January, in one such call to her, Shipman blew a romantic kiss down the phone at Primrose and told her, 'I love you too. Don't forget. I will always look after you.'

It was his final goodbye.

CHAPTER THIRTY

Self Medication

'DOCTOR DEATH HAS THE LAST LAUGH' read the headline, which seemed to sum up the world's reaction to Shipman's last murderous act – the taking of his own life.

Shipman, the ultimate control freak, hung himself in Wakefield Prison on January 13, a day before his 58th birthday and in doing so escaped the long years of punishment which would have seen him imprisoned for the remainder of his life.

His death once again brought fresh anguish for the families of many of his hundreds of victims who had clung onto the hope that one day he might explain why he so cold bloodedly murdered their loves ones.

Shipman's death at a top security jail was the biggest embarrassment for the UK Prison Service since serial killer Fred West committed suicide in his cell on New Years Day 1995.

It soon emerged that Shipman had been planning his 'big farewell' for at least two weeks. Prison staff had become concerned by Shipman's apparent anxiety about sorting out his financial affairs and, in particularly, whether his pension fund would pay out a salary to Primrose. But, despite his obvious stress, Shipman was never officially put on suicide watch.

Shipman, who'd also been working on a fresh appeal against his conviction for the previous few months, had even asked prison managers to allow a prison visit by Primrose on his birthday. But the day before, Shipman waited in bed in his single cell until an officer looked in at 5am – all 27 inmates on the four landings of Wakefield's D-wing were checked every hour.

Once the spy hole in the door to Cell 36 closed, Shipman frantically tore up his bedsheets to make a rope. Then he pushed open the window, tied the sheet to the bars and stepped up on to a heating pipe some feet above the level of the floor.

Before jumping off, Shipman pulled the orange and green curtains around him as an extra precaution against anyone looking in and saving him. The alarm was raised at 6.20am as Shipman was cut down and there were desperate attempts to revive him, but a prison doctor pronounced him dead from strangulation two hours later.

Rumours circulated that Shipman had been recently depressed by threats of sexual violence from other inmates in the showers and the theft of his radio, but the Prison Service insisted there had been no obvious indication he was preparing to kill himself. The *Daily Mirror* reported that Shipman had mentioned suicide on a number of occasions since his arrest.

At her cottage, Primrose stayed locked indoors. Her son Christopher looked furious as he arrived and fought his way through the hoards of journalists before telling them, 'Let me make it very clear, there will be no comment here today.' A brief scuffle then broke out between Christopher and a cameraman. Shortly afterwards, two policemen arrived and entered the property.

Not long afterwards, one of the officers emerged from the cottage to tell newsmen and women, 'Mr Shipman's son and mother will not be making any comment. This is a very upsetting time for them.'

Just after Shipman's suicide, it was also disclosed that probation officer Diane Sanderson had warned of the possibility Shipman might try and take his own life when he was still in Frankland Prison, in Durham. Her report said, 'There have been concerns while Mr Shipman was preparing his appeal, and when there were discussions about the possibility of his pension being forfeited, that he might attempt to take his own life. He has indicated that, should his appeal fail, this is what he might do.'

Again, the question was asked: if these warning signs were so apparent why wasn't something done?

Not surprisingly, relatives of many of Shipman's victims said they felt cheated by his suicide and branded the former GP as 'cowardly and selfish'. Danny Mellor, who's mum Winifred Mellor, 73, was killed in May, 1998, summed up their attitude when he said, 'I have been left feeling cheated. He's responsible for hundreds and hundreds of murders, but has taken the coward's way out. I had always harboured the desire to meet him face to face and ask him why he did it and I think secretly 99 per cent of the other relatives wanted to do the same. But now we will never know why. He has never shown any remorse or even accepted that he'd done it. He never thought of what other people were going through because of his appalling actions. It is a complete coward's way out. We are left with an empty void because of his appalling actions.'

Father Denis Maher, the parish priest at St Paul's Roman Catholic Church in Hyde, was surprised at the news of Shipman's death. 'From what I knew of Harold Shipman, his character, his bearing and his arrogance, I would never, ever have thought he would actually commit suicide. It was the furthest thing from my mind. But when I sat down and reflected further on it I can now understand it a bit more. After all, committing suicide is the ultimate act of selfishness.'

Detective Superintendent Graham Shaw, of West Yorkshire police, launched an investigation into Shipman's death. A report was due to eventually be made to the West Yorkshire coroner, David Hinchcliff, who was conducting an official inquest.

But perhaps the biggest question surrounding Shipman's death was his motive. Within days of his suicide, reports began emerging that Shipman had killed himself in order to guarantee his wife Primrose a generous pension. The Department of Health confirmed she would receive a lump sum and a widow's pension. But it could not confirm whether she would have been entitled to this if Shipman had lived longer. The amounts involved were said to be a lump sum of £100,000 and an annual pension of £10,000.

Nearly a week after Shipman's death, Primrose was given a chance to bid farewell to her husband by visiting the mortuary where his body was being stored. Primrose emerged from her cottage in County Durham with her eldest son Christopher to join two police officers for the 53-mile drive to the mortuary at the Medio-Legal Centre, in Sheffield. It was the first time Primrose had left the property since Shipman's death. One of her neighbours voiced a hint of sympathy for her when he told reporters, 'Harold Shipman fooled a lot of people and maybe that included her,' said Geoff Sharp. 'He's done all these terrible things and now he's killed himself and left the family to live with it.'

Shortly after viewing her husband's body in that mortuary in Sheffield, Primrose was questioned by West Yorkshire detectives about the six-minute phone call she received from Shipman at 8pm the night before he killed himself.

Meanwhile outside her cottage, a florist delivered two bunches of flowers and handed them to another son, David, before he closed and locked the door. At Wakefield Prison, Stephen Shaw, the prison and probation ombudsman, began his independent inquiry into the death of Shipman by meeting the governor and talking to staff.

No date had yet been set for an inquest and the coroner's office said that the body would not be released until a hearing was formally opened. Only then could a proper funeral be held. And Shipman's recently appointed high profile lawyer Giovanni di Stefano announced he was abandoning the ex-GP's appeal against his conviction. The lawyer commented, 'This stinks to high heaven. They could and should have prevented his death. He wasn't getting letters and had no one to relate to. That can do your mind in. I think he said to himself, "What's the point of living if I've got to live like this?"'

Once again, Tony Blair was obliged to talk about Shipman during Prime Minister's questions when he promised MPs they would have a proper opportunity to debate the findings of the third part of Dame Janet Smith's inquiry due out later that year. He also once again expressed his deepest sympathy to the relatives of victims of Britain's most prolific serial killer.

But his Home Secretary David Blunkett raised a few eyebrows when he publicly admitted he had felt like 'toasting' Shipman's death. Blunkett admitted, 'You wake up and receive a phone call telling you that Shipman has topped himself. And you think, is it too early to open a bottle?' But he did add, 'Then you discover that everybody's really upset. So you have to be very cautious in this job, very careful.'

On January 27, 2004, Shipman's body was made available to his family after the formal opening of an inquest into his death. West Yorkshire coroner David Hinchcliff issued a burial/cremation order and interim death certificate following ten minutes of evidence which confirmed that the former GP had hung himself on January 13.

It was expected that Shipman's body would be cremated in a private ceremony and his ashes scattered at a secret location. One local funeral director had already refused to handle the serial killer's body and whichever crematorium was chosen would probably have to open at night to avoid offending other mourners.

However by the middle of February, Shipman's corpse still remained in cold storage in Sheffield while his family haggled over what to do with him. His widow Primrose wanted to bury him in her home village of Walshford, West Yorkshire but was told this was impossible because his grave would attract sensation seekers. Other family members wanted to donate the body for medical research – Shipman's own wish – but that was rejected because of the post mortem, which had been carried out on the corpse.

On February 24, 2004, Shipman was finally laid to rest when he was cremated at a secret service attended by a handful of family and friends. No details were released of where the service took place.

In April, 2004, it was disclosed that Shipman had left his wife Primrose £24,000 in his will. The document had been written in April 1979 and was formally issued at Newcastle Upon Tyne High Court. The final amount only covered Shipman's own personal assets. If Primrose had not survived him, Shipman appointed his bank to hold his estate in trust to be divided between his children.

Then in August, 2004, confirmation finally came that Primrose had been awarded a bumper pension package at the taxpayer's expense. She'd already received a lump sum of £100,000 following Shipman's suicide the previous January. She was also getting an index-linked pension of £1,207 a month, leaving her financially secure for life. Ironically, her income dwarfed the amounts paid out to families of Shipman's victims. The NHS confirmed that if Shipman had lived beyond the age of 60, then his wife would only have received an annual pension of half that amount and no lump sum.

So Shipman really had kept to his promise to look after Primrose whatever happened.

Norman Brennan, director of the Victims of Crime Trust, said, 'It is absolutely staggering that one of the most prolific murderers in history has left his wife better off than any one of his victims' families. Who says crime doesn't pay? For Mrs Shipman, it appears to have paid very well indeed.'

Postscript

Only one man ever came close to unlocking the secrets of Dr Shipman's twisted mind. Dr Richard Badcock was the psychiatrist who spent an hour with the mass murderer after being called in by Greater Manchester Police shortly after his initial arrest.

Shipman, then 52, had suddenly broken down while being interviewed by two detectives at Ashton-under-Lyne police station. He'd asked for a break and moments later collapsed sobbing on the floor in front of his solicitor, Anne Ball. He never spoke any further to police so it is only now, after his death, that it is possible to appreciate the significance of Dr Badcock's meeting with Shipman during those early days following his arrest.

Dr Badcock, a psychiatrist at Rampton Special Hospital, near Retford, in Nottingham, believes he got close enough to Shipman to diagnose him as a 'classic necrophiliac', a man obsessed not with having sex with the dead, but with the act of inducing death, and controlling and observing the moment when life leaves the body.

353

Dr Badcock remains convinced to this day that Shipman's choice of career was influenced by his developing necrophilia, probably originally triggered by the death of his mother from cancer when he was 17.

'In sexual homicides and serial killings it is clear that there is something other than ordinary passions at work. The killing makes sense in terms of how the murderer organises his life and in the kind of relationships he expects to make, both with other people and with himself.'

Shipman's difficulty in forming relationships, especially when he was younger, may also have contributed to the state of mind which led him to kill. 'We need relationships with other people. If we don't have them, we don't progress as human beings. There are lots of people to whom this concept of interaction and mutuality in relationships simply doesn't mean anything. As often there is a huge fear of feeling vulnerable. The feeling of being in control wipes out that vulnerability, but the flipside is that you can't develop as a person. The most you can achieve is self-gratification.'

Deep inside himself, Shipman was, according to Dr Badcock, 'a shell of a person.' He had to reinvent himself in the outside world. Inevitably, his over focus on control led to him forcing others to do things against their will and a form of sadism took over.

Dr Badcock explained, 'They might humiliate them in ways that you know are demeaning. They might inflict pain and torture on victims and see them take it. They end up manipulating and sometimes even torturing people because that is the only way they can see they've got control.

'It can become quite seductive, especially if the person begins from a point where they feel inadequate. It is quite a potent buzz. If you push it to the limits, the only thing they can ultimately control is their own destruction.'

Dr Badcock is convinced that Shipman's necrophilia was a psychological disorder rather than an illness. But he insisted, 'Equally you could make a case for it being a spirited disorder that transcends the conventional disciplines of medicine, psychology and religion. It is something that presumably many could get into but don't. I think evil comes into it.'

So there you have it from one of the few people to get inside Shipman's murderous mind. It answers just a few of the important questions, but thanks to Shipman's last act of murder (on himself) we will never get a more accurate assessment of the demons that drove this apparently ordinary man to become one of the biggest mass murderers of all time.

Right to the end, Shipman played God. His suicide allowed him one final opportunity to exercise power over life or death and he took it, making a deliberately timed exit from a life dominated by a need for control.

EPILOGUE

Epilogue

An astounding catalogue of errors allowed Fred Shipman to kill undetected for more than 25 years. Many victims died because of the arrogance of his colleagues who refused to believe that his drug addiction could seriously impair his abilities as a GP. These blunders gave Fred Shipman a free run at turning murder into a full-time hobby. There were seven key areas that should have helped bring him to justice many years earlier:

- **Criminal Record**

Police initially completely failed to check whether Shipman had any past convictions which would have uncovered his drug addiction in Todmorden.

- **BMA Checks**

Investigators also failed to check whether the British Medical Association had a file on Shipman, which it had held since that first conviction.

• Death Certificates
Police requested from local authorities all death certificates relating to Dr Shipman's cases over a six-month period. They only saw 19 when there were actually a total of 30.

• Victims' Records
Medical files on only 14 of the first 19 suspected victims were provided by the local health authority. Nobody even bothered to try to locate the missing five.

• Softly Softly
The police were so over-sensitive to the relatives of the victims that they completely failed to grasp initially the sheer numbers involved.

• Relatives
Officers were reluctant to upset victims' relatives by interviewing them, so vital information was not gathered quickly enough.

• Prescriptions
No checks were run on Shipman's prescription records, so the huge amount of diamorphine he was prescribing went unnoticed. Shipman was, in fact, the sixth-highest prescriber of the drug among more than 90 locals GPs.

* * *

Never has a story unfolded with such horror. The chilling conclusion of this account is that Fred Shipman may have murdered upwards of 400 patients. That is the number of unexplained deaths which occurred under his 'care'. He truly is amongst the worst serial killers in history.

For hundreds of families in Todmorden, Yorkshire, and Hyde, Lancashire, the nightmare continues. Did their loved ones die of natural causes, or were they cold-bloodedly murdered by the doctor they all trusted with their lives? Many will probably never know the truth. All they can be certain is that Shipman got away with his killings for years, right under the noses of the authorities. The British Government were finally forced to agree to a public inquiry after relatives of the victims successfully challenged its original, short-sighted refusal.

What I hope my book has established is how Shipman got away for so long with his career of mass murder, and why no one noticed what he was up to. Inadequate medical checks and misplaced professional loyalties must share the blame. It beggars belief that such systematic evil could flourish undetected and unchallenged for so long. The case of Fred Shipman has exposed a catastrophic failure in our system.

And then there is Fred Shipman himself and the demons that drove him to commit such atrocities. Will he ever come to terms with the sheer scale of his murderous ways? In this book, I've tried to unpeel the mind of Fred Shipman, his wife Primrose and the life they led so quietly and so reservedly for more than 30 years. But Fred Shipman is not a two-headed monster, a freak-show exhibit. On the outside, he was a painfully normal middle-class family man. Some found him a tad boring, to put it politely. But inside that head of his, the darkest, most evil thoughts were taking shape from the day that his mother died.

He went on to murder many innocents, even including a mother and daughter, two brothers and two pairs of next-door neighbours. Two women even died on the same day. Shipman claimed the lives of at least five patients at his surgery.

His crimes were connected to power and status. Accustomed to godlike adulation and authority, he easily slipped into the role of playing God. Soon, his murderous desires became all-consuming, and the sick and elderly became the means of satisfying those aspirations. If many were close to death, then he was doing them a favour. Everyone was a winner in Fred Shipman's world.

Intriguingly, that was how prosecutors depicted the rationale which had driven another British medical killer, Dr Bodkin Adams, a GP who lived in the county of Sussex, in the south of

England. In the mid-1950s he murdered at least 21 of his female patients, after many of them had changed their wills in his favour.

Bloated, balding, bespectacled Adams, in his late fifties, had a taste for the good life. Wealthy elderly ladies made up the majority of his patient list. Adams's favourite type of treatment for many of these old ladies was a bottle of barbiturates and opiates. He prescribed such generous doses that many of them were soon addicted to the drugs supplied by this particularly attentive doctor. Most of his victims died because of either barbiturates or Fred Shipman's favourite method, diamorphine, which Adams fraudulently prescribed to himself. The similarities with the Shipman case are chilling.

Many of Adams's victims expired soon after naming him as major beneficiary in their wills. One of them had a Rolls-Royce that Adams wanted to get his hands on. Just like Fred Shipman, he was finally brought to justice thanks to the curiosity of the relatives of one of his victims. Adams eventually found himself facing 21 murder charges at the infamous Old Bailey criminal court in London. Another batch of cases was lying in wait in case prosecutors did not succeed.

Adams argued that he had, indeed, contributed to their deaths by giving them large quantities of painkillers so they could retain some dignity in death. His lawyer used the phrase 'easing the passing' in open court. The jury shook their heads in understandable agreement. The end of his lengthy trial in 1957 shocked the nation because the jury were unable to accept that a respectable doctor could commit such heinous crimes. The rotund doctor seemed a bumbling, innocent character and his victims had included some who were terminally ill. Less than an hour after retiring, the jury returned with a 'not guilty' verdict. Adams survived, although he was struck off as a doctor for prescription irregularities.

The case of Bodkin Adams seemed to prove that doctors could literally get away with murder provided they were careful, clinical and discriminating in their choice of victim. Whether this harsh reality even occurred to Fred Shipman, we will probably never know. Many believe he was so sloppy in the execution of many of his murders that he is not in the same league as Adams, but with at least 400 deaths to his name he certainly managed to be far more prolific.

The most recent UK case of a murdering health expert before Shipman was that of nurse Beverly Allitt, convicted of the killing of four children, the attempted murder of three others, and grievous bodily harm of six more. Health services must accept responsibility for protecting patients from such individuals. The public cannot be expected to have confidence in a system that fails to detect the murder of a large number of patients over a period of years by a doctor or other health professional.

Of course, there is no standard blueprint of the rogue, Fred Shipman-type killer doctor, but there are a number of common elements:

- They do not usually start killing until middle age.
- They abuse drugs, in particular diamorphine or its cognates.
- They are brusque and acerbic in their manner.
- They are arrogant with colleagues.
- They can command extraordinary loyalty from those close to them.
- Often self-made, they are over-conscious of their status as doctors.
- They have a complete lack of empathy.

* * *

The many new revelations I have uncovered in the towns and communities where Shipman worked and lived as a GP will add further anguish to those whose relatives died while under Shipman's care and may lead to fresh demands from some of them for a new public trial for one of the most notorious murderers of modern times. That desire for a new public trial is a natural response to an appalling series of crimes. But at the time of Shipman's original criminal trial, detectives were well aware of the potential number of victims but they chose to focus resources and attention on a limited number of murders in order to secure a conviction in court.

Fred Shipman now faces the rest of his life in prison; trying him for 400 other killings in order to pile life sentence upon life sentence would add nothing to his punishment. What is important is that the findings of the recent governmental report and my investigations are acted upon by the Shipman Public Inquiry which is expected to last a further two years. It is a disturbing fact that the extraordinarily high death rate among Shipman's patients, especially elderly women, passed unnoticed by his health authorities for many, many years. If statistical aberrations in the performance of general practitioners are now to be routinely checked, this will show, more than any number of retrials, that the lessons of Fred Shipman's horrific crimes have been taken to heart.

The British Government believed that by launching the Baker Inquiry and the public examination of all the Shipman deaths they could strengthen the bond of trust between doctor and patient. 'Patients' protection' seemed to be the key phrase. But the truth is that the entire medical profession needs to take a closer look at itself by examining the role of the General Medical Council, under whose rules Shipman remained a GP for years after his arrest. That seems to suggest that the GMC is not really interested in the protection of patients. They also need to examine most stringently the measures needed to safeguard against the risk of a lone doctor committing long-term malpractice, as well as carefully to review the policies on the handling of controlled drugs by doctors.

In the light of this, can we ever fully trust our doctors again?

Fred Shipman–
a career in Murder

	Born on 14 January 1946
1965–1970	Leeds University Medical School
1970	Gained MBChB
23 July 1970	Provisional registration with GMC (Number 1470473)
1 August 1970	Pre-registration house officer
31 January 1971	(surgery) Pontefract General Infirmary
1 February 1971	Pre-registration house officer
31 July 1971	(medicine) Pontefract General Infirmary
5 August 1971	Full registration with GMC, number 140473
September 1972	Diploma in Child Health (DCH)

September 1973	Diploma of Royal College of Obstetricians and Gynaecologists (DRCOG); Number A9640
1 March	Assistant general practitioner
1 April 1974	General practitioner, Todmorden Group Practice
September 1975	Practice, Todmorden
1976	Convicted of dishonestly obtaining drugs, forgery of an NHS prescription, and unlawful possession of pethidine. He was fined on each charge and ordered to pay compensation to the local Family Practitioner Committee. These offences were reported to the GMC, who told Shipman that if he offended again, these cases would form part of a subsequent hearing. Medical reports at that time said he was unlikely to offend again.
11 December 1975	Break in practice, 1 year and 294 days
1977	Clinical Medical Officer, South-West Durham. His responsibilities are reported as having been limited to examination of infants and advice about development.
1 October 1977	General practitioner principal at the Donnybrook House Group Practice, Hyde
1985	The GMC received a complaint alleging that Shipman had provided inadequate medical care for a young man who died from an undiagnosed illness. The complaint was referred back to the Family Practitioner Committee.

1989	A complaint was made that Shipman had prescribed the wrong dose of Epilim to a patient with epilepsy. The complaint was upheld, but there was no reducton in his salary. A civil case for negligence was pursued and settled for £250,000.
1 January 1992	General practitioner principal
31 May 1992	Donnybrook House, Hyde, operating as a single-handed GP
1992	A complaint for failure to visit was upheld.
1 June 1992	General practitioner principal, the Surgery, 21 Market Street, Hyde
1995	A complaint about inadequate/incorrect treatment was made but the patient did not pursue the complaint.
24 March 1998	Concerns about the excessive number of deaths among Shipman's patients reported by local general practitioners to Stockport coroner.
7 September 1998	Arrested by Greater Manchester Police.
31 January 2000	Sentenced to life imprisonment after being found guilty of murdering 15 of his elderly patients as well as forging Kathleen Grundy's last will and testament.
13 January 2004	Committed suicide in Wakefield Prison.

Notes of Gratitude

The idea of using a leaden, dispassionate word like 'Acknowledgements' for this section cannot begin to express the depth of my feelings for the many individuals who've made this book possible. I owe them my deepest and most heartfelt gratitude and I know that many in Hyde would rather I didn't mention their names in print.

However, to my literary manager and great friend Peter Miller and my editor Charles Spicer, I say many thanks. Without them, this book would never have happened. Their support and guidance has been very much appreciated. Then there is John Glatt, John Blake, Joe Smith, Bob Duffield, Fran Pearce, Dr David Walker, Adrian Pomfret and all the family, friends and associates of many of Shipman's victims and his own family.

About the author

Wensley Clarkson has been a writer and journalist all his working life. He is a bestselling true crime writer, whose books have sold over a million copies worldwide. His career has taken him into contact with many notorious criminals in the London underworld and beyond, giving his work a gritty realism that has seldom been matched. He divides his time between London and Spain.

ALSO BY THE SAME AUTHOR

Doctors of Death
The Mother From Hell
Hell Hath No Fury
Like a Woman Scorned
Caged Heat
Killer on the Road
Gangsters
Love You to Death, Darling
The Valkyrie Operation
Slave Girls